Samuel Joseph Agnon, Psychoanalysis and Jewish History

Samuel Joseph Agnon, Psychoanalysis and Jewish History: A Comparative Study compares the writings of Samuel Joseph Agnon (1887–1970) with other writers, including Gustav Flaubert, Franz Kafka, D.H. Lawrence, and Carl Gustav Jung, as well as his great Hebrew predecessors, Mendele Mokher Sefraim and Chaim Nachman Bialik, who drew on the ancient Jewish biblical and rabbinic tradition in creating a modern secular literature.

Through close readings of Agnon's fiction in comparison with some of his great contemporaries, the reader comes to a new appreciation of the richness and psychological depth of modern Hebrew literary art and its roots in ancient Jewish history and literature; of Agnon as a major figure bridging the traditional culture of the pre-1939 East European Jews with the modern world; of Hebrew fiction amid tumultuous historical change, as its centre shifted in the early 20th century from Eastern Europe to Tel Aviv; and of the centrality of Hebrew literature in the rise of modern Jewish nationalism as anti-Semitism grew.

This book is of particular value to students of Hebrew and Comparative Literature and of psychoanalysis and the sociology of literature, but it is written clearly and without jargon and has much interest to the general reader.

David Aberbach is Emeritus Professor of Hebrew and Comparative Literature, McGill University, Montreal, Canada.

Routledge Jewish Studies Series

Series Editor: Oliver Leaman, *University of Kentucky*

Jewish Studies, which are interpreted to cover the disciplines of history, sociology, anthropology, culture, politics, philosophy, theology, religion, as they relate to Jewish affairs. The remit includes texts which have as their primary focus issues, ideas, personalities and events of relevance to Jews, Jewish life and the concepts which have characterised Jewish culture both in the past and today. The series is interested in receiving appropriate scripts or proposals.

Jewish Hungarian Orthodoxy
Piety and Zealotry
Menachem Keren-Kratz

Jewish Women
Between Conformity and Agency
Katharina Galor

The Poetry and Essays of Uri Zvi Grinberg
Politics and Zionism
Tamar Wolf-Monzon

Hans Jonas
The Early Years
Edited by Daniel M. Herskowitz, Elad Lapidot and Christian Wiese

Expressivist Religious Zionism
Modernity and the Sacred in a Nationalist Movement
Shlomo Fischer

Samuel Joseph Agnon, Psychoanalysis and Jewish History
A Comparative Study
David Aberbach

For more information about this series, please visit: https://www.routledge.com/Routledge-Jewish-Studies-Series/book-series/JEWISH

Agnon as a young man, Jaffa, c. 1908

Samuel Joseph Agnon, Psychoanalysis and Jewish History

A Comparative Study

David Aberbach

Routledge
Taylor & Francis Group
LONDON AND NEW YORK

First published 2026
by Routledge
4 Park Square, Milton Park, Abingdon, Oxon OX14 4RN

and by Routledge
605 Third Avenue, New York, NY 10158

Routledge is an imprint of the Taylor & Francis Group, an informa business

British Library Cataloguing-in-Publication Data
A catalogue record for this book is available from the British Library

Library of Congress Cataloging-in-Publication Data
Names: Aberbach, David, 1953– author
Title: Samuel Joseph Agnon, psychoanalysis and Jewish history : a comparative study / David Aberbach.
Description: Abingdon, Oxon ; New York, NY : Routledge, 2026. |
Series: Routledge Jewish studies | Includes bibliographical references and index.
Identifiers: LCCN 2025008443 | ISBN 9781032976754 hardback |
ISBN 9781032976761 paperback | ISBN 9781003594802 ebook
Subjects: LCSH: Agnon, Shmuel Yosef, 1887–1970–Criticism and interpretation |
Psychoanalysis and literature | Judaism in literature | LCGFT: Literary criticism
Classification: LCC PJ5053.A4 Z543 2026 | DDC 892.43/5–dc23/eng/20250626
LC record available at https://lccn.loc.gov/2025008443

ISBN: 978-1-032-97675-4 (hbk)
ISBN: 978-1-032-97676-1 (pbk)
ISBN: 978-1-003-59480-2 (ebk)

DOI: 10.4324/9781003594802

Typeset in Times New Roman
by Newgen Publishing UK

Contents

Figures

Note on Agnon's Collected Works

Quotes from Agnon in this book, unless indicated otherwise, are translated by David Aberbach from the 8-volume *Kol Sippurav shel Shmuel Yosef Agnon* (Collected Works), 1953–62, referred to as 'CW' in the notes. This edition, authorized by Agnon, contains most of the stories cited, including the following, with dates of first publication:

Vol. 1: *Hakhnasat Kalla* (The Bridal Canopy, 1931)
Vol. 2: *Elu ve-Elu* (Of Such and Such): including 'Agunot' (1908), *Ve-Haya he'Akov le-Mishor* (And the Crooked Shall Be Made Straight, 1913), *Aggadat ha-Sofer* (The Legend of the Scribe, 1919), *Ha-Nidakh* (The Outcast 1919), *Ha-Mitpahat* (The Kerchief, 1932), and *Bilvav Yammim* (In the Heart of Seas, 1934).
Vol. 3: *Al Kapot ha-Man'ul* (At the Handles of the Lock): including (*Bi-Ne'arenu uviZkenenu* (*With Young and Old Together*, 1920), *Bi-Dmi Yameha* (In the Prime of Her Life, 1923), *Sippur Pashut* (A Simple Story, 1935), *Panim Aherot* (Metamorphosis, 1933), and *Ha-Rofe u-Grushato* (The Doctor's Divorce, 1941).
Vol. 4: *Oreah Nata La-Lun* (A Guest for the Night, 1939)
Vol. 5: *Temol Shilshom* (Yesteryear, 1945)
Vol. 6: *Samukh VeNire* (Near and Apparent): including *Sefer ha-Ma'asim* (The Book of Deeds, 1932–51), *Ha'Adonit vehaRokhel* (The Lady and the Pedlar, 1943), and *Shne Talmidei Hakhamim she-Hayu be-Irenu* (Two Torah Scholars in Our Town, 1946).
Vol. 7: *Ad Hena* (Thus Far): including *Shvu'at Emunim* (Betrothed, 1943), *Iddo ve-Enam* (Iddo and Enam, 1950), *Tehilah* (1950), *Im Kenisat ha-Yom* (At the Outset of the Day, 1951), and *Ad Hena* (Thus Far, 1952).
Vol. 8: *Ha-Esh vehaEtzim* (The Fire and the Wood): including *Ad Olam* (Forevermore).

Agnon's posthumous works cited are listed in the bibliography.

Introduction

This book compares the writings of Samuel Joseph Agnon (1887–1970) with other writers, including Gustav Flaubert, Franz Kafka, D.H. Lawrence, and Carl Gustav Jung, as well as his great Hebrew predecessors, Mendele Mokher Sefraim and Chaim Nachman Bialik, who drew on the ancient Jewish biblical and rabbinic tradition in creating a modern secular literature.[1] Agnon's outlook, style, and ambitions were determined by the extraordinary, changing social and cultural worlds in which he lived, as the centuries-old Eastern European Jewish way of life declined, ending in the Holocaust. By the early-20th century, Hebrew literature, previously imitative, became competitive and aimed, largely successfully, to become an important part of European literature, an instrument of expression in which nothing human was alien; with a new richness of style comparable to Marcel Proust and Thomas Mann, and in psychological insight and complexity, to Sigmund Freud and James Joyce.[2] Agnon was immersed in European literature, chiefly in German and German translation. This influence is seen in his portrayal of character, his attention to psychological detail and *le mot juste*, his use of images and symbols, often redolent of Freud and modern writers such as Gustav Flaubert, Knut Hamsun, and Franz Kafka, to hint at unconscious motives, and his habit of depicting troubled personal relationships with broader social and historical implications. Yet, much of the fascination of Agnon's writings comes from the ever-changing crosscurrents of history in which they flow. No storyteller could compete with the story of the Jewish people, in their homeland and in lands of exile, from the biblical age to their national rebirth in modern times.

Agnon's most devoted early readers (like those of his 19th-century Hebrew predecessors) tended to have a foot in two worlds, many being, like him, Talmudic scholars who read widely in European literature, and whose taste in Agnon was determined by this volatile combination. These readers constituted an elite, steeped in Jewish learning and widely read and discerning, though mostly self-taught, and familiar with European literature.[3] These were Agnon's core readers, for whom he wrote (despite his claim that he wrote only for himself), and who studied – not merely read – his stories with the intense analytic attention and reverence they had given to their abandoned Talmudic studies.

DOI: 10.4324/9781003594802-1

In the observant world of Eastern Europe Jewry into which Agnon was born, fiction was a heresy, and effectively banned.[4] Agnon's characters are frequently troubled with guilt. In a dream in *In the Shop of Mr. Lublin* (*Ba-Hahunto shel Mar Lublin*, 1974), the narrator recounts a dream:

> I saw my father, my teacher, in a dream. I greeted him but he did not return my greeting because he was in mourning. 'Father', I asked, 'for whom do you mourn?' He replied, 'For you, my son, I mourn.'[5]

In his stories, Agnon explores the guilt of abandoning Torah as a way of life and turning it into mere subject for study:

> People live by the Torah, they die for their ancestral heritage, then researchers turn the Torah into a subject of study, and the ancestral heritage – to folklore.[6]

Agnon questions faith, even the existence of God. As is the case with Kafka, his writings can be read as a quest for meaning.[7] In 'The Orchestra' (*Ha-Tizmoret*, 1946), the narrator attends a dream-like concert in which the musicians are all people the narrator knows or once knew, playing with no conductor:

> Each man and woman played separately, but the melodies formed a single song. All were bound to their instruments, fixed to the floor, and each thought he alone was bound, and was ashamed to ask his neighbor to free him. Perhaps they believed they had chosen to be so tied, and to play in this way. One thing was clear: though their eyes were set on their instruments, they did not see what their hands were doing, for all were blind. And I fear perhaps their ears did not hear what they were playing, for from too much playing they had grown deaf.[8]

Even so, from the viewpoint of the younger generation in the early-20th century, especially among assimilated German-speaking Jews such as Martin Buber, Gershom Scholem, and Max Brod (Kafka's biographer), Agnon was no heretic but an authentic voice of Jewish tradition, an irrefutable answer to the anti-Hebraistic and anti-Hasidic (some would say, anti-Jewish) streak in German-Jewish culture. To those alienated by anti-Semitism in supposedly rational secular states which had emancipated their Jews, such as France and Germany, Agnon spoke the language of a rich and ancient Jewish heritage. Through Agnon, many readers rediscovered the Hebrew language as a subtle instrument of modern culture. The idea of Agnon as a 'bearer of spiritual tradition',[9] as Gershom Scholem described him, originated chiefly in Germany.

Agnon as cultural bridge

Agnon's life and works bridged the great events of Jewish life in the 20th century: the end of a centuries-old, largely monolithic Orthodoxy in Eastern Europe – Agnon spent his formative years in Polish Galicia, then part of the

Austro-Hungarian empire before moving to Ottoman Palestine (1908–1912); the rise of racial anti-Semitism and anti-Jewish violence, and the concomitant growth of Jewish nationalism and of *aliyah* to the land of Israel under Ottoman, then British rule; the cataclysm of World War I, when Agnon was in Germany, and its troubled aftermath, when Agnon moved to Jerusalem (1924), where he spent the rest of his life; the political, social, and cultural upheavals in interwar Europe; the rise of Hitler and the Holocaust, with the destruction of the entire world of *shtetl* Judaism portrayed in Agnon's stories; and the growth of the Jewish *yishuv* under British rule, the establishment of the state of Israel in 1948, and the immense transformations in Jewish life which followed.

Agnon's life and works also bridge the pre-modern world of East European Jewry – in his Galician *shtetl* childhood, electricity had not yet arrived, and in his stories synagogues are still candle-lit – and the new industrial world of cars and machines, rapid transport and communication, and of modern warfare; the ideological divide between pious traditionalism and secular ways of life, including socialist Zionism and women's liberation, and the enormous educational and psychological changes which came about; the transition from a Yiddish culture with a doubtful future to a revived Hebrew culture – a linguistic leap from a world in which there were no native Hebrew speakers to a society in which Hebrew was spoken daily; and the aesthetic gulf between pre-1914 Romanticism and post-1918 modernism, spurred by the catastrophic effects of World War I and by the historical, ideological, and aesthetic changes which followed.

Agnon portrays the Galicia of his early years, prior to World War I, in stories such as *In the Prime of Her Life* (*Bi-Dmi Yameha*, 1923), 'The Kerchief' (*Ha-Mitpahat*, 1932), *A Simple Story* (*Sippur Pashut*, 1935), and *Two Torah Scholars in Our Town* (*Shne Talmidei Hakhamim she-Hayu be-Irenu*, 1946). Jewish life in Agnon's stories changes as secular education – including education for girls – becomes more acceptable, though maintaining until the Holocaust, when it was all swept away, its fundamental, increasingly attenuated, rabbinic character. The emperor, Franz Joseph, did not tolerate anti-Semitic violence, though the empire was full of suppressed ethnic rivalry and hatred, and Vienna had an anti-Semitic municipality with Karl Lueger as mayor (1897–1910), and an unknown Adolf Hitler, who lived in Vienna, an admirer.[10] Austro-Hungarian Jews were exceptionally upwardly mobile and tended to be patriotic and respectful of authority; the Galician Jews, living on the eastern frontier of the empire, near the Russian border, were not attacked in pogroms as the Russian Jews were in 1881–82 and 1903–06. Jewish life in the short-lived empire (1867–1918) was full of contradictions: of tolerance and intolerance, acceptance and rejection, success and insecurity, conservatism and radicalism, loyalty to the emperor and Zionism. Within the empire, Rabbi Moshe Sofer (the Chatam Sofer) founded the famous Pressberg Yeshiva, many of whose students became officers in the Austrian-Hungarian army; in the same empire, Klimt painted his 1907 portrait of Adele Bloch-Bauer, *The Woman in Gold*, and Austro-Hungarian Jews created an extraordinarily varied and revolutionary culture: including Mahler and Schoenberg in music, Kafka, Schnitzler, and

Joseph Roth in German literature, Freud in psychoanalysis, Herzl in politics, and Agnon in the creation of modern Hebrew fiction.

Agnon's younger contemporary, the novelist Joseph Roth evokes the Jewish reverence for Emperor Franz Joseph in *The Radetzky March* (1932). The emperor (one of whose titles was 'King of Jerusalem') visits a remote village in Galicia on manoeuvres, where he is greeted by a procession of pious Jews:

> Their coal-black, fire-red, and silver-white beards billowed in the breeze. The elder stopped three paces before the Emperor. He carried a large purple roll of the Torah in his arms, ornamented with a golden crown whose bell was tinkling softly. Then the Jew held up the Torah scroll to the Emperor. And his overgrown, toothless mouth began to mumble in an incomprehensible language the blessing that Jews have to speak when they see an emperor.[11]

Agnon recalls similarly, in a story written long after the emperor's death and the fall of the empire, the visit of an Austrian archduke, on manoeuvres to a Galician town, where he is greeted in the local synagogue in the presence of the entire Jewish community. The Jews in this provincial backwater speak Yiddish in daily life, and the rabbi normally preaches in Yiddish or Hebrew, and so there is apprehension that the rabbi will be unable at short notice to deliver his sermon in German. Using his formidable intellect, the rabbi prepares rapidly and preaches in German, with great success:

> It was no miracle, for the rabbi knew by heart Mendelssohn's German translation of the Psalms as well as most of Heidenheim's German translations from the Hebrew liturgy; and he had also picked up a bit from his wife, who knew German.[12]

Agnon's stories set in pre-1914 Ottoman Palestine, notably the novella *Betrothed* (*Shvu'at Emunim*, 1943) and the novel *Yesteryear* (*Temol Shilshom*, 1945) portray, among other things, the revival of vernacular Hebrew in daily life. Agnon's Hebrew fiction is set in a multilingual society, mostly in Jaffa and Jerusalem, in which many newly arrived immigrants still spoke Yiddish, Russian, German, and many other languages, but a growing number used Hebrew daily. At the time he wrote his story '*Agunot*' (1908) in Jaffa, Agnon recalled, 'my landlady spoke Ladino, my landlord who taught in an *Alliance* school spoke French, their daughters went to an English school and spoke English, the girl who cleaned my room was from Yemen and spoke Arabic, the women from whom I bought bread and olives spoke Lithuanian Yiddish, my cleaning lady, a Russian convert, spoke Russian.'[13] When he went into a shop to buy a hat and spoke to the shopkeeper in Hebrew, the reply was in French; but, as he found on returning in 1924, the same shopkeeper spoke Hebrew to his customers.[14]

Agnon's closest friend during his period in Ottoman Palestine was the Hebrew writer, J.H. Brenner, who, shortly after his arrival in Jaffa in 1909, a year or so after Agnon, wrote a story 'Nerves' (*Atzabim*), which sets out the parlous state of

Hebrew culture at this time. It opens in the bare, rocky, ruined landscape of the hills of Judea, with scattered, newly planted trees. The narrator, ideologically committed to the rebuilding of the land which he loves, almost despairingly, sees these trees as pathetic symbols of a modern Jewish culture far from maturity.[15] While the land of Israel, particularly Jerusalem, Jaffa, Hebron, and Safed remained, as in the past, a center for the preservation of Talmudic Judaism, the centers of modernity were overseas, in the great Western and Central European cities with their centuries of remarkable growth, of science, technology, and art. 'Nerves' makes clear why the greatest pre-1914 Hebrew writers lived in the diaspora – and why Agnon left Jaffa for Germany in 1912. Jaffa honed Agnon's style; Berlin made him a world-artist.

Between two worlds: generational conflicts

Agnon's art emerged in the early 20th century from the friction between two worlds, of Eastern and Western European Jews. In the transition from a largely Eastern European Jewish culture to Western European culture (and especially German *Kultur*), Agnon moved from a position of religious heresy to being representative of a religious culture largely shunned by Western European Jews. Agnon's family in Buczacz opposed his becoming a writer in the first place; and in Germany, his fiancée's family opposed the marriage and were not invited to the wedding in Berlin.[16]

Agnon's works are set against a vast, rapidly and radically changing historical panorama, but his narrative persona remains that of the Eastern European Orthodoxy of his youth. In his own literary world, Agnon maintains the fundamental consistency of Judaism and its moral values preserved by the rabbinic tradition from ancient times: change is tolerated, in fixed, pre-existing norms. Betrayal of tradition is a recurrent source of grief, anxiety, and disillusionment in Agnon's stories. In Agnon's lifetime, even before the cataclysm of World War I, serious generational conflicts opened up between the Orthodox Jewish mainstream and a growing minority disenchanted with rabbinic tradition, seeking alternative ways of life, such as secular Enlightenment (Haskalah in Hebrew), socialism, Zionism, and revolution. Similar conflicts appear at the same time in other cultures too, but are especially evident among the Jews as they had no territory, only culture.

Especially vulnerable were those who sought secular education leading to assimilation in their countries of citizenship, but exposed to anti-Semitic prejudice. By the end of the 19th century, Austrian Jews were disproportionately represented in trade, banking, and capitalist investment; in the professions, especially law and medicine; in literature and the theatre, as well as in the creation and promotion of the press and social organizations; and, in contrast with Germany, there were large numbers of Jewish officers in the Austrian army. However, as elsewhere in Europe, Jewish emancipation and assimilation severely tested the state-based national identities in which Jews, especially in German-speaking lands, sought acceptance. Jewish cultural prominence provoked anti-Semitism, revealing the fragility of Jewish emancipation. European Jews, most of whom had been initially hostile or indifferent to Zionism, became increasingly aware of their own national identity, more ancient and in some ways richer than most European cultures. Jews previously alienated from Judaism turned to the Hebrew language and literature to reconnect with their ancestral heritage.

Jewish generational tension in Agnon's stories has many parallels in other European literature. Freud, for example, writes of father–son conflict as a universal psychological phenomenon (the 'Oedipus complex'), but also as one linked among Jews to their extraordinary conditions in 19th century Europe and vast, rapid cultural and psychological changes undergone in the passage to modernity.[17] Freud's parents came from the same Galician world of rabbinic piety as Agnon. Freud's father, born into a Hasidic family in the town of Tysmenitz, found in the Haskalah and Hebrew literature a halfway house to the modern world; but Freud went much further in assimilating into Western culture, distancing himself from his father's Judaism. When Freud was eleven, in 1867, the united Austro-Hungarian empire emancipated its Jews, and Freud dreamed of becoming a cabinet minister. As a young man, Freud was a staunch German nationalist and admirer of Bismarck (as was Herzl). With the rise of anti-Semitism, he questioned his nationalism, as many Jews did (including Herzl) and became increasingly concerned with the future of the European Jews. After seeing Herzl's play *Das Neue Ghetto* (1895), Freud had the following dream ('My son, the Myops … '), which he related in *The Interpretation of Dreams* (1900):

> On account of certain events which had occurred in the city of Rome, it had become necessary to remove the children to safety, and this was done … I was sitting on the edge of a fountain and was greatly depressed and almost in tears.[18]

The dream alludes to the classic picture of the exiled Jews, 'By the waters of Babylon we sat down and wept' (Psalms 137), implying Freud's awareness of being in *golus* (exile), subject to the *geseres* [Hebrew and Yiddish for 'decrees'], the sufferings decreed by the gentile world:

> The Jewish problem, concern about the future of one's children, to whom one cannot give a country of their own [*Die Judenfrage, die Sorge um die Zukunft der Kinder, dene man ein Vaterland nicht geben kann*], concern about educating them in such a way that they can move freely across frontiers – all this was easily recognizable among the relevant dream-thoughts.[19]

Kafka wrote, similarly, in his *Letter to His Father* of the generation gap created by the move from Eastern to Western Europe, and the sense of a spiritual void felt by many sons of assimilated Jewish fathers, who were consequently drawn, as he was, to cultural Zionism.[20] Kafka and Freud, as we shall see, left a strong mark on Agnon's stories.

Agnon's pride in and creative use of Hebrew literature had particular attraction to German-speaking Zionists. Many of these came from thoroughly assimilated families, often contemptuous of *Ostjuden* and their allegedly primitive Hebrew and Yiddish culture and backward religious practices. The German-Jewish conception of German national identity was closely tied to German *Kultur*, to mastery of the German language, thorough knowledge of its literature, and appreciation of its unique folklore and poetic and mystical traditions. The rise of racial anti-Semitism in the late-19th and early 20th century was a massive blow, and a serious threat to the future of Jews in Germany. German anti-Semitism during World War I was a further disillusionment to German Jews, perhaps especially to those who served in the war, and their families. Some turned to Zionism and to Hebrew cultural nationalism, to Hebrew language and literature, delighting in their discovery of 'authentic' Eastern European Hebrew writers, such as Agnon.

In *Goodbye to Berlin* (1939), the English novelist Christopher Isherwood relates a not-atypical change in cultural affiliation among German Jews, typical of those to whom Agnon was close during and after World War I. He tells of the Landauer family in Berlin who lost a son in the war. His surviving brother, Bernhard, tells Christopher how their grieving mother sought comfort in Hebrew and Jewish history:

> After my brother had been killed, my mother scarcely ever left this house and its grounds. I think she tried to forget that a land such as Germany existed. She began to study Hebrew and to concentrate her whole mind upon ancient Jewish history and literature.[21]

At this historical juncture, during and after the war, Agnon spoke to German readers of Hebrew in the original or in German translation, with Jewish folk stories whose aesthetics bore the imprint of German literature. In Agnon, as in Peretz, Bialik, and Buber, German Zionists found a Jewish cultural force as compelling as German *Kultur*, if not more so.

Herder and modern cultural nationalism

Agnon's enchantment with Jewish folklore followed a cultural trend in Europe from the end of the 18th century, triggered by the French Revolution and the rise of secular nationalism, and associated particularly with the German thinker Johann Gottfried Herder (1744–1803). Until modern times, European folk culture – including Jewish culture, its languages, legends, myths, superstitions, history, and mystical literature – was generally looked down upon as inferior to the 'high culture' of the educated aristocracy. In Jewish society, the intellectual aristocracy was the rabbinic elite with its strict emphasis upon Talmudic study. In Herder's view, national cultures in their splendid variety owe much to the Hebrew Bible, a model of national distinctiveness. Herder taught that every age, tribe, people, and nation, are unfathomably and indestructibly unique; each individual folk culture in all its manifestations and detail expresses the original character of the Nation; it must be free to be itself, and valued on its own terms; a nation's folk literature preserves its deepest traits, its highest hopes, and its spirit; each culture – including and especially that of the Jews – is precious and must be preserved.

With the rise of Jewish secular nationalism in the late-19th century, this high valuation of folk culture, particularly that of the previously despised Hasidic movement, entered Jewish literature. Peretz's *Khasidish* (Hasidic Stories), came out in Yiddish in 1900, and *Folkstimlekhe geshikhtn* (Folktales), in 1909, with Hebrew versions. Martin Buber, whose grandfather was a noted midrash scholar, published the tales of Nachman of Bratslav in German (*Die Geschichten des Rabbi Nachman*) in 1906 and legends of the Baal Shem Tov (*Die Legende des Baalschem*), in 1908. *Aggadah* (Jewish legend) became a major element in Hebrew literature and Jewish scholarship. Writers such as Mendele, Yehuda Steinberg, Micah Yosef Berdichevsky, and Bialik retold and drew constantly on *aggadic* literature. Bialik and Ravnitzky edited the *Sefer ha-Aggadah* (Book of Legends) whose first volume came out at the same time as Agnon's story '*Agunot*' (1908). Agnon's close bonds with Bialik, Buber, and Scholem were due in large part to a shared interest in folk literature, for a variety of purposes but as part of a secular Jewish cultural national movement.

Agnon, though a master of Jewish folklore and of the narrative voice of tradition,[22] emerged as a modernist with close links to other major writers of the 19th and early-20th century. Although Yiddish was the main language of his Galician childhood, he was taught German and, as seen in Chapter 6, his concerns are in some respects close to those of German-Jewish writers. As a young man, Agnon was impressed by the fiction of Arthur Schnitzler and Jakob Wassermann, and he was later in contact with leading German-Jewish writers, including Franz Werfel and Richard Beer-Hofmann. He had modernist ambitions from the start. He slyly related how the great rabbi and mystic, Abraham Isaac Kook, later Chief Rabbi of Palestine, whom he knew in pre-1914 Jaffa, responded approvingly to his early fiction by pronouncing it kosher, for the modernist *tref* content was no more than one-sixtieth![23] At this time, Agnon recalled with a rueful dig at later Hebrew writers, no one could imagine a world in which Hebrew writers were unfamiliar – God forbid! – with the classic texts of Judaism, Chumash and Rashi, Mishna, Midrash, and Jewish legend (*aggadah*).[24] His move to Germany was as vital to his creative life as Ibsen's was from Norway to Italy, or Joyce's from Ireland to Trieste.

Rabbinic roots and modern Jewish nationalism

Agnon was born into a centuries-old Eastern European rabbinic world, in which Jewish religious observance was the daily norm and devotion to the sacred texts was absolute. Scripture defined Jewish identity and ensured Jewish survival. Outstanding among Jewish writers of Agnon's formative years were two humorists raised in the same tradition, both vital in pre-Holocaust Jewish culture – Mendele and Sholom Aleichem – whose writings appeared both in Yiddish and Hebrew.[25] Agnon began as a Yiddish writer following both Mendele and Sholom Aleichem. Like them, he used humor and satire to portray the decline of tradition and growing violent anti-Semitism in Eastern Europe. Their influence is clearest in Agnon's first novel, *The Bridal Canopy* (*Hakhnasat Kalla*, 1931), whose comic premise – travels in quest of dowries for daughters – combines the social satire of Sholom Aleichem with Mendele's quixotic parody.[26]

Agnon follows both also in portraying the close links between anti-Semitic violence and Jewish emigration from Europe.[27] In Sholom Aleichem's Tevye stories, the pogroms drive Tevye and his family to leave for the Holy Land. The rise of Jewish nationalism drew attention to the fact that the Jewish community in Palestine was one of the most heterogeneous in the world: only one language united its varied groups – Hebrew. In the short story 'Earthquake Days' (*Bi-Yme ha-Ra'ash*, 1890), Mendele gives a brilliant satiric picture of the time: a bedraggled *melamed* (a traditional teacher of Torah to children) attempting to escape the pogroms to Palestine via Odessa is converted literally overnight into a private tutor of modern Hebrew. Hundreds of Hebrew-speaking groups sprung up in towns and villages such as Buczacz, Agnon's birthplace, where Yiddish-speaking Jews had lived for centuries.[28] The upsurge of interest in modern spoken Hebrew and journalism increased the market for creative Hebrew. After 1881, the artistic standard of this literature rose impressively. Hebrew readers of writers prominent in the early 20th century, when Agnon began writing – including Mendele, Peretz, Bialik, Brenner, Gnessin, and Shoffman – rarely exceeded a few thousand, but this was far more than during the pre-1881 period.[29] Modern Hebrew became a major point of contact between Eastern and Western Jews. Jews such as Agnon, who knew Hebrew exceptionally well, found themselves in demand as tutors among Western European Jews. Agnon's entrée into German-Jewish society began as a tutor to devotees of Hebrew and admirers of his work, including his mentor in Jaffa, Arthur Ruppin; his future publisher, Salman Schocken; and his future wife, Else (Esther) Marx.

Agnon began writing at a time of growing national conflicts that led to the two world wars and the Holocaust. To Agnon, amid these changes, Hebrew was a rock of permanence, *leshon ha-kodesh*, the Holy Tongue, language of the Bible, the Mishna, and the 16th-century *Shulkhan Arukh*, the standard code of Jewish law used in daily life, and the *siddur*, the Hebrew prayerbook. In his stories, Agnon continued the tone of devotion to these texts in Jewish life through the ages, which at times balances precariously against his ambivalence toward his characters and the current of satiric mockery running through his works.

Agnon and German anti-Hebraism

When Agnon met Saul Bellow in the early 1960s, he warned the American novelist teasingly (in Yiddish) to ensure that his novels appear in Hebrew – otherwise, they were unlikely to survive. From ancient times, Jewish communities that forgot Hebrew tended to vanish from history. This threat existed in Agnon's childhood and youth. Yet, already in 18th century Western Europe, the Age of Enlightenment and the French Revolution, with their anti-theological ideology of the secular state, radically undermined the traditional Jewish attachment to Hebrew. In particular, among patriotic German Jews, from the time of Prussian Jewish emancipation in 1812,

Hebrew became a problematic issue. In a pamphlet dating from the same year, the founder of German Reform, David Friedländer (1750–1834), appealed to Prussian Jewry 'to undertake complete religious, social, as well as educational reforms for the sake of becoming fully integrated in the Prussian state'[30] – including the elimination of Hebrew from Jewish education and prayer. The reformers excluded the ancient Hebrew prayers for Zion and Jerusalem, in part as they genuinely believed them to be anachronistic, but also in reaction against the charge that Jews could not be loyal citizens. A recoil from Hebrew is evident also in Jewish communities that failed to establish schools in which their children learned Hebrew, or that provided second-rate education, putting the children off; in the massive insecurity leading to grotesque patriotism, above all among German Jews, for countries harboring genocidal impulses towards the Jews, and exaggerated attachment to their cultures in preference to Jewish culture; and in the ignorance of Hebrew, most strikingly among the Jewish or baptized Jewish intelligentsia.[31]

Assimilated 19th- and early 20th-century German-speaking Jews were in the forefront of a socio-psychological revolution among the Jews. For the first time, they revered non-Jewish culture as superior to their own. Karl Marx, a child-convert to Christianity, shared with Agnon a long line of East European rabbinic ancestors; his school report has favorable comments on his knowledge of Greek and Latin – the entry on Hebrew is blank. Sigmund Freud, who shared, similarly, a rabbinic ancestry in Eastern Europe, kept, as a young man, a diary in Greek but professed ignorance of Hebrew in his Hebrew preface to *Totem and Taboo* (1913) – in fact, he had studied Hebrew as a child.[32] Freud gave his children no Jewish education whatsoever. His son Martin recalled his maternal grandmother, Emmeline, as the end of the line, tradition-wise: 'She stayed with us occasionally and on Saturdays we used to hear her singing Jewish prayers in a small but firm and melodious voice. All of this, strangely enough in a Jewish family, seemed alien to us children who had been brought up without any instruction in Jewish ritual.'[33] Similarly ignorant of Hebrew was Theodor Herzl (1860–1904), founder of political Zionism. Herzl envisaged German as the language of high culture among Zionists. He only slightly exaggerated when he asked in *Der Judenstaat*, 'Who among us can ask for a railway ticket in Hebrew?'[34] He needed special coaching to undergo the ordeal of reciting the short blessings when called to the Torah at the time of the First Zionist Congress, held in Basel in 1897: 'When he was called up to the Torah, he found that the few Hebrew words of the benediction were causing him more anxiety than all the speeches he had delivered, more than the entire direction of the congress.'[35] Kafka was even more frightened of Hebrew than Herzl. In his 1919 *Letter to His Father*, Kafka tells that for years he was terrified that he would be called to recite the blessing in synagogue as his father had not troubled to have him taught Hebrew.[36] Shortly before his death in 1924, Kafka began studying Hebrew in preparation for emigration to the land of Israel. His last writings include lists of Hebrew vocabulary.[37]

Even during the interwar period – a time of Hebrew creativity unprecedented since the Bible, and when Agnon wrote some of his finest works – there was much denigration of Hebrew, particularly among German-Jewish intellectuals. In a well-known joke of the 1930s, a German-Jewish refugee walking in Tel Aviv is asked the time in Hebrew. Deeply offended, he replies, *Was meinst du, ich bin ein Kind*? (What do you think, I am a child?) – in other words, Hebrew was for children, not grown-ups. Hannah Arendt at this time expressed typically irrational contempt for Hebrew in first confessing her ignorance of the language, then echoing Heine's quip that Judaism was not a religion but a misfortune, describing Hebrew as 'no language, but a national misfortune.'[38]

Against this background of German-Jewish emancipation, assimilation, and rejection of Judaism, in an age of rising anti-Semitism, young assimilated German Jews, such as Gershom Scholem, discovered Agnon. They, perhaps more than most Orthodox East European Jews (to whom Agnon and his ilk had gone off the rails), valued his mastery of tradition, his superb Hebrew style, and his total commitment to Jewish cultural identity and creativity – an oasis in a German spiritual desert.

Agnon: 'bearer of spiritual tradition'

And indeed, despite the many forms Judaism has taken in its evolution over the centuries, Agnon spoke for the fundamental Bible-based spiritual unity and continuity in Judaism. Though immersed in European secular culture, he was widely read as an authentic voice of Jewish tradition, steeped in the sources, a scholar in fiction of the profundities of ancient Jewish literature, expressing the yearning for national renewal and for a lost land associated with the nation's childhood. In his acceptance speech for the Nobel Prize for Literature in 1966, Agnon declared with a typical mixture of naiveté and calculation:

> Because of the catastrophe of Titus's destruction of Jerusalem [in 70 CE] and the exile of the Jewish people from their homeland, I was born in exile. But I always imagined myself born in Jerusalem.[39]

Implicit in Agnon's works is the understanding that the seeds of modern Jewish nationalism are preserved in the Jewish religion. Secular Zionism is an empty shell when tradition is lost. Agnon in his lifetime was recognized even in translation as a writer of enduring worth, a leading Hebrew experimental modernist and, at the same time, a powerful link in modern Hebrew to the ancient world of biblical and rabbinic Judaism; he would meet such praise with ludicrous insistence that he was not an original writer but a scribe (*sofer*), writing by divine inspiration. Agnon follows in the Hebrew tradition of recreating in literature a world lost or destroyed. In the Bible, for example, the literary memory of the Israelite kingdoms survived, though the kingdoms were long gone. In the Mishna, the world of the destroyed Temple in Jerusalem – including many defunct laws pertaining to agriculture and the sacrificial rites – was kept alive, studied daily in the rabbinic tradition. Agnon's stories, too, are a record of a world in the process of spiritual dissolution, demographic upheaval in war, and ultimate destruction in the Holocaust.

Agnon draws creatively on the entire history and culture of the Jews from the Bible to modern times. In doing so, he – like other original Hebrew writers from ancient to modern times – indicts the historic basis of supersessionary anti-Semitism: that Christianity (and later, Islam) had replaced Judaism. In this prejudiced view, Judaism was a dead religion and culture, and Jews by definition were evil, deserving of persecution. In Agnon's hands, in contrast, Jewish life is intensely alive. Hebrew is a living force conveying inmost feelings. Jewish culture is not only not dead, but a live and powerful civilization, capable of renewal for the modern age. Agnon shows how immensely original modern Hebrew fiction can be, a potent, subtle instrument of expression, capable of portraying the most highly complex spiritual and psychological states and relationships. If Thomas Mann in *Joseph and His Brothers* could seek to recreate the ancient land of Israel for modern readers, why could a Hebrew novelist not do the same, all the better in the language of the Bible and Mishna, and set in the land where Hebrew continued to be spoken?

Hebrew more than most other languages has traditionally shunned the depiction of inner reality as pure art, for its own sake, detached from religious faith and social purpose. Hebrew writers from the Talmudic age were antagonistic towards the high Greek value attached to aesthetics, and tended to deny Hellenistic influence on Jewish culture.[40] Agnon could be considered a rebel, like other Hebrew writers, notably Tchernichowsky, in his aesthetic aims, insofar as these involved an outlook and standard associated with the non-Jewish world.[41] As we shall see in Chapter 3, among Agnon's main literary influences was Flaubert who struggled, virtually with every word, to get the effect he wanted.

Yet Hebrew at the time of Agnon's birth in 1887 had only a limited range. It was just starting to revive as a native spoken language, in the land of Israel and Eastern Europe. It had survived from the ancient world chiefly as the language of religious texts dominating Jewish life. Modern Hebrew was promoted by the Haskalah movement, with its educational program seeking to bring the European Jews into the modern world.[42] The Haskalah attracted only a small progressive minority, prepared to risk opprobrium and ostracism at the hands of the Orthodox majority and their rabbinic leaders. Hebrew fiction was, at first, largely confined to a small elite of devotees, mostly men with a strong Jewish religious education, who became heretics in the act of seeking a secular education. Agnon's readers often studied him with the devotion and intellectual fervor of lapsed rabbinic students. In Agnon's lifetime, the Hebrew language and literature underwent a transformation unique in cultural history: vernacular Hebrew became the everyday language of the Jewish community in the land of Israel; and Hebrew literature grew in sophistication. The Hebrew reader, once familiar with Agnon's distinctive style, its elegance and intellectual pressure, its allusiveness and tonal ambiguities, will recognize his voice instantly.

Agnon's literary persona has been subject to much critical discussion and debate. He gave the impression of being free and unorthodox in his thinking. Like other modernists of his generation, such as Franz Kafka and T.S. Eliot, Agnon was drawn not just to tradition but also to all that undermined tradition. Yet, Agnon was a practising Jew, presenting himself in his stories as an arch-conservative, quaintly naïve and idealistic, a wise spokesman for Jewish observance, for conformity, belief, and fulfillment of duty, and looking askance at the modern world.[43] Agnon is no more the naïve and pious teller of tales than the poet Robert Frost is the sensible, good-natured Farmer Brown. Both men were, in fact, highly sophisticated, and could be at times malicious, egocentric, and guilt-ridden, and both were hungry for success and fame. Like Frost, Agnon was a consummate performer who wore many masks and delighted in his 'uncatchability', as Frost called it.[44]

Rejection of influence

Agnon changed the Hebrew literary world with his *avant-garde* fiction, particularly the surreal collection, *The Book of Deeds* (*Sefer Ha-Ma'asim*, 1932–1951). Yet, he insisted that Jerusalem was his true spiritual home, his main influences the classic Jewish religious texts rooted in the land of Israel: the Bible, Talmud, Midrash, Rashi's commentary on the Torah, the later commentaries on the Talmud, and also the great medieval Hebrew poets and rabbis, especially Maimonides.[45] Agnon went so far as to suggest that his main works were not his novels or short stories but his anthologies on the High Holy Days and the giving of the Torah at Sinai.[46] Asked about the volumes of Kafka in his library, he said they were his wife's.[47] He was generally reluctant to acknowledge fully the influence of other European writers, even Flaubert whom as a young man he had virtually idolized for his striving after artistic perfection.[48] One might think Agnon had trained as a rabbi and was sidetracked into literature – only by a miracle had his pure rabbinic soul remained unsullied.

The present study highlights comparative elements in Agnon, showing how close he is to some of the great European writers of the 19th and early-20th centuries. In some cases, notably the writings of Gustav Flaubert and Franz Kafka, the similarities in Agnon are so extensive as to suggest profound influence, which Agnon, notoriously, did not like to acknowledge; this refusal is not out of keeping with the history of the Hebrew language. From its ancient origins to the present, Hebrew steals and borrows promiscuously. The biblical prophets and Talmudic rabbis warn against foreign influences; yet, these influences helped make Hebrew rich and expressive. Though rooted in the land of Israel, Hebrew is also part of the culture of the Fertile Crescent, the 'cradle of civilization', abundantly fertile and enriched by cross-fertilization of its rich cultures and linguistic heritages. Hebrew was enriched further, later, in the Jewish diaspora, by the Graeco-Roman empire, medieval Arabic civilization, and the European nations and empires to modern times. For all the wealth of these influences, Jewish religious culture traditionally presents itself as *sui generis*, a culture apart for a people apart, so that, for example, the clear links between the Epic of Gilgamesh and the book of Genesis, or those between Egyptian love poetry and wisdom literature and the Song of Songs and the book of Proverbs, are unacknowledged (and in any case are forgotten with time); rabbinic Judaism, which has thousands of Greek loan words, does not admit its debt to Hellenistic civilization, to Roman law, or to the Stoic tradition; and medieval Hebrew poets adapt Arabic poetics into a rabbinic world view while asserting a viable creative Judaism within a dominant Muslim world, and continuing the notion of Hebrew, and Judaism as a whole, developed purely within the boundaries of its independent, uniquely sacred culture. As monotheisms deriving from Judaism, both Christianity and Islam were influenced by Judaism in their refusal to acknowledge fully, if at all, the Jewish influence on their faith. In denying the influence of others, Agnon, in short, was in good company.

Only in post-1789 Jewish culture is there increasing awareness, acknowledgement, and welcome of external influences, especially of German *Kultur*, and an unprecedented belief that non-Jewish cultures might in some respects be more advanced than Jewish culture, and worthy of study.

Agnon had linguistic mastery of all the main forms of Hebrew prose style, from ancient to modern times, and throughout his life retained pride at writing in the Holy Tongue, though in a style all his own, 'cast in bronze', as Bialik put it.[49] Yet, European influences, both traditional and modernistic, were decisive in his writing, which might be characterized as traditional in style but modern, even revolutionary, in outlook and content.

Europe as vampire

The modern world forced itself painfully on Agnon, especially in the two world wars, when the world of the East European Jewish *shtetl*, his main subject, was destroyed; Jewish nationalism spread, and the State of Israel struggled into existence from British Mandatory rule. During the Holocaust, Agnon was in Jerusalem when news of the fate of the European Jews reached the free world. The Jewish communities in the Middle East and North Africa faced extermination if the Allies lost the war. At this time, Agnon wrote 'The Lady and the Pedlar' (*Ha-Adonit veha-Rokhel*, 1943), a bitter allegory of Jewish existence as it seemed to him then.[50] This story, which may have had its germination in Agnon's stay in Germany (1913–24), tells of a meek Jewish pedlar, Joseph, who wanders the isolated villages and forests of Eastern Europe, barely surviving. Caught in fierce winter storms, he is given shelter by Helena, a mysterious Gentile woman living alone in an isolated cottage in the woods, who hires him to do odd jobs. At first, she lets him sleep in the chilly, windswept barn, then among the junk in the house downstairs, and finally she takes him upstairs, into her bed, and they live together as husband and wife. Living with her, he gets used to his new life, gives up his Jewish customs, and hardly thinks of himself as a Jew any longer. But ominous hints slowly reveal the truth: Helena has had several husbands, all dead, and she has slaughtered them and drunk their blood – and she is sharpening her knife to slaughter him too. In despair, the pedlar goes out into the icy fields to pray. He returns to find the lady dying of self-inflicted knife wounds: momentarily losing her sacrificial victim, she has turned suicidally on herself. Astonishingly, the pedlar remains loyal to her. In her death-throes, a scene reversing the anti-Semitic image of the Jewish vampire, he lets her suck his blood. Then the pedlar, after disposing of the corpse, goes on his wandering way as though nothing has changed, marked for all we know for similar horrors in future.

The traumatic circumstances in which Agnon wrote this story accounts in part for its dark pessimism; yet, Agnon is, in fact, following earlier writers such as Peretz Smolenskin, in viewing Jewish history in the diaspora as a series of disasters and homicidal bed-mates. There is a cyclical pattern of imagined acceptance – notably in Germany, which Agnon evidently had chiefly in mind, where many assimilated Jews nurtured an illusory 'German-Jewish symbiosis' – ending in outbursts of pathological anti-Jewish violence, often on the part of erstwhile friends, acquaintances, and neighbors, even lovers.[51] At the same time, the subject of marital breakdown involving not physical violence but mental cruelty runs through Agnon's stories from '*Agunot*', the story from which he took the name 'Agnon', written at age twenty, until the novel *Shira*, unfinished at the time of his death.

Agnon evokes the richness and tragedy of Jewish life in its full historical perspective, with tales of anguished personal relationships resonant with national experience. In some stories, Agnon presents his characters as allegorical representations of conflict between the communal Jewish religious ideal and the individual artistic drive. The synthesis of personal and national grief is especially poignant in *Iddo and Enam* (1950), in which a love triangle recalls the tensions in Jewish spiritual identity, in the contrasting forms of love, traditional and modern, for a *Shekhinah*-like ideal, and the threat to Jewish survival if the wounded identity of the nation is unhealed. But the sense of spiritual conflict between tradition and individual creativity is present from the start of Agnon's career, in '*Agunot*'.

Agnon, Agunot

In '*Agunot*', the story of the betrayal of love and tradition is allegorized in the pseudo-midrashic opening, in which a 'hindrance' ruins the wholeness of the God-woven prayer shawl (Agnon's quest for wholeness, recurrent in his stories, is discussed in Chapter 7, in comparison with the writings of Jung). Agnon draws on familiar midrashic and kabbalistic imagery from the Song of Songs in portraying Israel as a bride beloved of God the Father. The shawl, created from the good deeds of Israel, adorns her in exile as in her Father's house, the Temple in Jerusalem. When the lover in the Song of Songs whispers, 'Behold thou art fair, my beloved, behold thou art fair', all Jews feel the love commanded in the Bible, for God, Israel, and all humankind.

> It is said: A thread of grace is spun and drawn out of the deeds of Israel, and the Holy One, blessed be He, Himself, in His glory, sits and weaves – strand on strand – a prayer shawl all grace and mercy, for the Congegation of Israel to deck herself in. Radiant in the light of her beauty she glows, even in these, the lands of her exile, as she did in her youth in her Father's house, in the Temple of

> her Sovereign and the city of sovereignty, Jerusalem. And when He, of ineffable Name, sees her, that she has been neither sullied nor stained even here, in the realm of her oppressors, He – as it were – leans towards her and says, 'Behold thou art fair, my beloved , behold thou art fair.' And this is the secret of the power and the glory which fills the heart of every man in Israel.[52]

The prayer shawl is the image of perfection, but at times a fault occurs and a thread breaks in the loom:

> Then the prayer shawl is damaged: evil spirits hover about it, enter into it, and tear it to shreds. At once a sense of shame assails all Israel, and they know they are naked. Their days of rest are wrested from them, their feasts are fasts, their lot is dust instead of luster. At that hour the Congregation of Israel strays abroad in her anguish, crying, 'Strike me, wound me, take away my veils from me!' Her beloved has slipped away, and she, seeking him, cries, 'If ye find my beloved, what shall ye tell him? That I am afflicted with love.'[53]

'*Agunot*' portrays heresy and disillusionment, but it draws on the richness of midrashic tradition and affirms the values of Judaism. In his use of midrash to portray contemporary experience, Agnon followed the lead of Mendele and Bialik, as we shall see in Chapter 2. Some in Agnon's generation felt strongly that the thread of tradition, though broken, could be mended through the building of Eretz Yisrael. Agnon's writings represent a summing up of the value of Hebrew through the ages and its capacity to function both as a Holy Tongue and also as a language of a modern secular state.

To the child in Agnon's fiction, Hebrew has the power to redeem the Jews from exile. The child in the story 'The Kerchief' (*Ha-Mitpahat*, 1932) associates a local beggar with the Messiah, as in the Talmud (*Sanhedrin* 98a), and imagines him in waiting to redeem the Jews. The image of the beggar-Messiah is parallel to the image of Hebrew itself prior to the 20th century – impoverished but capable of uniting and elevating a downtrodden people:

> Yesterday he sat unrecognized among the poor, and some treated him despicably. Then the Holy One, blessed be He, suddenly recalled his oath to redeem Israel and gave him permission to appear in the world.[54]

The hope for messianic redemption is linked with maternal love as the child gives her shawl to the beggar – the Messiah in his midrashic imagination.

Agnon spells out further the meaning of the mystical garment of divine grace and spiritual breakdown, in language deriving from kabbalistic sources and the Song of Songs, in his novel of the Second Aliyah, *Yesteryear*:

> This generation, distant from its ancient tradition, finds itself naked and, having created nothing new, tries to cover itself with a garment left by previous generations; it does not see that their ancestors had kept the garment like new,

> protecting it from moths and dust, so that it warmed the wearers in the cold and hid them from parching heat. But the sons did not protect it from moths or shake the dust off it.[55]

Agnon's writings are conflicted in head and heart, intellect and emotion: is Judaism best served as a rational-legal way of life or is it most authentic as an expression of emotion and faith? Agnon's characters are often torn between what they understand rationally to be true and the vagaries of emotion and imagination. In *Betrothed*, for example, the Jaffa-based marine biologist, Jacob Rechnitz knows his childhood oath of betrothal in pre-1914 Vienna to Susan, a consul's daughter, has no rational basis. Nevertheless, in dream and fantasy this oath has a powerful hold on him, directing his thoughts and actions. In a similar way, the ancient 'betrothal' of Israel to God has no rational validity, but has had the most profound influence on Judaism and Jewish history – and, by extension, on the monotheisms which emerged from Judaism: many Christians, for example, have felt themselves to be 'betrothed' to God in faith (this idea is found also in Sufism); and the crisis of faith in modern Christianity has similarly been felt at times as a kind of marital breakdown or divorce.

Triangles and divorce

The triangular, unresolved attachment of Agnon's characters to tradition and spiritual ideals on the one hand, and to art and secular values on the other, is paralleled by their relentless attraction to love triangles: here, too, they are almost always outsiders, *agunot*, waiting pathetically 'at the handles of the lock' – a phrase from the Song of Songs used by Agnon repeatedly in his works and also as the title of his love stories.[56] Agnon uses the word *agunot* not in its traditional meaning[57] but, already in his story '*Agunot*', in the sense of wandering souls, unwhole, unfulfilled, searching futilely for their true mate. Set in pre-modern Jerusalem, '*Agunot*' tells of the wealthy Ahiezer who betrothes his daughter, Dinah, to a great Eastern European scholar, Ezekiel, and builds a house of prayer for him. He commissions the artist Ben Uri to carve the Holy Ark. Dinah, secretly watching Ben Uri, is captivated by him and he is secretly inspired by her in his art. In the end, Dinah marries Ezekiel but the marriage fails and all the characters in the story remain in a state of *agunot* – this sets the pattern for Agnon's later stories telling of relationships between men and women. Ezekiel, the epitome of traditional halakhic Judaism, and Ben Uri, whose art is perhaps more an expression of sexual longing for Dinah than of the love of God, represent two conflicting forces in Agnon's stories.

Agnon's later portrayals of marital breakdown take on increasingly sadomasochistic elements, culminating in the mid- and late-1930s, in the novel *A Simple Story* (*Sippur Pashut*, 1935) and the story, 'The Doctor's Divorce' (*Ha-Rofe u-Grushato*, 1941): at this time, Agnon and his wife reportedly had severe marital difficulties.[58] In *A Simple Story*, Hirshl's suppressed rage at his wife, Mina, appears to follow from his troubled relationship with his mother, who manipulates him into this marriage at a time when he becomes attached to his ill-fated cousin, Blume Nacht. Mina senses his anger and accuses him of wanting her death:

> 'Why should I want you to die?'
> 'For no reason.'
> 'If for no reason, no man wants his wife to die.'
> 'This applies only if the man loves her.'
> 'And if he doesn't love her, he wants her to die?'
> 'That's just it, darling.'[59]

'The Doctor's Divorce' continues this exploration of suppressed rage as a threat to a marriage in the story of a Viennese doctor who falls in love with a nurse in the hospital where he works. His marriage proposal, glib and ominous, follows the cruel death of his professor in a concentration camp:

> One day the trooper ordered him to lie prone, arms and legs outstretched, and instantly to jump up. As he was slow, the trooper kicked at him with his hobnailed boots, mangling the old man's thumbnails. He died of blood poisoning. What more can I say? I liked this girl, like everyone else, and she liked me, but unlike the others who did not dare I dared, and I married her.[60]

The doctor's abuse of his wife, ostensibly as she has had a lover beforehand, with whom he becomes obsessed, leads to divorce.[61] In writing of troubled relationships, Agnon often echoes theological sources in Jewish literature, in the Bible, and rabbinic literature, in which the marriage of God and Israel breaks down – but always with hope of reconciliation and renewed love. In the book of the 8th century BCE prophet, Hosea, for example, the prophet marries a prostitute and is tormented by her unfaithfulness; but in his prophetic mission to Israel, it is the nation that has been unfaithful to God, and it is the nation that repents and returns to God in a renewal of the covenant. Similarly, in the private realm, the prophet's wife returns to him with renewed love.

This hope of return, rare in Agnon, glimmers in some stories, notably 'Metamorphosis' (*Panim Aherot*, 1933). This story, written at the start of the Hitler era, takes on rich allegorical implications in light of the unrequited love motif in interwar German-Jewish literature,[62] and the remarkable re-discovery of Judaism and Jewish literature by the persecuted German Jews after 1933. The story opens with a divorced couple, Michael and Toni Hartmann, emerging from the *beth din* of an unnamed German town and, walking into the countryside, they begin to rediscover their feeling for each other. As their intimacy grows, Hartmann begins to see himself, his cold egotism and obsession with work – perhaps he has made the mistake of his life. He tells Toni a dream of his: a friend takes him to see a rented apartment. It has no stove, except in the bedroom, and the study is made of glass. The friend asks, 'Do you want a place to live, or an observatory to watch the frozen birds?' The coldness here, and the stove, as in Thomas Hardy's poem, 'The Frozen Greenhouse', point to emotional coldness:

'There was a frost
Last night!' she said.
'And the stove was forgot
When we went to bed,
And the greenhouse plants
Are frozen dead!'[63]

'Metamorphosis' ends in irresolution, but Agnon reveals in the later work, *A Guest for the Night* (*Oreah Nata la-Lun*, 1939), that the divorced couple are now reconciled.[64] And indeed, the classic hope in Judaism, of reconciliation between God and Israel and the return from exile to Eretz Yisrael, is realized at the end of *A Guest for the Night*, when the semi-biographical writer-narrator returns from the ruin of his birthplace to his only true home, Jerusalem.

Four empires

Prominent among the creative contradictions which formed Agnon as an artist is his small-town origin in the Austro-Hungarian empire and his attraction to the wider world in which, until the 1914–1918 war, the imperial system dominated. At the time of Agnon's birth in 1887, the eastern part of the empire had only recently been linked by rail to the great European centers, Vienna above all. In 1908, Agnon left one empire for another, the Ottoman, which ruled the eastern Mediterranean, including Palestine, where modern Hebrew was starting to thrive and the young writer reached artistic maturity. In 1912, Agnon again left one empire for another, this time imperial Germany, where he struggled through the war years and, after, in the Weimar Republic. Finally, in 1924, Agnon moved to a fourth empire by returning to Palestine, now under the British Mandate; and from 1948–1970, lived as an Israeli in Jerusalem. In each of these stages, Agnon's style developed, adapting the cultural richness of a new environment to his own individual creative vision.

The settings of Agnon's stories are chiefly those he knew: Buczacz in *A Simple Story*, c. 1905, and *A Guest for the Night*, based on Agnon's return to his hometown in 1930;[65] Ottoman Palestine, where he wrote '*Agunot*', and recalled some thirty years later in *Yesteryear* and *Betrothed*; Germany, portrayed in *Thus Far* (*Ad Hena*) and *In the Shop of Mr. Lublin*, and stories such as 'Metamorphosis', 'The Doctor's Divorce', and 'Fernheim'; and Jerusalem before and after the creation of the state of Israel, in *Shira*, 'Tehilla', and *Iddo and Enam*.

Agnon once remarked that individual stories should be seen in the context of the entire output – as in the Talmud, 'words of Torah poor in one place are rich elsewhere'.[66] However varied the historical and cultural milieu, and however much Agnon's characters differ superficially, they are remarkably similar in psychological make-up and behavior.[67]

Though Agnon lived through some of the crucial events of modern European history, his main subject remained the small town of his birth. He appreciated Flaubert in particular for showing in works such as *Madame Bovary* and *Sentimental Education* that small-town life could be, improbably, the subject of great art.[68]

Roots

Agnon's roots and upbringing explain some of the contradictions of his life and art. Agnon was the pseudonym of Samuel Joseph Czaczkes, born into a family of furriers in the Galician town of Buczacz, then under Austro-Hungarian rule and therefore part of a community of Jews emancipated with the unification of the empire in 1867. In considering Agnon's close links to Kafka, in Chapter 1, it should be borne in mind that, as mentioned earlier, both had ancestral roots in Eastern European Jewry, and both belonged to a generation that had been emancipated but continued to experience anti-Semitic prejudice. Agnon's father and maternal grandfather, both fine rabbinical scholars, had high hopes, later disappointed, that he would follow in the footsteps of distinguished rabbinic ancestors. Agnon, in stories peppered with heresy, portrays the emotionally wrenching experience of the critical and sorrowful gaze of these exemplars of tradition: he is inclined, consequently, to portray himself (or his authorial image) as a naïve, pious teller of tales rather than the sophisticated artist he is. Agnon's grandfather, a hard, puritanical figure, appears in various dream-like stories as the embodiment of religious ideals, stirring up the narrator's guilt at being a traitor to his roots. In one such story, 'The Candles' (*Ha-Nerot*, 1932), the grandfather casts a shadow of disapproval over the narrator's literary endeavors. The narrator finds himself in a house crowded with people, including his grandfather. Though the table is set for the Sabbath, a bookseller persists in selling books written in the language of Jewish heretics – the Samaritans. Leafing through the books, the narrator finds, to his astonishment, that he himself is the author. The grandfather's bearing is a comment on his 'heresy':

> My grandfather stood silently on the side. His black skullcap rested on the middle of his head. An other-worldly sadness dwelt upon him. White fringes of his hair curled over his sunken cheeks like silver bells whose tones are held within.[69]

Agnon's first taste of 'heretical' secular literature might have come from his mother, Esther Czaczkes. Like many Orthodox Jewish girls from well-to-do families in Eastern Europe, she had been allowed to read the European classics which the men, for religious reasons, were forbidden to read. Afflicted with a heart condition, she was particularly close to her son, the eldest of five children, and he grew up with a strong sense of responsibility toward her. The intimate, troubled bond between mother and son – a major theme in Agnon's fiction – was tightened as the father was often away on business. Agnon claimed to have written his first poetry at the age of seven because his father was away.[70] Agnon's father did not mind his son writing poetry – he too wrote verse. But when Agnon decided during his adolescence to become a professional writer, the family was shocked. This was seen as the first stage on the road to heresy. But it was too late to stop him: his poems and short stories, mostly in Yiddish, had already begun to appear in the local Jewish press.[71]

In 1908, as his mother's illness worsened, Agnon was forced to leave home to evade conscription into the Austro-Hungarian army. He chose to go to Palestine, and he never saw his mother again: she died the following year in her early forties.[72] He spent the years 1908–12 mostly in Jaffa and Jerusalem, leading a semi-bohemian life, working for local organizations and writing Hebrew stories exploring his new life and his often-devastating grief for his mother, compounded by guilt at having left her in her final illness. Chapter 4 explores the effects of grief on creativity, in comparing Agnon and D.H. Lawrence, who also emerged as a mature artist in a time of grief for the lost mother.

In a society in which vernacular Hebrew, however awkwardly, was rapidly being adapted to daily life, Agnon's Hebrew style became psychologically richer and linguistically more expressive. His stories, notably '*Agunot*', from which he took his pseudonym, and the novella, *And the Crooked Shall be Made Straight* (*Ve-Haya he-Akov le-Mishor*, 1912), established his distinctive artistic voice, drawing on the full gamut of the Jewish literary tradition but open to modern influences. During this period, Agnon remained linked to Orthodoxy and admired the mystic Zionist, Rabbi Abraham Isaac Kook, who was in turn deeply impressed by his stories; but his best friend was the Hebrew novelist, J.H. Brenner, a brooding, impetuous, big-hearted Russian socialist, alienated from Judaism but devoted to the struggling, impoverished Jewish community in the land of Israel.

Mother image

A salient feature of Agnon's major works is the hero's inability to rid himself of the maternal presence in his involvements with women.[73] The mother is still alive within him, arousing his dependence and rage. In his attachments to women, he is governed by emotions and attitudes other than sexual desire. He might be drawn to a woman because of her baking, or out of sympathy for her, fears for her health, the desire to free her from shame, or because of a childhood oath, or a certain dominance on her part to which his passive nature submits, or perhaps because he associates her with religious purity. The Agnon hero tends to be attracted to a woman not for her own sake but because of the infiltration of the mother's image, a cause of sexual inhibition and paralyzed anger.

The fullest portrait of the Agnon hero, the causes and disastrous effects of his incestuous ties, is found in *A Simple Story*, first published in 1935, and set in early 20th century Buczacz. This novel, Agnon's most remarkable psychological study, clarifies many of his other works. The hero, sixteen-year-old Hirshl Horowitz, is first attracted to Blume Nacht, his orphaned cousin who lives with his family, by her baking. Her cakes remind him of his mother, Tzirl, who, for her part, is alarmed at the idea of his being in love with a girl without money or social status. Tzirl wants him to marry Mina, whose father is a wealthy merchant. Hirshl remains passive, clinging to the impossible hope that Blume will stand up to his mother, take the initiative that he should take, and be the active partner as his mother has been. Blume does not comply. Both he and Blume are deeply frustrated and angry, but they do not tell one another. Hirshl idealizes Blume as a kind of asexual mother figure forbidden to him (as suggested in her name, similar to the Hebrew *balum*, 'closed'). His idealization might indicate the way he would like to see his mother, without ambivalence: in thinking of her in this way, he keeps a firmer grip on his sanity. Mina, who later becomes the target for his suppressed violence, is the one to whom his darker feelings toward his mother are expressed.

The narrator of *A Simple Story* links Hirshl's passivity with Blume with the fact that his mother has never given him love which encourages independence. Tzirl has failed, Agnon shows with great subtlety and understanding, to respond to her son's emotional needs, much as her own emotional needs have been suppressed in her marriage to a man she does not love. Entrenched in bourgeois existence, she values possessions and status, what is 'seemly' (as Mina's family name, 'Tzimlich', suggests) – not what is best for Hirshl or what he would, ideally, want. As she has not loved her son, he remains dependent on her, and she can handle him virtually like a piece of wax, eventually manipulating him into marrying Mina.

The marriage is a disaster at first. Hirshl, tormented by suppressed rage at his mother, displaces it, as we have seen, on to Mina, then in madness turns it against himself. Agnon's portrayal of Hirshl's madness, with his nightmarish fantasies of being a sacrificial rooster, has remarkable parallels with Mendele's depiction of madness in his Yiddish and Hebrew novel, *The Mare*: the similarities are discussed in detail in Chapter 5.

Mendele

When Agnon began writing in the early years of the 20th century, Mendele was the preeminent Hebrew writer, and his influence on Agnon is clear.[74] This influence was not confined to style and narrative technique alone, but includes sharp historical insight and social criticism as well as psychological elements commonly put down to the impact of Freud or Kafka.[75] Mendele's works prepared the ground not only for *The Bridal Canopy* but also, to some extent, for *The Book of Deeds* and *A Simple Story*, works which might appear superficially a radical point of departure from anything written in Hebrew previously.

Though a number of largely forgotten 19th-century writers were instrumental in the evolution of modern Hebrew, Mendele was Agnon's chief model of literary excellence. Hebrew is not the spoken language of most of Agnon's characters, but he creates the illusion that it is – this he learned from Mendele, as was his use of biblical and rabbinic sources to create a new, distinctive style. The historian of modern Hebrew fiction, Gershon Shaked, rightly puts Mendele on a higher plane than Agnon in this regard: 'No Hebrew writer is more original [than Mendele] in the use of the riches of the Hebrew language'.[76] At the heart of both writers is satire of the Jewish town, Mendele's Kesalon (Foolstown) and Agnon's Shibush (Corruption).[77] The nature of Mendele's early influence on the young Agnon is seen in the picaresque heroes of Mendele's *The Travels of Benjamin the Third* (*Mas'aot Binyamin ha-Shlishi*) and Agnon's *The Bridal Canopy*. Cervantes' comic spirit in *Don Quixote* infuses both. Agnon's Reb Yudel in *The Bridal Canopy* is a more ambitious version of Mendele's Benjamin the Third: two *shtetl* characters, *luftmenschen* who abandon their families and set out on a comic, eventful quest through the villages of eastern Europe. Both are beggars on a quest, Reb Yudel to collect charity for dowries for his three unmarried daughters (*hakhnasat kalla*), Benjamin in search of the *aggadic* Ten Lost Tribes of Israel. In the countryside beyond his village on the day he starts his travels, Reb Yudel, overcome by the beauty of God's world, cannot help but sing:

> When he finished his prayers he stretched his legs out one on top of the other, looked at the world around him and began to sing *Adon Olam*, nodding his head to the passers-by, the circumcised and the uncircumcised alike, wondering at the great light that the Lord blessed be He, had spread out and adorned the world in His kindness.[78]

This moment is virtually lifted from Mendele's *Travels*: on the morning Benjamin leaves Batlon, he, too, overwhelmed by the world of nature, breaks into song:

> Benjamin was so happy that his lips opened of their own accord – and the poem *Melekh Elyon* came from his throat in a fine trill. His joyous soul blended with the chirping of the birds and crickets and the hum of flies, and rose loudly, a song to the King of Glory in the highest heaven.[79]

Mendele's frequent 'Judaization' of the natural world in the *Travels* – storks are like women at the *mikveh* (ritual bath) dipping modestly into the water, a horse and team of oxen naturally say the *birkat ha-mazon* (grace after meals), and so on[80] – is echoed by Agnon, for example in 'The Legend of the Scribe' (*Aggadat ha-Sofer*, 1919): 'The bird leaving for the land of Israel in *Parashat Ki Tavo* [i.e. the autumn] returns at Passover to hear the Song of Songs'.[81]

Mendele's portrayal of East European Jewish types, their way of life, beliefs and superstitions, legends and folklore, his brilliant adaptation of Hebrew idiom to portray an entire world uniquely his own, his use of satire, irony, and ambivalence, the mixture of mockery and empathy, the importance of memory, both collective and individual, of dreams and nightmares, superstition and folklore, the sensitivity for childhood and the theme of lost innocence, the disillusionment and psychological complexity in his writings, all permeate Agnon's style. Mendele frequently struggles with emotional confusion. In his memoir, *Of Bygone Days* (*Ba-Yamim ha-Hem*), he recalls that after his father's death, he returned home for the High Holy Days to find his father's seat in synagogue has been sold. Struggling to rejoice in the festival, he feels despair, a double-facedness; this image has many parallels in Agnon:

> A strange face, laughing and furious, like a wafer smeared with honey and vinegar, a sunbeam fighting to break through dark clouds and mists in the rain season.[82]

Mendele set the artistic standard for Agnon's satiric, pseudo-rabbinic depiction of a quixotic Jew, and for his use of the persona of an Orthodox Jew. For Mendele, the pious bookseller, is also a persona, a 'traveller disguised', a sophisticated, deeply divided artist: '[Mendele's] beard, sidelocks, and old-fashioned gaberdine are a mask'.[83] Many other features of Agnon's writings show that 'he too had studied in Mendele's school', as Bialik put it.[84] In some cases, the similarities between the two writers may be owing less to Agnon's reading of Mendele as to the shared influence of traditional or secular sources, or to coincidence. Both populate their stories with cripples and misfits, outsiders, and the emotionally disturbed. 'The extent to which life is not whole and pleasant' – writes Mendele in the 'Introduction' to *Of Bygone Days* – 'that, in the end, is the essence of reality.'[85] Most of Agnon's protagonists are *agunot*, in the distinctive sense in which Agnon uses the word – souls doomed in their search for wholeness and fulfilment, anchored to their emotional infirmity. In '*Agunot*', images such as the wandering souls or the broken thread, symbolizing human discord, trauma, and alienation, have parallels in Mendele.

Other elements in Agnon are foreshadowed by Mendele. There is, for example, Mendele's extraordinary analogy in a Hebrew story of 1894 between the urge to emigrate to the land of Israel and the urge of a rabid dog to bite:

> Pestilence afflicts not only men's bodies but sometimes also their souls. Some are plagued like mad dogs, God protect us – foaming at the mouth, stinking, full of fury, burning to bite... Some lose their minds. They see things upside down, they change good for evil, light for darkness, white for black... This plague, which the Lord, blessed be He, brought upon us, drove us, in a relentless, extraordinary way. It made our imagination fly off, like an arrow from a bow, until it seemed a trifle to cross the sea, no harder than lifting a hair out of milk.[86]

Mendele's portrayal here of the emotional impact of the Russian pogroms of 1881 and the panic-stricken wave of emigration to Palestine which followed, encapsulates Agnon's nihilistic account of the Zionist dream over a half-century later, in *Yesteryear*, culminating in death from the bite of a rabid dog. Similarly, in Mendele's novel, *In the Valley of Tears* (*Be-Emek ha-Bakha*), the comparison between a longed-for father and the messiah in the mind of an anxious child looks forward to Agnon's story, 'The Kerchief' (*Ha-Mitpahat*, 1932): 'Hirshl imagined all the Kislonites waiting for his father, as if for the messiah.'[87]

Germany

After his father's death in Galicia in 1913, Agnon settled in Germany and stayed there until 1924.[88] His writings on this period, particularly the novella *Thus Far*, portray a shiftless and confused life in wartime, an abandonment of Orthodoxy, and affairs with Gentile women, recounted with relish and guilt. Agnon met Martin Buber and Gershom Scholem, who remained friends and supporters for the next 50 years, and Salman Schocken who became his publisher, encouraging him to keep writing by paying him a regular salary.[89] As German anti-Semitism spread during and after the war, and nationalistic German sympathizers such as Buber became disillusioned with the ideal of a German-Jewish 'symbiosis', Agnon's fame increased as a symbol of a Jewish culture richer and more ancient, and more authentic to the modern Jewish experience than newfangled European secular cultures inimical to Jews. After Mendele's death in 1917, Agnon was recognized as the leading Hebrew writer of fiction. Translated into German, he was read relatively widely. His literary reputation was established firmly in an outpouring of serious German criticism on his work. Marrying into a prominent German-Jewish family in 1920, he moved to Bad Homburg; by 1922 he had two children. In 1924, a fire wrecked his home and, to his lifelong grief, destroyed his large and valuable personal library and many manuscripts, the product of years of work. Agnon saw this catastrophe as an evil omen and, soon after, returned to Palestine, deciding on the way to return to Orthodox Judaism. He confessed on the way in a letter to Schocken that he lacked peace of mind: disillusioned with European culture, he felt he ought to live permanently among Orthodox Jews. A few days later, he made his decision: 'If a man is privileged to live in the Land of Israel, he should observe the mitzvot and continue in the way of his ancestors.'[90] When he arrived in Jerusalem, he went to the Western Wall and wept.[91]

Until his death in 1970, Agnon lived with his family in Jerusalem, dedicated to his art, an inconspicuous Orthodox Jew, short, compact, quizzical, praying three times each day, studying a daily portion of the Talmud, while writing both of the joy of communal observance, of piety and study, and the modern crisis of faith, disillusionment and guilt at betraying tradition. For all Agnon's apparent ambivalence to tradition, no writer has recreated with greater insight the religious life of Eastern European Jews (particularly in the novels *The Bridal Canopy* and *A Guest for the Night*) or, with the possible exceptions of Mendele and Bialik, has made better use of biblical, talmudic, and later rabbinic idiom. (Bialik said that Agnon wrote the way the Hasidim ought to write, if only they knew how.[92]) Some of Agnon's most ardent disciples were convinced that by reading him one virtually fulfilled one's duty to study the Torah. Judging from some of his stories, this was an impression Agnon was aiming at: in the story, 'At the Outset of the Day' (*Im Kenisat ha-Yom*, 1951), the narrator sees an original scroll of his in a synagogue ark alongside of Torah scrolls.[93]

Many scholars and students of Agnon share the admiration expressed by Edmund Wilson who proclaimed Agnon a genius and supported his candidacy for the Nobel Prize for Literature in 1966. They admire his pruned, lucid, inimitable style, his psychological sharpness, his gifts for satire and understatement, his encyclopedic knowledge of traditional Jewish texts and customs, his utter devotion to his art. Yet, as Agnon can be read for his affirmation of the wholeness of Jewish tradition, he can also be read for his evident conviction that life has little or no meaning: it is as though the joyous brilliance of Isaiah's vision of national return were tempered by the grief and misery of Job.

The quest for meaning

In the semi-biographical novella, *Thus Far* (*Ad Hena*), set in Germany during the war of 1914–1918, the narrator, convinced of the futility of his life, tells a parable recalling both the tales of Nachman of Bratslav and Kafka, of a man's quest ending with his discovery of a scroll, and the recounting of his journey:

> Briefly, as there were seven hills one on top of the other, seven caves each inside the other, seven doors, steps, barrels, and boxes, so also there were seven scrolls. He rolled out each in turn and found on the seventh scroll a clear inscription: 'Fool! What have you put here that you're searching for?'[94]

Agnon's world is filled with a sense of emptiness, uselessness, coldness, numbness, and futility. His characters often lack the warmth of loving bonds with others that give meaning to life.[95] The emotional torment in Agnon's stories may be attributed in part, not unjustly, to the catastrophic history Agnon witnessed, particularly the effects of World War I and the Holocaust. Like Flaubert, Ibsen, Kafka, and Thomas Mann, among others, Agnon is drawn to imagery of then-incurable illness, such as rabies (*Yesteryear*) or leprosy ('Forevermore', *Shira*), as emblematic specifically of the Jewish condition, and more generally of humanity as a whole. In *Yesteryear*, written during the Nazi era and the Holocaust, Agnon plumbs the depth of despair. The entire final section of the novel is a portrayal of pre-1914 Jerusalem, virtually street by street, through the eyes of a rabid dog. This allegorical representation derives in part from the extraordinary passage in the Mishna depicting the deterioration of Jewish life after the Roman destruction of the Temple in 70 CE: 'The face of this generation is a dog's face'.[96] The despair in Agnon often recalls Kafka.[97] In their writings, too, a childhood sense of weakness, inferiority, and dependence appears to coexist with an uncommon self-centeredness and conviction of superiority. The futility permeating *Yesteryear* and many other works of Agnon, the sense of being cut off from the human race, evidently underlies the parallel longing for the wholeness of tradition. This longing was felt by Kafka, too, with his final jottings in Hebrew before his death in 1924.

Tradition as therapy

Agnon gives his fullest account of tradition as therapy in *A Simple Story*, when Hirshl, having suffered a breakdown in his Galician hometown after marrying a woman he does not love, is treated by a psychiatrist, Dr. Langsam in Lemberg (Lviv). Though, as seen in Chapter 7, Agnon was steeped in the world of psychoanalysis, his conception of tradition does not look kindly on conventional psychiatry and Freudian thought.[98] Langsam never confronts the crux of Hirshl's illness, as a Freudian would do, not once asking about his mother, wife, or the woman who obsesses him. Instead, he spends hours spinning tales of the *shtetl* of his youth, putting the silent Hirshl once again in touch with a world of order and stability in which communal unity can enable one to survive personal maladjustment. This act of healing in passive silence is the essence of Agnon's art: illusory but with the power of reality, an effective salve for the wounded individual life and the scarred collective history.

In Agnon's stories, the grandfather represents the stern face of an intensely pious, puritanical, highly legalistic Judaism associated with 19th-century Lithuanian *mitnagdim*, opponents of the Hasidim. 'Another *Talit*' (*Talit Aheret*, 1943), originally dedicated to Max Eitingon, disciple of Freud in Vienna and founder of the Palestinian Psychoanalytic Society – and Esther Agnon's psychoanalyst – depicts a typical sense of guilt toward the grandfather as representative of tradition. The story opens as the narrator arrives late at his grandfather's house of prayer on Yom Kippur and finds, perhaps as he has hoped, that there is no room. He is upset to see his grandfather's disappointment with him. Outside, the narrator is tempted, by the rabbi's son of all people, to drink on the holy day. Returning indoors, 'again my grandfather looked sorrowfully at me. Did he sense what had happened? I pretended his sorrow had another cause. "You must be unhappy to see me standing here without a *talit*. I shall take this one here and wrap myself in it."'[99] This attempt to pacify the grandfather fails as the *talit* is missing a fringe and cannot be worn. Agnon may be hinting here that the '*talit*' of his art, as portrayed in the imagery opening '*Agunot*', is somehow invalid – as is the damaged Ark in '*Agunot*'.

For all the conflict and guilt roused by the grandfather, he remains a powerful link with the world of wholeness and faith which the narrator seeks to recreate. The grandfather evidently represents the faith of centuries-old mainstream Judaism. It is he, or his memory, or surrogates such as Mr. Klein in the story 'The Letter' (*Ha-Mikhtav*), who can restore the wholeness of a lost world and make the bogus real. 'The Letter', the last story in *The Book of Deeds*, ends with Klein recreating the House of Study of the narrator's childhood and letting him re-enter it:

> He drew six marks with his cane, raising a house like the House of Study. I tried to go in but could not find the door. The old man lifted his cane and knocked twice on the wall. The wall opened and I went in.[100]

Kafka and Agnon

To the dying Kafka yearning for a new life in Palestine, Agnon's portrayal of an authentic Jewish culture was a desired ideal; while to Agnon, Kafka's uncompromisingly tormented vision was a model for his own artistic dedication and ambition: each had what the other sought. Kafka's emotional turmoil, in his fiction as well as in his letters and diaries, particularly in relation to authority and women, has many parallels in Agnon's writings.[101] Kafka's 'marriage' to his art and his difficulties in relationships are, in some ways, similar to Agnon's *agunot*,[102] and often bring to mind the emotional dilemmas portrayed by Agnon: an overriding self-absorption and concern with inner reality, usually expressed in an obsession with work;[103] difficulty in breaking away from childhood and launching out into life, particularly in relations with women; creation of distance from people despite superficial gregariousness, by means of love triangles, detachment of outward behavior from inner feeling; and a chronic sense of unwholeness, guilt, and futility.[104]

These are universal difficulties, but the literary voices with which Kafka and Agnon approach them are unique, in German and Hebrew respectively, using the full resources of language to probe and dissect and reveal coldly and dispassionately the invisible, immeasurable, often-inexpressible suffering which humanity is heir to, individually and in the nightmare of history. In this world of sorrow, Judaism – and, to both writers, Hasidism in particular – is a religion of joy giving release in a collective religious-national identity.[105]

Both Kafka and Agnon portray the fear of loving and being loved on equal terms with women. Whether conscious of it or not, they seem to look for or even create circumstances in which attachments to women must go unrequited or end in failure. In both, there is a quest for distance from the 'beloved', usually through love triangles or through interminable work. Sickness and madness threaten if these methods fail. The very name 'Agnon', as Agnon uses it, refers, as we have seen, to those unfortunate souls, *agunot*; and Kafka, similarly, writes of the allegedly combined personal and social basis of sickness, as 'matters of faith, efforts of souls in distress to find moorings in some maternal soil.'[106]

Kafka shares with Agnon a troubled quest for optimal distance. In a diary entry of February 13, 1913, he tells of a dream he had of being on his way to see his fiancée, Felice Bauer, in Berlin. 'In Berlin, through the streets to her house, calm and happy in the knowledge that, though I haven't arrived at her house yet, a slight possibility of doing so exists; I shall certainly arrive there.'[107] This dream encapsulates the desire, familiar in Agnon, to be in transition toward involvement with a woman without ever quite getting there.[108] In an entry the following day, on February 14, 2013, Kafka contemplates suicide: 'I can't live without her and must jump, yet – and this F. suspects – I couldn't live with her either.'[109] In a letter of July 8, 1913 to Felice, Kafka, tormented by the prospect of marriage, confesses his fears of destroying her:

> Can you not see by now that if disaster – yours, your disaster, Felice – is to be averted, I have to remain locked up within myself… if need be, I can live as I am, my rage turned inward, tormenting only by letter, but as soon as we lived together I would become a dangerous lunatic fit to be burned alive.[110]

And two days later:

> I have a definite feeling that through marriage, *through the union, through the dissolution* of this nothingness that I am, I shall perish, and not alone but with my wife, and that the more I love her the swifter and more terrible it will be.[111]

Engaged to marry Felice in 1914 (the first of four failed engagements, to three women), Kafka began an overly intimate correspondence with her friend, Grete Bloch, unburdening himself of his fears of marriage. Greta, seeing that Kafka was seeking her love, informed Felice, and the engagement fell through, as Kafka had probably hoped.

In its twisted psychological dynamics, Agnon's *A Simple Story* is close in some ways to the world of Kafka. Hirshl Horowitz, in love with his impoverished cousin, Blume Nacht, but manipulated by his mother into a marriage with Mina Tzimlich, is driven mad with suppressed rage and the torment of murderous fantasies toward his wife. Even when he has supposedly recovered, he is not free of thoughts of her death:

> Hirshl thought: if Mina died, Blume might marry me. God forbid that he wanted his wife to die, but what does a widower do if he does not remarry? As he knew no one apart from Blume, he decided on her. If she would not marry him for love, she would out of pity.[112]

Sadistically in Mina's hearing, he calls his son 'my orphan', as though his wish for Mina's death had been fulfilled. When the baby falls sick and is taken away to recuperate with Mina's parents, Hirshl's first genuine desire for Mina is aroused: he takes the child's place in his wife's affections.

Agnon's close acquaintances, such as Dov Sadan and Gershom Scholem, were generally agreed that Agnon's writings constitute the fullest biography of the man.[113] According to Sadan, Agnon despised his own creations: he would have liked to create a totally different type of character, finding to his dismay that he could not escape his troubled creations, projections of his own inner life. Scholem noted Agnon's detachment from others and his loneliness, characteristic of the stories; and the theme of divorce in stories such as 'Metamorphosis' and 'The Doctor's Divorce', had biographical origins in Agnon's marital difficulties.[114] 'The Doctor's Divorce', one of Agnon's most bizarre and troubling stories, is set in post-1918 Vienna; it tells of a doctor besieged on his wedding night by thoughts of his wife's former lover, and although the affair is long past, he persists in tormenting her with this 'sin', filled with inexplicable rage at her. Tormented by guilt, the doctor cannot control his inner violence. When the lover by chance enters his hospital for treatment, the obsession becomes unbearable. The doctor – in a startling echo of Hawthorne's *The Scarlet Letter*, in which Chillingworth, Hester Prynne's former husband, becomes the doctor of Dimmesdale whom he suspects, rightly, of fathering Hester's child – treats the patient with exquisite, malicious care. The patient is totally unaware that his doctor is seething with murderous rage, but the doctor's wife, a nurse in the same hospital, is not so fortunate. His sadism wears her down, and she obtains a divorce.

Marital troubles in Agnon's fiction are occasionally echoed in his wife's letters. For example, when in 1924 he left her and their children in Germany while he went to Palestine, Esther Agnon confessed her doubts that the marriage would last, and suggested that they live apart: 'A life closer together – so I understand your feelings – will bring no good to either of us':[115] he would be better off with someone else.[116] Since their marriage in 1920, she wrote, 'you have not budged from your reservations towards me. In your heart of hearts you still feel yourself to be deprived.'[117] Scholem observed that Agnon, despite his superficial gregariousness, was a deeply lonely man.[118]

Agnon's stories are littered with troubled relationships often resonating with the deteriorating condition of the Europeans Jews in the early-20th century, and with symbols of disturbance and breakdown: the frayed garment, the locked door, the ruined house, the deserted garden. The garden in *Iddo and Enam*, appears to sum up the futility of life: 'the garden and all that was in it, every tree and shrub, seemed detached and unconcerned with its neighbor's affairs.'[119] The temporary shelter – an inn, a rented room, a hotel – is frequently the epitome of individual loneliness and heartbreak and also of the decline of faith, the fragmentation of morality, and the absence of religious wholeness. The extraordinary portrayal of the rabid dog, Balak, the words 'mad dog' painted on his back, in *Yesteryear*, appears as a terrifying vision of impending breakdown:

> At times his eyes were wrapped in a terrible sadness, at times his eyes emptied, at times his heart was crushed, at times his heart was ground, as if he were put in a wood or stone crusher, crushing and grinding, grinding and crushing.[120]

Agnon's failed relationships are set against a background of increasing anti-Semitism, culminating in the Holocaust. It is doubtful if in this grief-stricken world unambiguous love can be felt even for tradition, for the Torah, the land of Israel, or Jerusalem. In his writings, Jewish life in the land of Israel is the main hope for the future. Amid the dark despair at the end of *Yesteryear*, Agnon added a ray of hope – 'The creator of souls allots each soul its share of love. Some souls have their portion of love in life, others after they depart...'[121] – which he later omitted. Moments of grace in his stories celebrate, nevertheless, the splendor of Jewish ritual and learning and the beauty and richness of the Hebrew language. At such moments, Agnon speaks as though from the living heart of Jewish life through the ages.

Notes

1 Agnon in a witty, untranslatable wordplay, acknowledged that modernism had influenced him, however unwillingly: 'Even though I didn't want to be modern, modernism rebels and rules in me' – *ve-afilu eini rotze le-hitmadren ha-moderniyut mitmaredet ve-roda vi* (Agnon 1976: 43). On modernist elements in Agnon's traditional-seeming style, see for example Band (1968), Hochman (1970), Barzel (1975), Aberbach (1984), Shaked (1989), Hoffman (1991), Werses (2000), and Laor (2008).

2 Agnon shared with his intellectual soulmates, Martin Buber and Gershom Scholem, the aim of achievement in the world of secular culture, not just among Jews (as was the case with rabbinic intellectual accomplishment which prior to 1945 had little recognition outside the Jewish world) but also in the non-Jewish world. The growing competitiveness of European Jews after 1789, as a result of their emancipation and the spread of mandatory secular education, was driven by not only by economic factors and strong patriotism, but also by the powerful anti-Semitic reaction to emancipation which sought to preserve medieval anti-Jewish prejudices and disabilities and the belief in the fundamental

and unchanging inferiority of 'the Jewish race'. The 18th- and 19th-century Haskalah (Hebrew Enlightenment) movement fought these pernicious beliefs, but for patriotic motives, to encourage secular education and assimilation. (On the Haskalah, see p. 5f.) Cultural Zionism, in contrast, was a creative Jewish national liberation, enabling scholars such as Scholem, poets such as Bialik, novelists such as Agnon, and philosophers such as Buber to make their mark in the world, particularly in the revelation of Jewish folklore, legend, mysticism, and philosophy as part of a national culture which had grown continuously from biblical to modern times. Their work showed that Jewish culture is comparable to other European cultures, and influenced them, being older and, in some ways, richer and more profound. On Jewish cultural nationalism, see Aberbach (2008a).

3 Agnon's stories, themselves a product of careful study of Jewish life and culture, illustrate the traditional rabbinic view of learning as a value in itself, and also – in stories such as *In the Prime of Her Life* (*Bi-Dmi Yameha*, 1923), *Two Torah Scholars in Our Town* (*Shne Talmidei Hakhamim she-Hayu be-Irenu*, 1946), and *Iddo and Enam* (1950) – how this exclusively religious learning, mostly done for its own sake, could be applied productively to the world of secular learning. These stories also show – in stark contrast with the hagiographic tendency in rabbinic literature – how an excess of learning can be associated with harmful psychopathology. On the sociology of *shtetl* life, see Zborowski and Herzog (1974).

4 Orthodox women from well-to-do families were sometimes allowed to read novels, which was prohibited to men. This was the case with Agnon's mother. See p. 20. The most detailed study of Agnon's major fictional works, with essential biographical background and bibliographic information and discussion of the texts, is that of Band (1968); see also Laor (2008), who has also written the most thorough biographical study so far (1998).

5 Agnon (1974: 184). For parallel fantasies of guilt, in 'The Candles' (*Ha-Nerot*, 1932), and 'Another *Talit*' (*Talit Aheret*, 1943), see pp. 27, 48 in the present volume.

6 *Iddo and Enam* (1950) in Agnon (CW vii 382). On Agnon's use of 'folklore' in his stories, see pp. 2, 7, 8, 23: several of those closest to Agnon, including Bialik, Buber, and Scholem, were engaged, similarly, in transforming an exclusively religious culture into a secular national culture. In *Iddo*, Agnon gives a fictional portrait of Scholem, exploring the paradox of rational academic study of an subject irrational by nature – mysticism, folklore, legend, superstition. A similar paradox is evident also in the use of 'folklore' in creative literature, such as that of Peretz, Agnon, and Buber. Agnon tells of his period in Germany, when he visited Franz Rosenzweig. 'I would be astonished', said the eminent philosopher, 'if [Scholem] does not become a victim [lit. a 'sacrifice'] to the bibliography of kabbalah' (Agnon 1976: 276). Rabbinic literature is clear in its disapproval of those who 'make the Torah a crown for their ambitions, a spade to dig with' (Mishna *Avot* 4: 7). In this traditional perspective, Bialik was evidently at times a greater heretic than Agnon. He reportedly told the eminent Jewish scholar, Shimon Rawidowicz in Berlin in 1923: 'I didn't come to open – but to stop, to seal, to end, to finish *aggadah* off' (Rawidowicz 1983: 67). The poet took a similar view of Hasidic lore (Rawidowicz 1983).

7 On the quest for meaning in Kafka and Agnon, see pp. 26, 137–9; also see p. 77.

8 Agnon (CW vi 200–01).

9 Scholem (1976: 60).

10 Anti-Semitic propaganda in the Austro-Hungarian empire 'had no equal in other European lands in the liberal era, either for quantity or virulence' (Katz 1980: 229). On anti-Semitism in the empire, see Pauley (1992) and Levy (2010). Rabbi Dr. Joseph

Samuel Bloch (1850–1923), elected to the Austrian Parliament in 1883 by an overwhelmingly Jewish constituency in Eastern Galicia (including Kolomea, Buczacz, and Sniatyn), was a lone voice exposing, ridiculing, and denouncing anti-Semitism – and Jewish self-hate (Wistrich 1990). Bloch was a dominant political figure in Agnon's Galician childhood, an Austrian patriot who believed that the future of the Austrian Jews was in Austria, but he was also a realist who saw the limitations of political liberalism and Jewish emancipation. Bloch had much insight into the paradoxes of the Austro-Hungarian empire into which Agnon was born, its superficial tolerance hiding a world of ethnic hatreds. In this world, the Jews, unusually vulnerable ('adoptive children' in Bloch's phrase), were drawn to Zionism. In 1886, Bloch published a pamphlet, *Der Nationale Twist und die Juden in Osterreich* (The Strife of the Nationalities and the Jews in Austria), observing that the Jews, excluded by racial nationalism, especially in nationally mixed territories, were hated all the more as they tried to assimilate among the Germans, Czechs, Poles, or Ruthenians. Neither Germans nor Slavs would admit even the most selfless, self-sacrificing Jews to be their equals despite their chauvinist devotion to the adopted national cause. Bloch argued that the Jews should do more to defend their interests as Jews, elect their own representatives, and not rely on political parties vulnerable to Jew-hatred. To defend Jews against anti-Semites and Jewish self-haters, in 1884 Bloch founded a weekly newspaper, *Osterreichische Wochenschrift*, and in the following year, the *Osterreichische-Israelitische Union*, the first modern Jewish self-defence organization.

11 Roth (2002: 243). Even Austrian Zionists tended to be patriots; and on the outbreak of war in 1914, declared that they were second to none in their 'readiness to sacrifice for Kaiser and Empire' (Rechter 2001: 24). Agnon, a draft-dodger, strongly opposed this kind of patriotism, of Jews fighting for anti-Semitic countries. See pp. 110–11.

12 In *Two Torah Scholars Who Lived in Our Town* (Agnon, CW vi 15). Moses Mendelssohn (1729–1786): German Jewish philosopher, principal founder of the Haskalah, the Jewish Enlightenment, which aimed to encourage secular learning among the Jews, whose education until the 19th century was almost totally religious. Mendelssohn's German translation of the Pentateuch (the *Bi'ur* [Commentary], 1783) was instrumental in the transition from Yiddish to German among the German Jews. Wolf (Benjamin Ze'ev) Heidenheim (1757–1832): German Jewish scholar and translator of Hebrew liturgical texts, including the *siddur* (prayerbook), into German. On secular education among Jewish women in well-to-do Orthodox Jewish families, see pp. 20, 31 note 4; and on the Galician Haskalah, see p. 33 note 26. Agnon in *Two Torah Scholars* subtly builds a picture of Galician society before his birth (his grandfather appears in the story), undergoing slow but inexorable change.

13 Agnon (1976: 340). These reminiscences date from the late-1960s.

14 On Agnon's delight on his arrival in Jerusalem in late-1924 and hearing children speaking Hebrew in the streets, see Agnon (1983: 39). The linguistic diversity of pre-1914 Palestinian Jews was an obstacle to the growth of vernacular Hebrew. Hebrew was accepted as the *de facto* national language after the Zionist Organization was established by Theodor Herzl in 1897. Hebrew was universally read, though rarely spoken at the time, and no other language was possible (though German Zionists pushed for German and French Zionists for French). By the time the British conquered Palestine in 1917–18, Palestinian Jewish teachers and their students had won the battle for Hebrew as the language of instruction in their schools (German and French were commonly used until World War I), and the children spoke Hebrew among themselves. When, in 1918, the foundation of the Hebrew University was laid, there were over

thirty thousand native Hebrew speakers; no-one doubted it would be the first Hebrew-speaking university. On the 'language war' in the pre-1914 Palestinian Jewish community, see Rabin (1979).

15 Brenner (1960: 10–12). For a translation of *Nerves* by Hillel Halkin, see Lelchuk and Shaked (1983).

16 The sociological 'in and out' movements experienced by the young Agnon, in contrast with the relatively stable Orthodoxy of the pre-modern age which he most admired, is mirrored in many of the relationships which Agnon depicts in his stories, notably *Yesteryear* and *Iddo and Enam*. See pp. 40 note 108; 137–8.

17 On Freud's Jewish problem, see Robert (1976) and Aberbach (1980); the latter is reprinted as Appendix 2 below. On Freud's influence on Agnon, see Chapter 7. Generational conflict is a major theme in East European Hebrew literature, notably in the writings of Berdichevsky, Gnessin, Brenner, Bialik, and Feierberg whose novella *Whither?* (*Le'an*, 1899) is the classic example, of a rabbi's son who becomes a heretic.

18 Freud (1976: 572).

19 Freud (1976: 573).

20 On Kafka and Agnon, see pp. 44–8, 138. Though Kafka was uncommitted to Zionism until the end of his life, when he planned to make *aliyah*, he was for many years a serious student of Hebrew and Jewish history and literature, and several of his closest friends, including his literary executor and first biographer, Max Brod, were Zionists.

21 Isherwood (1958: 168).

22 For a brief bibliographic overview of Agnon and Jewish folklore, see Band (1968: 544–45).

23 Agnon (1976: 190). In Jewish dietary laws, a one-sixtieth smidgen of unkosher food (*tref*) is nullified (*batel be-shishim*). Among the *haredim* (ultra-Orthodox Jews), however, this *hekhsher* had little effect; and Agnon is read in Hebrew chiefly by a minority of secular and moderately Orthodox Jews, and he is included in school and university courses on modern Hebrew and/or Jewish literature.

24 Agnon (1976: 192). Similarly, in pre-modern Europe generally, it was hard to imagine a literature in any language whose authors did not know the classics of antiquity, particularly the Bible.

25 Mendele Mokher Sefarim (Mendele the Bookpeddler) was the *nom de plume* of Shalom Ya'akov Abramowitz (1835?–1917); Sholom Aleichem ('How do you do?' in both Yiddish and Hebrew) was the popular name of Shalom Rabinovitz (1859–1916). Both writers were key figures in the development of Yiddish and Hebrew literature, both as popular culture (Sholom Aleichem wrote the Tevye stories, on which the musical *Fiddler on the Roof* is based) and as an increasingly secular Jewish literature which, in Hebrew, became the basis for Israeli culture.

26 Agnon's penchant for satire and social criticism may be traced further back, to the Galician Haskalah of the early-19th century, with its two major Hebrew literary figures, the satirists Joseph Perl (1773–1839) and Isaac Erter (1791–1851) and the social critic Nachman Krochmal (1785–1840). Satire, the most highly developed 19th century Hebrew genre, was directed mostly at the Hasidim (Davidson 1966). The writings of Isaac Leib Peretz marked a change in the image of Hasidim among enlightened Jews in the early 20th century, no longer a laughing-stock but a repository of profound folk wisdom. This trend was continued in German by Martin Buber, in his much-admired reworkings of tales of Nachman of Bratzlav and the Ba'al Shem Tov. Agnon, whose family included both Hasidim and their opponents, *Mitnagdim*, continues the satiric tradition but essentially follows Peretz and Buber (who became a close friend and collaborator) in his sympathy and respect for Hasidism.

27 In particular, the shadow of anti-Semitism falls over *A Guest for the Night*, written in the late-1930s and set in Buczacz shortly before the rise of Hitler. See also 'The Lady and the Pedlar', pp. 14–15 above; and 'At the Outset of the Day', pp. 138–9 below. Agnon's early short stories, 'In the Depths' (*BiMetzulot*, 1917) and 'On the midget, Rabi Gadiel' (*Ma'aseh Rabi Gadiel ha-Tinok*, 1920), depict medieval blood libels.

28 Buczacz at the time of Agnon's birth had a population of about 10,000, of which two-thirds were Jewish. The town is setting for many of Agnon's stories and is the subject of his collection of tales, *Ir uMelo'ah* (A City in its Fullness, 1973). On the phenomenal increase in Hebrew journalism and in Hebrew readers, which may have reached 100,000 already in the 1880s, see Miron (1987: 59ff.). For the first time, Hebrew writers could, in theory, make a living from their writings, and publishers could make substantial profits.

29 Details of Agnon's early reading are sketchy: 'Of the titles of the books Agnon consumed during late childhood and adolescence with such intense and free-ranging curiosity, we know next to nothing' (Mintz 2022: 29). In a speech in honor of the distinguished scholar, Dov Sadan, in 1962, Agnon acknowledged his joy at reading Homer, Cervantes, Balzac, Gogol, Tolstoy, Flaubert, and Hamsun – but not Kafka, the writer with whom Agnon is most often compared, whom he claimed not to have read (apart from 'Metamorphosis') at the time he began writing the experimental stories in *The Book of Deeds* (Agnon 1976: 245). In his esteem for Hasidic tales, Agnon owed much to Peretz and Buber (Agnon 1976: 257f., 262) and also to the stories of Nachman of Bratzlav (Agnon 1976: 42, 366). Agnon was aware of the popularity of Hasidic stories as told and retold by Peretz in Yiddish and Buber in German. He gave his own versions of Hasidic stories an added dimension of authentic tradition, in an unusually aesthetic Hebrew style. Agnon's Hasidic retellings were highly attractive to the increasing number of young early-20th century assimilated Jews who sought to recover in East European Jewish civilization the living creative force of Judaism which they felt they were losing or had lost.

30 Barzilay (1959: 168). Also see Aberbach (2006). The preface to the 1817 *siddur* of the Berlin Reform congregation states that however holy Hebrew had been to the Jews in the past, German was more important now: 'seven times more holy unto us is the language which belongs to the present and to the soil whence we have sprung forth' (Petuchowski 1968: 135).

31 On Agnon's critique of German Jewry in the context of pre-Holocaust German Jewish fiction, see Chapter 6.

32 On Freud's Jewish background, including his knowledge of Hebrew, see Aberbach (2003: 122–8). For points of similarity between Agnon and Freud, see pp. 131–2.

33 M. Freud (1957: 14).

34 '*Wer von uns weiss genug Hebräisch, um in dieser Sprache ein Bahnbillet zu verlangen*?' (Herzl 1896: 75).

35 Elon (1975: 237).

36 Kafka (1978: 56–7). Kafka might be alluding to his own childhood ignorance of Scripture in the story, 'In the Penal Colony', when an unnamed Voyager visiting a penal colony from a foreign country is shown the 'Scripture' of its laws and is inexplicably asked to read it as though it were an easy matter, though he does not know the language. Unlike some modern Jewish writers who seem almost proud of their ignorance of Hebrew, Kafka evidently felt this to be a failing, which he sought to remedy in intensive study of Hebrew which was ongoing at the time of his death.

37 Other Jewish writers with the shared Galician family origins of Agnon and Kafka, in the Austro-Hungarian empire –including writers such as Arthur Miller and Philip Roth – had scant knowledge of Hebrew and tended to write of Jewish identity with little reference

to the wealth of Jewish literary culture of which Agnon is a master. Of the Newark Jews of his childhood in the 1930s and 1940s, Roth wrote in *The Plot Against America*, 'Their being Jews didn't issue from the rabbinate or the synagogue or from their few religious practices... Their being Jews issued from their being themselves' (2004: 220). In Agnon's world of East European piety and learning, a person of such limited knowledge of Jewish tradition would be dismissed as an ignoramus and, worse, a heretic; a Jew empty of Torah had correspondingly lower status. In Agnon's stories set in Germany, however, this is not the case; Agnon's German Jewish characters, such as Fernheim and Michael Hartmann, are not judged by their Jewish learning, of which they evidently have little.

38 In Aschheim (200: 6). Arendt's contemporary, the philosopher and mystic Simone Weil (1909–1943), was even more extreme in her rejection of Hebrew and the entire Jewish tradition. Though educationally outstanding and saintly in her compassion for suffering humanity, Weil had the ignorance of Judaism and the self-hate characteristic of many highly assimilated French Jews prior to and even during the Holocaust. The only admission in her writings of her Jewish origin was in a letter she wrote in Marseilles in 1940 to the Vichy minister of education complaining about the French anti-Jewish laws. Rather than express outrage at France's betrayal of its Jews or compassion for their suffering, Weil protests that she has no connection with Jews and Judaism. She has never set foot in a synagogue. She feels no connection with the Land of Israel. She is a French patriot. Her education is French. Her 'patrimony' is the French Catholic tradition: '*la tradition hébraïque m'est étrangère*' (the Hebrew tradition is foreign to me). Quoted by Plessix Gray (2001: 155).

39 Agnon (1976: 85).

40 On the ambivalent relationship between Jewish nationalism and Hellenism as reflected in literature, see Leoussi and Aberbach (2002).

41 Saul Tchernichowsky (1875–1943): a leading Hebrew poet of the late-19th and early-20th century, known as 'the Greek' (*Ha-Yevani*) for his love of Greek culture. Tchernichowsky was among the rare pre-1914 Eastern European Jews with a classical education, and he translated Homer to Hebrew. Tchernichowsky's spirit is felt in Agnon's *Betrothed* (published in 1943, the year of the poet's death), with its many allusions to Greek culture. See pp. 92–3 below.

42 Agnon's writings present the Galician Haskalah in various stages, for example in the mid-19th century in *Two Torah Scholars in Our Town*, and c. 1900, *In the Prime of Her Life*. In both works, Jewish women from well-to-do homes are given a secular education. This seems to have been the case with Agnon's family in Buczacz. *Two Torah Scholars* is notable, too, in its depiction of the enormous socio-economic gap between the common impoverished teacher and the talmudic scholar. The tragedy in this story derives from a few inadvertent words of insult directed by a wealthy rabbi, Rabbi Shlomo, against a poor scholar, Moshe Pinchas. Moshe Pinchas later achieves renown as a great Talmud scholar, and is provided for by the local working people, to the last detail, without his even knowing, as in 'The Elves and the Shoemaker'. He visits the bathhouse, and his old hat is silently replaced by a new hat, his old shoes by new shoes, his old suit by a new suit, every item to the highest standard. The transformation is reminiscent of a scene in Solomon Maimon's 18th century autobiography, in which Maimon who in his early years was often destitute, wanders into a small Polish town where the local Jews, delighted to find that their visitor is a Talmudic prodigy, treat him virtually as royalty. Moshe Pinchas likewise belongs to the elite. Then Rabbi Shlomo, seeking to atone for his sin, arranges a distinguished rabbinic position for him, which he declines – he cannot

forget Rabbi Shlomo's insulting words – knowing his behavior is irrational. (In this respect, Moshe Pinchas may be compared with other Agnon characters, tormented by their own nature – see p. 103.) He and his family are reduced to poverty, and he is forced into the ignominious drudgery of *heder* teaching. Despite Agnon's idealization of the pre-modern world, 'when Torah was king', what emerges between the lines is a somewhat mean and petty world in which *pilpul* is extolled at the expense of social justice. As is generally the case in Agnon (who in this regard was a disciple of Flaubert), the ideal is unsustainable; and the author's underlying cynicism is all the more remarkable in *Two Torah Scholars* as it was published immediately after the Holocaust. On the puncturing of illusion in Flaubert and Agnon, see Chapter 3.

43 Band (1968: 102) suggests that 'Perhaps Agnon's greatest achievement lies in his maintaining the illusion that the narrator is a guileless believer simply spinning a pious tale while he is really an accomplished artist, well in control of his subject matter.'

44 On the 'false face' in Agnon's fiction, see Aberbach (1984: ch. 5) and, in the present volume, pp. 43, 132.

45 Agnon (1976: 26).

46 See, for example, Canaani (1971: 34). Agnon made similar claims, for example that, given a choice, he would have lived in the 18th century, when Torah study still dominated Jewish life; and that he would have chosen to write the magnificent *Ata Zokher* (Thou remembrest) prayer, attributed to the 3rd century Amora, Rav, and included in the *Musaf* (Additional) Prayer on Rosh Hashana, rather than any of his stories.

47 Agnon (1976: 245). Ibsen, asked after the publication of *Ghosts* (1881) his opinion of Zola, replied that he did not read books, 'I leave that to my wife and son' (Ibsen 1973: 21).

48 On Flaubert's influence on Agnon, see Chapter 3.

49 Bialik (1935: ii 21).

50 For a translation of 'The Lady and the Pedlar' by Robert Alter, see Alter (1975).

51 On the '*agunot*' theme, of unrequited love, in German-Jewish literature, see Chapter 6.

52 Transl. Baruch Hochman, in Agnon (1970: 30).

53 Transl. Baruch Hochman, in Agnon (1970: 30–1).

54 Agnon (CW ii 257). On the image of the beggar-Messiah in 'The Kerchief', see pp. 56–7.

55 Agnon (CW v 560). For similar imagery of the damaged garment, see pp. 50 note 6; 133–4. In *A Guest for the Night*, Agnon appears to poke fun at his own use of garment image to portray a spiritual state: Aaron, a non-observant childhood friend of the writer-narrator, Samuel, tells him that 'the Holy One, blessed be He, will not make a warm coat from Israel's righteous deeds' (iv 292).

56 For a study of major psychological themes in Agnon – the love triangle; the passive, immature hero; the lost mother; depression, loneliness, the 'false face', and repeated distortion of body-image in fantasy; and the quest for wholeness in tradition and art, and other repeated elements in Agnon's fiction – see Aberbach (1984). Avner Falk, a psychiatrist, has written a psychoanalytic biography of Agnon (2018), attributing the dearth of detailed published documentation, even a half-century after Agnon's death, to the reluctance of the writer's family to make public his difficult private life. On the fundamentally autobiographical nature of Agnon's fiction, see p. 29.

57 The word *agunah* denotes a widow unable to remarry in Jewish law as there is no proof that her husband is dead. If she did remarry, she would be regarded as an adulteress. *Agunah* is linked to *ogen* (anchor), the widow being, in effect, 'anchored' (or 'chained') to her marital status.

58 For details on Agnon's marriage, see Laor (1998) and Falk (2018). In *A Guest for the Night*, the narrator-writer, Samuel, moves in with Ya'akov Milch, the mad doctor who narrates 'The Doctor's Divorce', whose sadistic behavior leads to divorce. This link between the writer and Milch hints at an identification with a man unable to live in harmony with a woman (Agnon, CW iv 389–90, 420). Agnon felt early in his career that that his creative life was driven by emotional troubles. After reading the Swedish playwrite, August Strindberg's autobiography telling of his singularly repressed childhood, and his adult existence never far from madness, his weak character, and the lack of a will of his own, Agnon wrote to his publisher, Salman Schocken, 'Most of [Strindberg's] sufferings with people (except women) I have felt and still feel in my skin and bones' (Shaked and Weiser 1978: 100 note 5). Stories, such as 'The Doctor's Divorce', with their pathological idealization of women and suspicions of infidelity, have Strindbergian echoes. On Agnon and Strindberg, see Mazor (1987). Agnon may have identified with Hölderlin, too, as an image of the tormented artist; on Agnon's interest in the German Romantic poet, which he shared with Scholem, see Agnon (1976: 279). On Agnon's description of Scholem's first wife as a character out of Strindberg, see p. 40 note 114.

59 Agnon (CW iii 172). At the end of *A Simple Story*, Hirshl's murderous rage against his wife is evidently still not fully resolved, despite therapy. See p. 29. In *Shira*, Agnon returns to the subject of a man tormented by suppressed, inexplicable rage against a woman. See pp. 71, 100–01, 107 note 2.

60 Agnon (CW iii 469–70). One of the many links between Agnon and Kafka is the impulse toward psychological sadism in sexual relations and consequent need for distance from women. See p. 47.

61 On the similarity between 'The Doctor's Divorce' and Hawthorne's *The Scarlet Letter*, see p. 29.

62 On unrequited love in German Jewish literature, see Chapter 6.

63 For a comparative discussion of loss and creativity, including Hardy's poems of 1912–13, written after the death of his wife, and Agnon's stories of loss, including '*Agunot*', see Aberbach (1989: 29–36). In Agnon's 'Metamorphosis', Hartmann is linked emotionally, through a complex of symbols, with the dead mother of his beloved.

64 Agnon (CW iv 392).

65 For a substantial collection of stories on Buczacz, see Agnon (1973). In his stories, Agnon satirizes Buczacz as 'Shibush', in the sense of 'corrupt', 'confused', or 'disturbed'. On Buczacz in the interwar period, the setting for *A Guest for the Night*, see Aberbach (2009b). Agnon's deep anxiety in this novel for the future of Polish Jewry is mirrored in interwar Polish Jewish literature (e.g. Singer's *Satan in Goray* and Tuwim's *A Ball at the Opera*), but there was at the same time growing Jewish assimilation into Polish society and Polish Jewish patriotism, as in Western Europe.

66 Canaani (1971: 77); *Rosh Hashana* 83b.

67 The basic outline of personality portrayed by Agnon from the start to the end of his career is consistent with what is known of Agnon himself (Aberbach 1984); and Agnon's acquaintances were generally agreed that the fullest biographical account of Agnon may be found, albeit in disguised form, in his fiction.

68 On Flaubert's influence on Agnon, see Chapter 3.

69 Agnon (CW vi 117). For a similar fantasy of guilt, in *In the Shop of Mr. Lublin*, see p. 2. Agnon's use of the grandfather as symbol of the stern, unyielding, even fanatical devotion to the strict observance of Jewish Law (Halakhah) recalls a similar use of the grandfather-figure by Bialik (e.g. in *The Scroll of Fire*). Bialik and Agnon had in common strictly devout, guilt-inducing grandfathers, who also evidently encouraged

their profound respect for rabbinic lore and wisdom, their love of books and diligence in study.

70 Agnon (1976: 26). On the father's absence as a theme in Agnon, see p. 56ff.

71 On Agnon's early writings, see Bakon (1989).

72 For biographical details on Agnon's mother, see Laor (1998); on the fictional image of the mother in Agnon, see Aberbach (1982; 1984: ch. 1).

73 See Aberbach (1984).

74 Mendele's 3-volume *Collected Works* in Hebrew (1909–1912), published when Agnon was living in Jaffa, is a landmark in Hebrew literature; and his *Collected Works* in Yiddish (1911–13) has equal significance in modern Yiddish literature. On the complex nature of Mendele's influence on Agnon, see Chapter 5 below. Agnon quotes Brenner who revered Mendele above all other Hebrew writers (with the possible exception of Bialik) as the great artist not just of Eastern European Jews but of the entire Jewish experience of national exile, from ancient to modern times (Agnon 1976: 116). In seeking to recreate in panoramic scope the entire world of the Eastern European Jews, Agnon followed Mendele; however, unlike Mendele, who was born over a half-century before Agnon, Agnon was also immersed in Western European Jewish life and in German *Kultur*; and whereas Mendele died in the year of the Balfour Declaration, Agnon lived to see the creation of the State of Israel.

75 On parallels in psychological descriptions in Mendele and Agnon, see p. 24 above and p. 98ff. below.

76 Shaked (1977: 99).

77 For meanings of 'Shibush', see p. 37 note 65 above and p. 67 below.

78 Agnon (CW: i 11).

79 Mendele (1947: 65). Mendele's nature descriptions tend to be richer and more precise than Agnon's, the consequence of the many years Mendele labored on his three-volume *Natural History* (*Toldot ha-Teva*, 1862–72); both, however, also are in constant contact with, and draw directly from, biblical and midrashic sources.

80 Mendele (1947: 101, 105). For other examples of Mendele's 'Judaization' of Nature, see Aberbach (1993: 77–8).

81 Agnon (CW ii 136). Agnon may be alluding here to Bialik's poem, 'To the Bird' (*El ha-Tzippor*), which established the poet's reputation already in his teens, in the 1890s.

82 Mendele (1947: 297). Parts of *Of Bygone Days* were published sporadically, both in Hebrew and in Yiddish, from 1894, and the autobiography remained unfinished at the time of Mendele's death in 1917. On the 'double face' in Agnon, see pp. 43–4.

83 Miron (1973: 148). For Agnon as for Mendele, the mask was a means by which the truth could be expressed: 'Man is least himself when he talks in his own person. Give him a mask and he will tell you the truth' (Wilde, 'The Truth of Masks', 1889 in Wilde [1891]). On the 'false face' in Agnon, see Aberbach (1984: ch. 5).

84 Bialik, speech in New York, 1926 (Bialik 1935: ii 21).

85 Mendele (1947: 258).

86 In 'Earthquake Days' (*Bi-Yme ha-Ra'ash*, 1894), Mendele (1947: 407). Physical and psychological sickness in Mendele is generally a reflection of a wider social malaise; in this respect, Mendele may be compared not just with Agnon but also with Ibsen (*Ghosts*) and Thomas Mann (*The Magic Mountain*). On Mendele's portrayal of psychological sickness and its influence on Agnon, see Chapter 5.

87 Mendele (1947: 161). On 'midrashic' childhood memory in 'The Kerchief' in comparison with stories of childhood by Mendele and Bialik which also draw on midrash, see Chapter 2.

88 On Agnon in Germany, see Laor (1998).

89 In some respects, it seems, Schocken behaved toward Agnon as a devoted patron in awe of a rare gift, giving practical help (including a fixed salary) toward the goals of an independent creative existence and widespread public recognition; the initial difference of status and wealth constituted not a mark of social superiority but a privilege and obligation. This pattern of relationships, familiar in the sociology of the Talmudic world going back to ancient times (see p. 31 note 3), may have been first formalized in the medieval Hebrew literary world in imitation of the patrons of Arabic poetry, and it carried over into secular life, in the world of music, art, and literature. On the importance of culture (or *Kultur*) to European Jews, lacking territory, see p. 5 above.

90 Haberman (1976: 91).

91 Agnon and Schocken (2003: 167).

92 Bialik (1935: ii 21). Bialik regarded Agnon as a great artist but faulted his work for being stylized, imitative, and self-absorbed. See p. 40 note 103. On Bialik and Mendele's influence on Agnon in the use of *aggadah* (Jewish legend and folklore) and in the depiction of loss, see Chapter 2.

93 On 'At the Outset of the Day', see p. 138–9.

94 Agnon (CW vii 51). Agnon's stories, 'The Orchestra' and 'A Whole Loaf', are similarly Kafkaesque encounters with futility. See pp. 2, 104–05.

95 For a detailed literary account of the emotional world of Agnon's characters, see Aberbach (1984). Agnon's close acquaintances, such as Gershom Scholem, felt that behind his superficial gregariousness was a lonely, self-absorbed man tormented by the feeling that he was cut off from others. To Scholem, Agnon's approachability masked his need for distance from others, and he wondered if Agnon had not set up 'something theatrical, or like a circus show as a blind to his loneliness' (Scholem 1976: 465). Scholem was one of the few living scholars for whom Agnon seems to have had genuine respect, as founder of the modern study of Jewish mysticism. In particular, he was impressed that Scholem, who came from a totally assimilated German-Jewish family, devoted to secular German *Kultur,* and, largely ignorant of Hebrew and Jewish learning, was mostly an autodidact. He had learned Hebrew from scratch. He was also a fervent early admirer of Agnon's Hebrew style and an outstanding translator of Agnon's stories into German. Agnon was drawn to Scholem, too, as a critic of German-Jewish patriotism, and as a draft-dodger. In speaking of Scholem, though, Agnon, typically, confessed his self-preoccupation, 'I am enslaved to myself' (*meshubad le-atzmi ani*) (Agnon 1976: 278).

96 Mishna *Sotah* 9:15.

97 On Kafka and psychological similarities with Agnon, see Chapter 1 and pp. 137–8.

98 On psychoanalytic elements in Agnon, see Chapter 7. The reader might wonder how Agnon's implicit rejection of Freudian analysis in *A Simple Story* was taken by his wife, Esther, who was in analysis with Max Eitingon, a disciple of Freud, in the 1930s, when the marriage came under severe strain. Wives of some writers, such as Joseph Conrad and James Joyce, had relatively little interest in their work; this seems not to have been the case with Esther Agnon, for whom Agnon was, in effect, writing, and who could trace the vicissitudes of their marriage in his stories. (One is reminded of Robert Frost's tribute to his wife, Elinor, as 'the unspoken half' of everything he wrote.) As she would prepare Agnon's writings for publication from manuscript (being among the few able to decipher his handwriting), she would have been his first reader. As an art student in Munich at the end of World War I, she was first drawn to Agnon by his stories, like Desdemona, a relationship haunting later stories, such as *In the Prime of Her Life* and *Iddo and Enam*, in which a woman is drawn to a man by the power of words. Band (1968: 9) points out that Agnon in Buczacz read *Othello* in Hebrew translation.

99 Agnon (CW vi 203).

100 Agnon (CW vi 249). In *Thus Far*, the narrator tells a parable of a king who commissions an architect to build a palace but is presented with a painting of a palace instead. When the king accuses him of deception, the architect 'knocked with his finger on the drawing of the door, the door opened, and the architect entered and never came out again' (Agnon, CW vii 55).

101 For detailed discussion of parallels between the emotional problems portrayed by Agnon and Kafka, and the different ways in which both seek insight and resolution in Judaism and Jewish history, see Aberbach (1984).

102 The difficulties in Joseph K's relationships with women, for example those leading to his broken engagement in *The Trial*, have parallels in Agnon, notably in *A Simple Story*, in which Hirshl is tortured both by his excessive proximity to and his distance from his wife, Mina. See p. 138.

103 According to Dov Sadan, Bialik likened Agnon to a fragrant *etrog* (citron) lying in a bed of pure wool inside a beautifully carved cedar box, placed in yet another box made of silver; this *etrog* spends its time sniffing itself (Aberbach 1984: 65).

104 On these 'schizoid' characteristics in Kafka, see Storr (1976: ch. 5) and in comparison with Agnon, see Aberbach (1984). Both Storr and Aberbach draw on insights on artistic motivation by the Scottish psychiatrist, W.R.D. Fairbairn (1937–38, 1938–39, 1952), who in his 'object-relations' theory built on the insights of Freud and Klein.

105 Agnon and Kafka both admired and were influenced by the combination of spirituality and aesthetics of Martin Buber's masterful German retelling of Hasidic tales, though they came to Buber from opposite directions, Agnon from Eastern European Orthodoxy, Kafka from the total assimilationism sought by many Western and Central European Jews. Agnon and Kafka never met, but by the time of Kafka's death in 1924, they had a similar ideological direction in which Jewish culture, especially in Hebrew, was paramount.

106 Kafka (1953: 217–18).

107 Kafka (1975: 258).

108 The mad doctor in 'The Doctor's Divorce' recalls: 'Things were never so good for me as during the time between my betrothal and marriage' (Agnon, CW iii 472); marriage takes him downhill. On the typical oscillation, 'in and out', in the relations of the sexes as portrayed by Agnon, see Aberbach (1984: 148–52). Agnon's friends and acquaintances observed a similar pattern in Agnon's marriage (Falk 2018).

109 Kafka (1975: 259). 'The Judgement', dedicated to Felice, ends with George Bendemann leaping to his death from a bridge. In Agnon's *Betrothed*, Jacob Rechnitz feels he cannot possibly marry Susan, yet 'without her the world was nothing to him' (Agnon, CW vii 270).

110 Kafka (1978a: 409). For comparable examples of irrational and uncontrollable anger at women in Agnon's stories, see pp. 17–18.

111 Kafka (1978a: 411).

112 Agnon (CW iii 262). On earlier, more violent manifestations of Hirshl's desire for his wife's death, see pp. 17–18 above and p. 99 below.

113 On alleged similarities between Agnon and his characters as observed by Agnon's acquaintances, see Aberbach (1984).

114 Agnon's stories of *agunot*, with their marital incompatibility, psychological illness, and divorce, reflect also the unusual number of couples in his circle with similar difficulties, to whom he occasionally refers in his letters (see, for example, Agnon 1983: 39). He describes Scholem's first wife as a character out of Strindberg (Agnon 1983: 82). (See

p. 37 note 58.) Buber, to whom Agnon was close, both personally and intellectually, for 50 years, had a background of traumatic family disruption, as did Bialik. When Buber was three, his mother 'disappeared without leaving a trace'; he saw her only once afterwards, many years later (Friedman 1981: 4, 11). This was 'the decisive experience of Martin Buber's life, the one without which neither his early seeking for unity nor his later focus on dialogue and on the meeting with the "eternal Thou" is understandable' (15). On Agnon's quest for wholeness in his writings, see Chapter 7.

115 Agnon (1983: 122).

116 Agnon (1983: 121). Earlier in 1925, Esther Agnon related a dream of finding Agnon with a blonde, which he strenuously denied, claiming to be living the life of a Nazirite (Agnon (1983: 70).

117 Agnon (1983: 121).

118 Scholem (1976: 465); see also Canaani (1971: 107).

119 Agnon (CW vii 368).

120 Agnon (CW v 478).

121 Agnon (1971a: 213).

1 The crying child in Agnon and Kafka

Agnon's earliest recorded memory, of the Day of Atonement in Buczacz in the early 1890s, was set down over 50 years later in the introduction to his anthology on the High Holy Days, *Days of Awe* (*Yamim Nora'im*, 1946). In describing this memory, Agnon confesses childhood roots of his creative preoccupation with the tension between idealism and disillusionment, purity and corruption, ecstasy and despair:

> The heavens were pure, the earth tranquil, all the streets were clean, and there was a fresh breeze. I was about four, dressed for the fast day with my father and grandfather. A relative took me to the synagogue, packed with men wrapped in prayer shawls, silver crowns on their heads, their clothes all white, and prayerbooks in their hands. Candles gave a wonderful light and fragrance in long boxes filled with sand. An old man bent before the Ark, his *talit* coming down beneath his heart, sweet melodies rising from behind it. By the window I stood, trembling, awestruck by the sweet sounds, the silver crowns and the candle-smell of honey. The earth I had walked on, the streets I had passed, the world itself, seemed nothing but a vestibule to *this*. I could not yet think in abstracts, and *hadrat kodesh* (glory of holiness) I did not know. But I felt then the holiness of the place and the people there. I had never felt anything like it, and I didn't think it would ever end. I looked around and could not distinguish one man from the next, for all – and the House of Prayer itself – were a unity. My heart filled with joy and cleaved in love to this house, to these men and their songs.

The songs ended and the child burst into tears, startling everyone. Nothing would comfort him. No one knew what made him cry. Fifty years have passed, and the writer finally puts his childhood misery into words:

> Now I will tell you what made me cry. Suddenly, just when the prayer came to an end, the unity was broken. Men took off their prayer shawls and spoke to one another like every day. I had loved them, and suddenly their faces and the whole house had changed. I was sickened by this, and I cried. Many years have

DOI: 10.4324/9781003594802-2

> passed, and the same wonder stays with me, together with the pain. Each year on the Day of Atonement, when I see Jews 'standing robed in white to glorify you as do the winged seraphs' [*Imatzta asor*], changing pained faces to faces of everyday, I feel the same sadness as on that day.[1]

As part of an introduction to a work on the holiest days of the Jewish calendar, Agnon's memory is a plea for seriousness and consistency in worship: fathers should not disappoint their children. On a deeper level, the memory goes to the heart of Agnon's works, with its characteristic distance from, and ambivalence toward, Jewish tradition. Though a highly accomplished artist, he typically presents himself as a simple teller of pious tales. The first perception of the double face in others contains the seed of later artistic two-facedness. Agnon's characters have a tendency to double-perception as, for example, in *Betrothed*, when Jacob Rechnitz suddenly realizes why since childhood he has been drawn to the sea: 'Jacob went all wide-eyed, and a second face joined his visage, like an artist seeing something new and trying to grasp it.'[2] The moment of truth in Agnon's childhood memory foreshadows his ambiguity toward his tradition, for his trademark is the shattering of illusion.[3]

Agnon's passion for coherence could be seen as a response to incoherence and emotional chaos caused in childhood by unpredictable adult behavior. And indeed, when Agnon spoke, one was never entirely sure whether he was expressing real feelings or hiding behind a mask. In the story 'The Night' (*Laila min ha-Lelot*, 1951), Agnon describes a Jewish clown whose voice and actions are at cross purposes: 'Was he doing this intentionally? It seemed a great art, to be amusing in a sad voice and sad in a comic voice.'[4] The Agnon narrator is fascinated by truth and consistency, but his means of reaching this truth are ironically superficial, even childish. Objects such as clothes or mirrors, rather than the deeper psychological processes, are alleged to be tools for the exposure of human motives and feelings. The narrator of the novella *Thus Far* and the unfinished novel *In the Shop of Mr. Lublin* is writing a book about clothes (which he never finishes). By looking at a man's clothes – so he claims – he has x-ray vision into his buried life.[5] The narrator of *A Guest for the Night* believes that the torn or unfinished garment, not the whole one, shows a man as he is.[6] Fascination with false truth reflects the tendency to avoid seeing things as they are, perhaps for fear of confronting uncontrollable chaos, such as that experienced by the child on Yom Kippur.

In the story, 'The Face and the Image' (*Ha-Panim la-Panim*, 1942), the narrator comes face to face with his own slipperiness. His ambition is to write a book on mirrors which, like the book on clothes, is never done:

> It was a great book I wanted to do, to write down in a book my thoughts about polished mirrors… They are flat and thin and smooth as ice, and there is nothing inside them. But they store up whatever you put before them, and before them there is no cheating or partiality or injustice or deceit. Whatever you show them they show you. They do not expunge or amplify, add on or take away – like the truth which neither adds not takes away.[7]

The narrator in this story tries to reach his mother after hearing she is ill. As he rushes to the train station, his flesh creeps with fear at the childhood memory of playing hide and seek with his friends: 'I hide from them and they hide from me. We stand and wait, and none of us knows whether he wants to be found or not.'[8] This game, too, appears to prefigure the ambivalence of Agnon's art, for the artist, like the child, does not know 'whether he wants to be found or not', and has two faces, one hidden, the other revealed. In the end, the narrator finds himself sitting in front of a mirror, eating a large supper, thinking:

> Perhaps while I was filling my gullet they were sealing her grave. I turned my head aside so as not to look at what I saw. My image rose before me from the mirror in the wardrobe, which the carpenter fixed on an hour before. The mirror stared at me face to face, reflecting back every movement of the head and quiver of the lips, like all polished mirrors, which show you whatever you show them, without partiality or deceit.[9]

This rather sinister double face can be taken as that of the artist, stripped of illusion.

That the memory of disillusionment in *Days of Awe* should take place on Yom Kippur is not surprising in the light of other works by Agnon. Agnon attached the highest significance to the Days of Awe. He devoted two and a half of his most productive years to the compilation of *Days of Awe*; and the idea of penitence, of making the crooked straight and the unwhole whole, of trying futilely to right something wrong, runs throughout his writings. Several of Agnon's major stories, including the opening chapters of *A Guest for the Night*, are set on Yom Kippur. As in the childhood memory, the emotions associated with Yom Kippur in Agnon's stories are ecstasy and disillusionment. In one story, the narrator takes almost masochistic joy in fasting for two consecutive days. In another, he is disgusted by a man who puts on a chef's hat and sings vulgar songs in the middle of the service.[10]

Kafka, Letter to His Father

An early childhood memory of Kafka, the only one, he claimed, that he retained in adult life, is recounted in his most complete attempt at autobiography, *Letter to His Father* (1919). This memory is like a window into his inner world, particularly his relationship with his father:

> Once in the night I kept on whimpering for water, not, I am certain, because I was thirsty, but probably partly to be annoying, partly to amuse myself. After several vigorous threats had failed to have any effect, you took me out of bed, carried me out on to the *pavlatche* [balcony] and left me there alone for a while in my nightshirt, outside the shut door.[11]

The memory recalls the dark mood and several dominant themes in Kafka's writings and in his life: the cruel, unjust dislocation between feeling and the responses of others, a sense of smallness and helplessness, the perpetual state of being an outsider. In the *Letter*, Kafka insists time and again that his father's overbearing behavior has stifled his self-assertiveness, leaving him frozen in a filial state, unable to launch out into life, remaining dependent on his family: he did not leave home until he was 32. Kafka evidently believed his troubled bond with his father lay behind the nightmarish quandaries of his creations, such as Joseph K., when attempting to deal with authority or form new relationships: 'My writing was all about you.'[12] Parental control felt to be dominant but unreliable, inconsistent, and unpredictable, and occasionally terrifying in its harshness, has this result in later life, Kafka writes in 'Resolutions' (1913):

> Perhaps the best resource is to meet everything passively, to make yourself an inert mass, and, if you feel that you are being carried away not to let yourself be lured into taking a single unnecessary step, to stare at others with the eyes of an animal, to feel no compunction, in short, with your own hand to throttle down whatever ghostly life remains in you, that is, to enlarge the final peace of the graveyard and let nothing survive save that.[13]

This death-in-life Kafka appears to blame for the most part upon his father.

The memory of being abandoned on the balcony, Kafka writes in the *Letter*, was typical of his father, with lasting harm:

> What was for me a matter of course, that senseless asking for water, and the extraordinary terror of being carried outside were two things that I, my nature being what it was, could never properly connect with each other. Even years afterwards I suffered from the tormenting fancy that the huge man, my father, the ultimate authority, would come with almost no reason at all and take me out of bed in the night and carry me out on to the *pavlatche*, and that therefore I was such a mere nothing for him.[14]

This fear, Kafka suggests in the *Letter*, is the basis of *The Trial*. The father's overwhelming influence muted outward blame for his 'dreaded personality', his 'mania for domination', his 'hectoring temperament', 'antagonistic nature', 'harsh and dogmatic judgements', the 'strangling ring' of his influence, and for having an emotionally crippling effect on him, discouraging his relationships, making him feel shame, guilt, mistrust, and coldness. Kafka insists, 'you are entirely blameless in the matter of our estrangement'. He excuses the terrifying experience of being left alone on the balcony: 'I am not going to say that this was wrong – perhaps at that time there was really no other way of getting peace and quiet that night.'[15] The acquittal of the father while simultaneously accusing him can be explained by Kafka's resentful fear of him. The father himself points out this discrepancy, in a reply written by Kafka:

> Whereas I [the father] then attribute the sole guilt to you [Kafka] as frankly as I mean it, you are at the same time trying to be 'too clever' and 'too affectionate' and to acquit me too of all blame. Of course in this latter you only partly succeed

> (and you do not want more, either), and what appears between the lines, in spite of all the 'turns of phrase' about character and nature and antagonism and helplessness, is that actually I have been the aggressor, while everything you were up to was only self-defence.[16]

Typically of Kafka, even the attack on his father 'between the lines' is turned by the father-in-Kafka into a self-condemnation. The father is too strong within him. Kafka is doomed to carry the burden of sole guilt. The letter was never read by the father.

Hermann Kafka was a burly butcher's son, successful in business, toughened physically and mentally by a harsh childhood and army experience, which his son was spared. Franz was cushioned against the slings and shocks of life, with the greater anxiety, especially on the part of his mother, as his two younger brothers had died in childhood and his eldest sister was six years younger than himself. His weak and sickly constitution made him all the more vulnerable to over-protection, stoking his own excessive worry about his health, and leading to real illness. The physical inferiority implicit in the memory manifested itself agonizingly in Kafka's childhood. When his father took him swimming,

> There was I, skinny, weakly, slight, you strong, tall, broad. Even inside the hut I felt myself a miserable specimen, and what's more not only in your eyes, but in the eyes of the whole world, for you were the measure of all things.[17]

The physical contrast between father and son prefigures the sense of smallness of the Kafka hero in relation to authority figures. In *The Trial* (1925), K. sits at his desk as the manufacturer and Deputy Manager stand over him discussing a transaction: 'it seemed to K. as though two giants of enormous size were bargaining over his head for himself.'[18] Of his father, Kafka wrote in the *Letter*, 'You were so huge, a giant in every respect.'[19] He likens himself to a trampled-on worm whose top end has broken away. Tormented by a sense of inhumanity, of belonging to a lower order of species, Kafka often wrote about animals and identified himself with them. His empathy with Eastern European Jews, whom his father loathed as vermin, grew with this identification.

The tragedy of being left helpless on a balcony by an insensitive, giant-like father is no greater, perhaps, than the mother's failure to intercede. At times his fight for independence was evidently as much hampered by his mother as by his father.[20] His mother seems to have regarded his infirmities as a license for well-meaning nosiness. In the correspondence with Felice Bauer, Kafka's first fiancée, one witnesses the spectacle of Franz, 30 years old, with a doctorate in law, having his mail secretly read by his mother. Max Brod had to explain to Felice that between Franz and his mother there was a total lack of understanding: this lack emerges in Kafka's diaries. The mother's silence as her son lay crying on the balcony is emblematic of this failing.

Kafka remained on the *pavlatche* of life, in relation to his family and to marriage. His creations exist in this state, outside, mysteriously belonging and not belonging, trying to get in. The *pavlatche* is a long balcony running around the inner courtyard of houses in Prague, and shared by a number of apartments. Banishment to the *pavlatche* does not mean total rejection and being thrown out, as the balcony is not public domain. Full acceptance and welcome are denied within, but escape from the *pavlatche* directly into the outside world is impossible.

To be neither in or out, trapped and struggling to escape, is Kafka's lifelong dilemma. Soon after meeting Felice, he wrote to her, 'All parents want to do is drag one down to them, back to the old days from which one longs to free oneself and escape; they do it out of love, of course, and that's what makes it so horrible.'[21] The resulting weakness, lack of self-confidence, and a sense of guilt drew a cordon between Kafka and marriage, driving him into himself and his writing. He professed indifference to his parents. Faced with the ordeal of telling them about his forthcoming engagement to Felice, he admitted that for years he had hardly spoken to them. The 'greatest terror' of his life was independence through marriage. In the end, he was unable to go through with it. The *Letter to His Father* was practically the epitaph to his marital hopes. Kafka compares his attempts at marriage to a children's game in which one holds onto the other's hand while insisting, 'Oh, go away, go away, why don't you go?'[22] Apparently the only time Kafka lived happily with a woman was in his final months. The remarkable Dora Diamant nursed him and made plans with him to emigrate to Palestine: both knew he was dying.

Kafka and Agnon: the anxiety of influence

Even if there were little or no direct influence of Kafka on Agnon – Agnon claimed to have read only Kafka's 'Metamorphosis' and, in later life, *The Trial*[23] – the childhood memories of being outsiders, of disillusionment and tears, point to striking similarities. He uncharacteristically defended the frequently attacked rough and unaesthetic literary style of the Hebrew novelist, J.H. Brenner – the opposite of his own – as being right for Brenner, for his style grew organically from his suffering.[24] The same might be said of Agnon and Kafka – the cry of a child echoing in their writings and inscribed upon them: in the child-like behavior of their characters, the sense of detachment from others, the quest for optimal distance from others, the egocentric devotion to work, the difficulty in expressing genuine feeling, the sense of smallness and inferiority, the passive aggression, the sado-masochism, the cold indifference, the sense of being outside in relationships both physical and spiritual; the susceptibility to love triangles; the vulnerability to insomnia and illness, guilt, suppressed rage and madness, and to frequently overbearing, tactless, unpredictable, overweening, inconsistent, and even downright irresponsible authority figures.[25] In both Kafka and Agnon, a particular brand of suffering underlies their distinctive style.

Agnon and Kafka's memories of childhood tears reflect failings on the part of the grown-up world to comprehend and respond to the child, though both writers portray the child as knowing parental love. These memories, in different ways, reflect states of dependence, or of striving for independence, evidently screening emotions and experiences which are later prominent in their writings. They also mirror in some ways the crisis of faith pervading Jewish life in the late-19th and early-20th centuries, when the uniformly Orthodox world of Eastern Europe began to break up under pressure of assimilation. In Agnon's Buczacz, as in Kafka's Prague and Freud's Vienna, all under Habsburg rule, Jewish emancipation in 1867 was a major event. In *The Interpretation of Dreams*, Freud describes the optimism of the Jewish community at that time, the hope that the younger generation, including himself, would make the most of the educational and professional opportunities which had opened to them in the Austro-Hungarian empire. Unprecedented access to secular education and social mobility accelerated the shift away from traditionally insular Orthodoxy: these changes are stamped in the writings of Agnon and Kafka – and of Freud. Agnon portrays a superficial conformity to tradition but also the impulse to blaspheme and subvert, though more in thought than in deed. In the story 'Another Talit', the mood of sacredness on the Day of Atonement is lost in the narrator's guilty fantasies:

> Benches were brought to the house of prayer and stacked to the left of the Holy Ark, one on top of the other, like levels in the bathhouse. A man whom I will not name stood at the top, with a kind of baker's hat on his head, singing songs that had nothing to do with the Day of Atonement. A little boy, his son or grandson, stood by him making faces as he sang, and half the congregation watched in amusement.[26]

Kafka describes a similarly blasphemous scene on the Day of Atonement in Prague: the Ark containing the Torah scrolls opening like a shooting-stand at a fair, 'a cupboard door would open in the same way whenever one got a bull's-eye, only with the difference that there something interesting always came out and here it was always just the same old dolls with no heads.'[27]

This debasement of religion signifies the rift with Kafka's father who has failed to give his son a meaningful way of life, while in Agnon's story the singing 'chef' on Yom Kippur, like the *talit* with missing fringe, suggests, too, heretical rebellion and alienation from tradition and community.

Painful and bewildering awareness of the crumbling of a tradition that had seemed to many Jews until the French Revolution, and even after, as cast in bronze, fixed and final, underlies Freud's unexpected feeling of guilt before the Moses of Michelangelo in the church of San Pietro de Vincoli in pre-1914 Rome, long after the optimism engendered by emancipation had faded and anti-Semitism was growing alarmingly, and long after the young Freud's remarkable confession to his future wife, 'I have often felt as though I had inherited all the defiance and all the passion with which our ancestors defended their Temple and could gladly sacrifice my life for one great moment in history.'[28] Now, standing in front of Michelangelo's snarling Moses confronted with the great blasphemy, the Israelite worship of the golden calf precisely at the moment of receiving the Torah at Sinai, Freud seems to have felt most acutely the extent of his break with his rabbinic ancestors. He identifies himself not, as one might have thought, with the lawgiver but, as Agnon's characters often do, with the rabble who abandon the true God and his eternal Word:

> Sometimes I have crept cautiously out of the half-gloom of the interior as though I myself belonged to the mob upon whom his eye is turned – the mob which can hold fast no conviction, which has neither faith nor patience, and which rejoices when it regains its illusory idols.[29]

The memories of both Agnon and Kafka are moments of illumination, 'spots of time' as Wordsworth called them, preserved for a lifetime in their first intensity, the image of alienation, of being outside, of *agunot*, pervading their writings. In them, the reader senses the essence of the writer, the intertwined psychological and social sources of his creative motivation by means of which his art may be encountered and understood.

Notes

1 Agnon's biographical introduction to the 1946 edition of *Days of Awe* is included in his posthumous autobiographical collection, *Me-Atzmi el atzmi* (From Myself to Myself, 1976: 448–9). The first edition of *Days of Awe* appeared in 1937; at this time, Agnon was writing his novel, *A Guest for the Night* (1939), which opens with the narrator's return to his hometown on the eve of Yom Kippur. On 'screen memories' such as those of Agnon and Kafka, see Aberbach (1983). In the depiction of childhood and childhood memory, Agnon was deeply influenced by Mendele and Bialik (see Chapter 2), especially by Mendele who, following Enlightenment thinkers such as Rousseau and the Romantic movement, introduced the subject of childhood into Hebrew literature. As is the case with Agnon's childhood memory of Yom Kippur, Mendele's memories of childhood tend to shift from idealization to disillusionment. See, for example, Mendele's Introduction to *Of Bygone Days* (Mendele 1947: 257–8). Agnon seems to have been drawn to Flaubert in part, similarly, as the French author sought to puncture ideals and illusions. See pp. 67–8.

2 Agnon (CW vii 277).

3 Agnon (CW iv 66). On a parallel with Jung, in which a 'sense of union' with the Church is shattered, see p. 135f. Agnon's childhood memory of disillusionment might be linked to parallel intimations of disillusionment in stories written about children and ostensibly for children, such as 'A Pleasant Story about my *Siddur*' (*Sippur Na'eh al Siddur Tefilati*, 1931) and 'The Kerchief' (*Ha-Mitpahat*, 1932). On the latter, see pp. 56–8. In the former, the author recalls the prayerbook given to him by his father when he was a child and how proud he was of its contents, its binding and printing and decoration, which impress even his unruly friends. Then someone asks if it was printed in Jerusalem and, upon checking, the child finds to his disappointment – and amid the mockery and insults of his 'friends' – that it was printed in the unromantic Polish town of Piotrkow (CW ii 247)! The mature artist would have appreciated, however, how remarkable it was that in an obscure Polish town with fewer than 10,000 Jews, there was a Hebrew printing press which produced such a labor of love; and that his artistic identity had its roots in an extraordinarily rich, largely forgotten Polish-Jewish culture.

4 Agnon (CW vii 214). Freud's patient, the Wolf Man, related a story told by Freud, 'How once a little, insignificant-looking man had come into his office complaining of severe depressions. When Freud inquired as to his work, it turned out that he was the greatest contemporary Viennese comedian, the late Eisenbach' (Gardiner 1972: 42).
5 Agnon (1974: 40). An acquaintance of the young Agnon once reportedly found him stark-naked on the floor of his room surrounded by rabbinic texts, scribbling fine phrases into his notebook for use in his stories.
6 The damaged garment image begins in the opening of 'Agunot' and appears periodically in Agnon's stories, reaching its fullest allegorical form in 'The Garment' ('*Ha-Malbush*', 1950). As Gogol's 'The Overcoat' can be read as a representation of Russia and its atrophied social stratification, so also 'The Garment' can be read as a meditation of the quest for wholeness and redemption in Jewish life; both works, however, end in failure and the death of the protagonist. In a number of Agnon's stories (e.g. 'The Legend of the Scribe' [*Aggadat ha-Sofer*,1919], *A Guest for the Night*, and 'At the Outset of the Day'), a garment catches fire, evidently as symbol of spiritual vulnerability (Aberbach 1984: 166–7).
7 Agnon (1970: 163). The first known Hebrew printed book of prayers was, in fact, also printed in a small town, Piove di Sacco, in Padua around 1475.
8 Agnon (1970: 165).
9 Agnon (1970: 168).
10 On this passage, with a parallel in Kafka, see p. 48.
11 Kafka (1978: 33). On *Letter to His Father*, see pp. 45–7, 138.
12 Kafka (1978: 60).
13 Kafka (1978: 93).
14 Kafka (1978: 34).
15 Kafka (1978: 33).
16 Kafka (1978: 73).
17 Kafka (1978: 35).
18 Kafka (1977: 145).
19 Kafka (1978: 43).
20 The biographical torment underlying Kafka's writings is described by Canetti (1978).
21 Kafka (1978a: 160).
22 Kafka (1978: 69).
23 Agnon (1976: 245).
24 Agnon (1976: 112).
25 The parallels, taken together, build a picture of a schizoid character similar to that described in the writings of W.R.D. Fairbairn, discussed at length by Aberbach (1984). See Chapter 7 below.
26 Agnon (CW vi 203).
27 Kafka (1978: 56).
28 E. Freud (1960: 202).
29 Freud (1914: 213).

2 Jewish nationalism and midrashic autobiography: Agnon and his contemporaries

Prior to 1914, almost all modern Hebrew writers had their cultural roots in the Orthodoxy of Eastern European Jewry and its rabbinic tradition. Their core knowledge of Hebrew derived from this background of prayer and study. Even so, what success they had as writers owed much to the secular world – and to the Zionist movement that promoted the Hebrew language. It is hard to imagine the successful revival of modern Hebrew language and literature without the rise of Jewish nationalism. At the time of Agnon's birth in 1887, Hebrew writers took a risk in writing in Hebrew. The ultimate success of the Hebrew revival was at that time by no means certain. Native Hebrew speakers were practically nonexistent, though many Jews, particularly in Eastern Europe and Muslim countries, were able, if the need arose, to communicate in Hebrew. As we have seen, emancipation (and hoped-for emancipation) and assimilation, in Germany above all, were generally associated with the decline in knowledge of Hebrew. In the mid-19th century, some German synagogues tried to do away with Hebrew entirely.[1] Hebrew was essential to Jewish religious life. What purpose could it serve to emancipated patriotic German citizens devoted to the Fatherland and to German *Kultur*? This question is implicit in a well-known, possibly apocryphal joke, involving the leading Hebrew poet of the 19th century, Judah Leib Gordon, and the leading Jewish historian, Heinrich Graetz, author of *History of the Jews* (12 volumes in German, completed 1871). Meeting for the first time in a German spa, they introduce themselves. Graetz asks Gordon what he does: 'I am a Hebrew poet', to which Graetz quips, 'When did you live?' Hebrew poetry, in other words, belonged to Jewish history, not to the present. Gordon himself had good reason to doubt if Hebrew literature had a future – 'For whom do I toil?' (*Lemi ani amel*), was his lament, echoed by Bialik.

The rise of Jewish nationalism in response to anti-Semitism changed the image of Hebrew from being a language of the past, or a transient educational tool leading to a better secular education, to a dynamic and highly creative modern language, both written and spoken. Agnon was born and came to maturity during this period of transition in the generation prior to 1914. Hebrew by the time of the outbreak of World War I was the language of instruction in many Jewish schools, in the land of Israel and the diaspora. Hebrew literature, too, took a great leap forward, notably

DOI: 10.4324/9781003594802-3

in the fiction of Mendele Mokher Sefarim (1835?–1917) and the poetry of Chaim Nachman Bialik (1873–1934). By the time Agnon moved to Jerusalem for good, in 1924, Hebrew had a small but firm base. Under British rule, Hebrew became the language of the *yishuv*. The daily life of schools, businesses, local government, and the press, was conducted in Hebrew.[2] Agnon at this extraordinary moment was in his late 30s and approaching the height of his power as a creative artist – and he was widely recognized as such.

Agnon's art is wedded to the ideals and values of religious Zionism, with a clear view of the religious basis of Zionism, tolerant of the mundane secular purposes of a national language. Agnon depicts with a critical eye the metamorphosis of the traditional Jewish spirit into a potent political force. Still, Agnon was not overtly political. Politics and world events gave him material, but his main interest was his art. Agnon, like Bialik, weaves his life story into the history of the Jews, often using midrashic material. In a charming reminiscence about his childhood prayerbook (*siddur*),[3] he describes the whole thrust of Hebrew prayer as being in the direction of the Land of Israel. He recalled how, as a boy of five living in the Galician town of Buczacz, then in the Austro-Hungarian empire, he set out for Jerusalem, having no idea that it was so far away, and headed eastward through the forest. After a while he lost his way, the sun set, and he wandered in darkness until he saw the lights of the town. He ran home to find his family frantic with worry about him. He was astonished at the tumult he had caused, but much worse, was bitterly unhappy that he had not seen Jerusalem.

To the end of his life, Agnon felt, as Orthodox Jews do traditionally, that his spiritual being belonged to Jerusalem.[4] Zionism had little purpose as a secular movement if divorced from the rich intellectual heritage and ritual traditions of Judaism. Unlike many Zionists of his generation who were ideologically committed to atheist socialism, Agnon believed that the religious – not just the historical – link of the Jews with the past must be kept. Some of Agnon's sharpest satires are aimed at secular Zionists.[5] In his view, they betrayed the religious and moral ideals of Zionism and tainted the movement with corruption. Yet he also believed that religious fanatics were equally self-serving and pernicious. He mocked them with the same contempt with which he attacked Zionists.

Despite his love for Eretz Yisrael and for Jerusalem in particular, Agnon was never what one would call an ardent Jewish nationalist. As a teenager in Buczacz, he was involved with the local Zionist movement, but even then his writing mattered more to him than politics. Still, the traditional cultural bond of wandering diaspora Jews to Eretz Yisrael – a 'culture on wheels', as Isaiah Berlin called it – is central to his writing. The idealization of the land of Israel in midrash reaches its finest expression in Agnon's stories. Agnon recasts talmudic sources in portraying the land of Israel as superior in all respects to all other lands: in 'The Good Years' (*Ha-Shanim ha-Tovot*, 1927), for example, the inhabitants of Jerusalem enjoy greater longevity than elsewhere and retain their youth longer;[6] in *Tehilah* (1950), the Jews of Jerusalem reach a higher level of purity and holiness than in the diaspora; the man or women who travels to Eretz Yisrael becomes like a newborn child.[7]

Among Agnon's so-called 'pious' tales, the novella *In the Heart of the Seas* (*Bilvav Yammim*) stands out for the beauty and charm with which Eretz Yisrael is idealized, following biblical and midrashic sources. Agnon had worked on this story since his arrival in Jerusalem in the mid-1920s and completed it at the time when Hitler came to power in Germany. By 1933, even the mostly anti-Zionist German Jews had begun to see the land of Israel as a potential place of refuge from persecution. Set in the early 19th century, *In the Heart of Seas* tells of a group of Hasidic Jews travelling to Eretz Yisrael. In this framework, Agnon weaves a magical tapestry of legends, stories, and superstitions, many of which reflect traditional praise of Eretz Yisrael. Shortly before they embark for Jaffa, the travellers are greeted by a messenger whose information about the land of Israel is culled mostly from rabbinic legends which for centuries were (and still are) a staple of Jewish education:

> Let's say you live in Safed, which is built on hilly land and has finer air than any town in Eretz Yisrael. When you die, your soul immediately flies to the Cave of Machpelah and from there to the Garden of Eden… Hebron is better than Safed as the Patriarchs chose to be buried there. Over their tombs, King David, of blessed memory, built a huge shrine, but because of our sins we are prohibited from entering it. Near these graves lie the graves of Nachmanides, of Jesse, father of King David, and of other righteous men. The dwellers of Hebron are strong and virtuous, and noted for hospitality, for which Abraham our father was praised… And how good it is to live in Tiberius where even empty-headed men are filled with *mitzvot* (good deeds) like a pomegranate… and which is surrounded by the sea of Galilee which God loves more than any other sea… And the resurrection of the dead will begin there, and there the redemption will begin, as it is written in the Talmud (*Rosh Hashana* 31). But who could diminish the holiness of Jerusalem where our Temple stood, for it faces the gate of heaven.[8]

Though the story is set several generations before his birth, Agnon includes himself and his wife, Esther, among the travellers, and he regales them with legends about Jerusalem, opening its gates as it were to encounter, for the first time, Sephardic Jews conversing in Hebrew and joining in among the author's audience. He tells them *aggadot* telling of the overwhelming grief felt by Jews though the ages for Jerusalem, and the perennial hope of its rebuilding:

> Rabbi Samuel bar Nachmani said: in *aggadic* tradition, Jerusalem will not be rebuilt until the exiles return to the land of Israel. Don't believe the man who tells you that if the exiles return Jerusalem will not be rebuilt, as Scripture states, 'God builds Jerusalem, He will gather the scattered of Israel' (Psalms 147: 2). Rabbi Yohanan says, Jerusalem will one day become a metropolis for all countries. Rav Nahman asked Rav Yitzhak, what does Scripture mean by 'Holy within you, I will not enter the city' (Hosea 11: 9)? Rav Yitzhak replied by quoting Rabbi Yohanan: The Holy One Blessed be He said, I will not enter

> the earthly Jerusalem until I enter the celestial Jerusalem. Is there a celestial Jerusalem? Yes, as Scripture says, 'Jerusalem upbuilt, a tight-knit city' (Psalms 122: 3).[9]

Such legends, retold by Agnon, are treasured in both the Ashkenazic and Sephardic traditions and, in a flight of audacious fancy, the Sephardim in Jerusalem are eager to hear the master storyteller weave his magic:

> They too wanted to hear these stories, and Rabbi Shmuel Yosef continued in Hebrew, like the angels on high, telling the praise of Jerusalem and the Shekhnah's joy in them. For since the destruction of the Temple, every day is a vexation seeing as the Holy One, blessed be He, swore that he would not enter celestial Jerusalem until Israel would enter earthly Jerusalem. Our Sephardic brothers, hearing this, could have kissed him on the mouth in joy.[10]

Jewish children were traditionally raised to believe – or at least to half-believe – in legends such as these. The hold of Eretz Yisrael on their imagination was far stronger than any cultural expression in the lands in which they lived, though in some countries, such as England, the influence of the Bible was sometimes felt in a profound empathy with the ancient Jewish longing for the land of Israel. Especially in times of hardship and persecution, *aggadah* helped to sustain the romantic image of the land of Israel as the true home, a land of miracles, where the redemption would take place and where there would be no religious intolerance.

Agnon's nationalism had less to do with the growing militancy of his generation than with the traumatic events of the distant past, particularly the destruction of the Temple and the exile. As if to underscore his role as a Jew of the old world, Agnon claimed falsely that he was born on the Ninth of Av, the anniversary of the destruction of the Temple; and that, given a choice, he would have been born in 18th century Poland – the time of the rise of Hasidism, in his view the golden age of orthodox Judaism. The yearning of many of his central characters for a woman out of reach, notably Hirshl Horowitz for Blume Nacht in *A Simple Story*, recalls the 'age-old, sad and hopeless love of Israel for that divine presence which once dwelt in the Temple whose destruction is mourned on the Ninth of Av.'[11]

Agnon lived in Jerusalem for most of his eighty-two years. Among Jerusalemites who knew of no life other than their orthodoxy, he was regarded, despite his adherence to custom, as something of an outsider, even a poseur. Nevertheless, after the fall of the old city of Jerusalem into Jordanian hands in 1948, he could best express the mood of loss felt particularly by orthodox Jews who could no longer pray at the Western Wall. The story *Tehilah* is both an elegy and a tribute to the old city as embodied in an extraordinary old woman who speaks these words of praise:

> The eye accustomed to see the city of Jerusalem never regarded what was built outside the walled city as the real Jerusalem. All the land of Israel is holy and, needless to say, the outskirts of Jerusalem. But the city within the walls is of a higher holiness.[12]

As in ancient rabbinic literature, Agnon takes for granted the right of Jews to live in the Land of Israel, and the recognition of this right by other peoples – including Muslims who accept Jewish Scripture as sacred and the Jews as the 'people of the Book' (*ahl al-kitab*).[13] Agnon has scant respect for secular Zionists who allegedly lost the traditional feeling of the sacredness of Eretz Yisrael and betrayed the ideals of the movement through their immoral behavior. In the satirical novella *With Young and Old Together* (*Bi-Ne'arenu uviZkenenu*, 1920), Zionists in Buczacz are portrayed as rash, self-righteous cowards, saved from a gang of drunken gentiles by Alexander, an anarchist, who is then arrested by the police. While Alexander is in custody, the leader of the Zionist faction seduces his fiancée.

Superficial reverence of Zionist leaders and philanthropists in Agnon's stories masks disillusionment and disgust with them. In the story, 'The Letter' (*Ha-Mikhtav*, 1951), a wealthy businessman, Gedalia Klein, boasts that if not for his generosity, Jerusalem would barely be able to survive. The narrator discovers the extent of Klein's 'help' from an impoverished tenant in a Jerusalem slum who is about to be evicted as he is too poor to pay the rent:

> Master Gedalia Klein was a great man and meant to help the builders of the neighborhood. He came forward when they were in trouble and got them a loan at the rate of eight per cent when people pay nine or ten or up to twelve. But anyone who gets into debt has to leave his house in the end.[14]

Though Agnon's political satire has a contemporary setting, his portraits of bureaucrats, speechmakers, and party hacks with their pompous self-importance, their meanness and ineffectuality, and their lack of idealism, have universal interest. In the story 'The Kidnappers' (*Ha-Hotfim*, 1942), set in Mandatory Palestine, a local hack, mockingly named Shreiholtz, is kidnapped by a group of yeshiva students. They accuse him of taking up too much time with his speeches, which prevent people from spending time with their children and studying the Torah. In captivity, Shreiholtz, formerly a student like them, comes round to their point of view, agreeing not to press charges and even offering to pay their expenses… on condition that they kidnap other speakers whom he hates as much as they.[15] In Agnon's view, Jewish communal officials, pompous and self-serving, had betrayed the religious ideals fundamental to Zionism.

In another of Agnon's satires, the state is plagued by drought. Committees are formed, speeches are made, opinions discussed, but no one does anything. A pious man goes out and, like the legendary Honi in the Talmud, prays to God for rain. The committees are shocked. Who gave the man permission? What right did he have to take matters into his own hands? If his prayers are answered and the rains fall, others will follow his example. Where will the committees be then? They agree there is only one solution: they have a huge canopy built over the entire state to prevent the rain from illegally getting through.[16]

Other stories illustrate Kafka's saying that 'The chains of tormented mankind are made out of red tape.'[17] In their inefficiency and lack of concern, Agnon's officials invariably arouse a sense of helplessness and, at times, something more sinister, as in the story *Hefker* (1945), recalling Kafka's *The Trial*, in which the narrator is arrested for no reason and detained overnight.[18]

Agnon's fiction prior to the creation of the State of Israel reflects his doubts whether a Jewish state could survive the incompetence and absurdities of its own citizens. Immersed in Jewish religious culture, Agnon evidently had a traditional diaspora Jewish aversion to power and distrust of armies. His response to military service in Buczacz and in Berlin was to dodge it. In questioning Jewish ability to organize or rule, he underestimated Jewish nationalists even more than he underestimated the Arabs. In fact, he was opposed to Israel's declaration of independence in 1948, preferring at the time to remain under the British Mandate. He said that, given a choice, he would have waited thirty years. Still, in keeping with his religious beliefs, after the 1967 war, he regarded the Israeli conquest of the West Bank in response to the Jordanian attack as a unification of territory which was part of the ancient land of Israel: he did not want to be denied the right to pray at the Western Wall or at the Cave of the Patriarchs in Hebron.

Autobiographical aggadah

Agnon, steeped in *aggadah* – he edited rabbinic texts pertaining to the giving of the Torah and the Days of Awe – was thoroughly familiar with the *aggadic* writings of his older contemporaries, Mendele and Bialik, and they were among his main influences in stories such as *Ha-Mitpahat* (The Kerchief, 1932).[19] Like them, Agnon reconstructs a world of wholeness and innocent faith in which the child is certain of the historic truth of *aggadah*, in this case of the 2nd century CE Rabbi Joshua ben Levi, Elijah, and the Messiah:

> Rabbi Joshua ben Levi found Elijah standing by the cave of Rabban Simeon bar Yochai. He asked: Will I enter the World to Come? Elijah replied: If this Master [God] wills it. Rabbi Joshua ben Levi said: There are two of us here, but I hear three voices. When will the Messiah come? Elijah replied: Go, see for yourself. Where is he? asked Rabbi Joshua. Sitting by the gate of the city [of Rome], replied Elijah. How can I recognize him? asked Rabbi Joshua. Elijah replied: He sits among the diseased poor. Everyone else bandages and unbandages his wounds in a cluster. He bandages and unbandages each wound one by one, thinking, if I am wanted I must not be delayed.[20]

'The Kerchief', based on Agnon's memories of the town of Buczacz in Galicia at the end of the 19th century, tells of a child distressed by the absence of his father, a businessman whose work takes him each year to the great fair in Lashkowitz. The *aggadah* of Rabbi Joshua ben Levi permeates the child's imagination, and his longing to bring his father home becomes entangled with the age-old Jewish yearning for messianic redemption:

> Throughout the time father was in Lashkowitz, I slept in his bed. Right after saying the *Shema*, I would stretch myself out in the long bed and cover myself

> up to my ears as usual, so as to get up in case I heard the shofar of the Messiah. I loved thinking about the Messiah the King. I often contemplated and laughed heartily at the future astonishment in the world on the day when he would appear. Yesterday he was sitting binding and unbinding his wounds – and today he is king. Yesterday he sat unnoticed among the poor, some of whom treated him despicably, when the Holy One, blessed be He, suddenly recalled his oath to redeem Israel and gave him permission to appear in the world. Others might be angry with the poor for not treating the King Messiah with respect, but I felt love for them seeing as the King Messiah had chosen to sit among them. Others might feel disrespect for the poor, as they ate cheap black bread even on the Sabbath and wore filthy clothes, but I loved them as some of them had the merit of sitting with the Messiah.[21]

In a nightmarish dream, the child flies to Rome in search of the father-Messiah and finds him, as the *aggadah* relates, sitting by the city gate binding and unbinding his wounds:

> As my eyes closed, I would take my *tzitzit* and count in its knots the number of days father would be in Lashkowitz. Green, white, black, red and blue lights whirled round, like those seen by wayfarers in the fields, forests, valleys and streams, and all sorts of treasures glittered and shone in them. I felt mischievous with joy at all that treasure hidden for us until the day the Messiah appeared, speedily in our time. Then a great bird came and pecked the light away. Once I took my *tzitzit*, tied myself to its wings and said: Bird, bird, take me to father. The bird spread its wings and brought me to a city called Rome. I looked down and saw a group of poor people by the city gates. One of them was sitting binding and unbinding his wounds. I looked away so as not to see his suffering, and a great mountain towered up full of thorns and briars, with wild animals grazing, unclean birds flying and repulsive crawling things. Suddenly a great wind came and tossed me onto the mountain. The mountain started to crumble and I was about to be crushed. I tried to scream but did not for fear that the unclean birds would peck at my tongue. Father came, wrapped me in his *talit* and carried me to bed.[22]

The significance of 'The Kerchief' and its *aggadic* source in Agnon's development as an artist is clear in his account of how, while still a child, he began to write. For his first poem was done in a state of longing for his father who, like the father in 'The Kerchief', was away at the Lashkowitz fair:

> When I was a child of six or seven, my father of blessed memory went to the fair in Lashkowitz. I missed him terribly and was sad all the time. One evening I came home from *heder* and pressed my head against the wall and cried: 'Father, father, where are you/ I love you deep and true!' I was amazed to write this poem, by accident – my first Hebrew poem. After, I wrote many poems and stories but they seemed lightweight alongside those two lines rhymed out of longing for father.[23]

This longing was complicated by the mother's illness – she had a heart ailment from which she eventually died – and her consequent difficulties in caring for Agnon, the eldest of five children. In 'The Kerchief', both parents are distant from the child, in contrast with the fantasy world of *aggadah* offering intimacy and the promise of salvation or release, if not through religious faith then through the power of art. In using *aggadah*, Agnon follows Mendele and Bialik in synthesizing past and present, portraying individual creative imagination as an outgrowth of ancient national culture. These writers showed that ancient Hebrew creativity could be adapted to modern Jewish nationalism, at a time when anti-Semitism gave this nationalism urgency and force.

Mendele and autobiographical aggadah

For all Mendele's *maskilic* ambivalence to *aggadah* as a world of fantasy, useless in the modern world, he depicts the first stirrings of his artistic instinct much as Agnon does, in *aggadic* symbolism, alluding several times to the following *aggadah*, set after the destruction of the Temple in Jerusalem in 70 CE:

> Rabbi Yose said: Once I was walking among the ruins in Jerusalem and entered one to pray. Elijah, of blessed memory, appeared and guarded the entrance… Why did you come here? he asked when I finished. To pray, I replied. He said: You should have prayed on the road. I said: I fear distraction by wayfarers. He asked: what did you hear in the ruin? I answered: I heard a heavenly voice moaning like a dove: Woe! I have destroyed my house, burned down my sanctuary and exiled my children among the nations! My son, Elijah said, I swear by your life the voice said this not just when you were praying but repeats it each day three times. Moreover, each time Jews in synagogues and houses of study say 'Amen, may the name of God be blessed…', the Holy One, blessed be He, shakes his head, as it were, and says: Happy the king so highly praised! What will be of the father who has exiled his children! Woe to those exiled from their father's table![24]

Mendele draws on this *aggadah* in portraying a childhood friend, an eccentric carpenter named Hirzl who, among other talents unusual in the *shtetl*, knew how to draw. One work of his stuck in the child's mind – a picture of Rabbi Yose and the dove based on the talmudic legend. The wonder of the child's mind is tempered by the gentle irony of the satirist:

> He drew Rabbi Yose following the talmudic account, with Rabbi Yose (wrapped in *talit* and crowned with *tefillin*, face plaintive, beard short, sharp and gray) praying in a Jerusalem ruin, hearing a heavenly voice moaning like a dove (a creature shaped somewhat like a dove, mouth agape) saying: Woe! I have destroyed my house, burned down my sanctuary and exiled my children among the nations! This work astonished the village mavens: words they could find in

> praise of Rabbi Yose, but as for the dove – their mouths hung ajar in speechless wonder – *Ribbono shel olam*, what can we say at this marvel?[25]

The picture and the *aggadah* of Rabbi Yose struck a chord in the child's heart, for he was determined to copy Hirzl's work, but in an Eastern European *shtetl*, artists' materials were hard to come by:

> Shloyme wanted very much to imitate Hirzl and do work similar to his drawing of Rabbi Yose and the heavenly voice moaning like a dove. However, it didn't turn out, and he excused himself, saying he didn't have proper artist's materials. For carving he needed a sharp chisel, while the one he had, won in a raffle, was soft and notched; and as for painting, he needed all sorts of colors…[26]

The *aggadah* takes on deeper significance in the final chapters of *Of Bygone Days*, written shortly before Mendele's death in 1917. These chapters are a moving portrait of the author after his father's death when he was 13 or 14. Separated from his mother, who could not support him – the parallel with Bialik is striking – he lived in a village a few miles away. In his loneliness, childhood memories returned, including those of Hirzl and his picture and the *aggadah* of Rabbi Yose:

> Hirzl the carpenter, too – that old man childlike in his walk, his talk and crazes – came to him with his violin and the picture he had done of Rabbi Yose, old, thin, wispy-bearded, wrapped in *talit*, crowned with *tefillin*, praying in a Jerusalem ruin, above his head a dove moaning in misery, abandoned, dejected.[27]

In the context of Mendele's life, as of Bialik's, *aggadah* becomes virtually symbolic of his own ruin. Bialik was Mendele's chief poetic disciple as Agnon was his chief disciple in fiction. Bialik's adaptation of *aggadah* to modern Hebrew has a strongly Mendelesque stamp. Bialik worked many years on the *Sefer ha-Aggadah* (Book of Legends), first published 1908–10, and knew Jewish myth and legend better than any Hebrew poet before or since. As a poet, Bialik had especial interest in the imaginative qualities of *aggadah*, which he recast as part of a viable modern national culture in ways comparable to the work of other national poets, such as Shevchenko in Ukraine, Lönnrot in Finland, Mickiewicz in Poland, or Yeats in Ireland: all collected and studied legend in the national language and sought to adapt it to modern national identity. *Scroll of Fire* is Bialik's quintessential *aggadic* poem, interweaving national and personal concerns; and *Safiah* (Aftergrowth 1903–23), his *aggadic* autobiography. In his use of myth and legend to interweave a traumatic personal and national past, Bialik is comparable with other poets who suffer severe trauma or disability, especially in childhood,[28] and seek to revive and unify a wounded, humiliated, divided nation; but his use of talmudic *aggadah* in Hebrew recalls Mendele and anticipates Agnon. Each of these masters of Hebrew literature speaks to national concerns through the use of *aggadic* fragments, creating a mythical world of wholeness and stability prior to family disruption.

Aggadah in Bialik's poetry

Exile haunts modern Hebrew poetry, drawing on biblical memories as well as the ancient homiletic tradition. Yet, victimhood and persecution are felt more strongly in modern Hebrew and the tendency to self-blame far less than in the Bible. Hebrew enlists the past, including legend and folklore, in national struggles. Hebrew poetry preserved in exile helped the Jewish people survive. The Bible and rabbinic literature acted as massive quarries for wisdom, heroism, and warnings of moral danger and catastrophe. Much 19th- and early 20th-century Hebrew literature might be described as modern Midrash, of which Bialik was the outstanding practitioner in poetry. Bialik sets Jewish legend against the background of rising assimilation among the young generation of Russian Jews and their rejection of both traditional Judaism and Jewish nationalism:

> You'll raise Pithom and Rameses for your oppressors,
> using your children as bricks;
> when their cry lifts from the wood and the stone –
> it will die before reaching your ears.[29]

Pithom and Rameses were cities built by Israelite slaves in Egypt.[30] Bialik recasts legends of the slavery to convey his bitter anger at the younger generation of contemporary Jews who ignored their own heritage and enslaved themselves (as he saw it) to foreign and hostile cultures (Germany, for example, or Russia). In a talmudic legend, an Arabian merchant offers to show Rabba bar Bar Hanna the Israelites who died trying to force their way into the Promised Land. The dead warriors lie in gigantic shapes where they fell in the desert:

> 'Come and I will show you the Dead of the Desert.' I went with him and saw the dead men looking as though they were ecstatic. They lay supine and the knee of one was lifted. The Arabian merchant passed under the knee riding on a camel and holding a spear erect – and he did not touch it.[31]

Bialik turns this *aggadah* into a magisterial allegory of the somnolent condition of the Jews of his time and of their immense latent power. The warriors in Bialik's poem are not a few desperate fighters, as in the biblical story, but 'sixty myriads', i.e. the entire nation. The climax of the poem was often read as virtually a declaration that the Jewish exile was over. Yet the poem does not support this interpretation. True, the warriors wake amid a desert storm, as at Sinai, and ready for battle they chant in unison –

> We are heroes!
> The last generation of slaves,
> the first to be free![32]

– but they remain frozen where they lie in the desert, and the poem ends in despair.

Bialik's *Scroll of Fire*, with its portrayal based on talmudic *aggadah* of Jerusalem's destruction by the Romans in 70 CE, conveys a parallel disaster in Bialik's life, after his father's death in Zhitomir, when the child was separated from his mother. Here are the opening lines of *Scroll of Fire*, the grief-stricken God and his Temple in flames:

> All night seas of flame boiled,
> tongues of fire leaped on the Temple-mount,
> starry showers of sparks flew
> from charred heavens earthward …
> Cloaked in pillars of smoke,
> footstool dust and ashes,
> head buried in arms,
> in mountains of grief,
> silent, desolate he sat
> staring at the ruin,
> eyes black with eternal wrath,
> silence frozen in his eyes -
> did God smash his crown,
> kick his throne away? …[33]

Like the ruined natural world in Nerval's *Aurélia*, or the lost Atlantis in the writings of Tolkein and C.S. Lewis, this image of total destruction appears to reflect the poet's chronic sense of personal loss: a child who has just lost his father and is about to be separated from his mother, as Bialik was at the time of the fire, might well feel that 'the whole world was being destroyed'. *Scroll of Fire* is, on one level, a personal *aggadah* of ruin, depression, and anger, and the distorted sexual relationships following catastrophic loss. The ambivalence of the central character toward his 'prophetic' role – his guilty awareness of private as well as national motivations – is a key to the poem and to Bialik's artistic life.

In *Scroll of Fire*, Bialik combines two *aggádot* on the *hurban* (destruction) of the Temple: that of the sacred fire saved from the ruined altar and of the captured children on a boat to Rome who leap to their death to escape their fate as sex slaves to Roman masters.[34] In Bialik's retelling, an angel rescues the sacred fire and carries it to a clifftop on a desert island where the children are shipwrecked. The boys, separated from the girls, search the island for water and after a few days they find a black river, an allegorical image of corruption, particularly of the growing violence against Jews at the time of the poem. The poet curses the nations, echoing the Psalms and the book of Lamentations:

> From deep destruction take a song of ruin,
> black like the brand of your heart;
> bear it among the nations,
> empty its coals over their heads,
> scatter it with the wrath of God![35]

At the time of writing *Scroll of Fire*, in 1905, Russia itself was on fire with revolutionary violence. The immediate event behind *Scroll of Fire* was the naval mutiny in June 1905 when Odessa was shelled for several days by the sailors on board the battleship *Potemkin* (the event depicted unforgettably in Eisenstein's film). Bialik was there when the oil refineries were hit and the entire harbor was set ablaze, and he recalled many years later, 'The daily cannon fire and gun shots stirred up a storm in me.'[36] The poem draws on a combination of public and private sources to become, for most of its readers, a national allegory, recast from *aggadic* sources, expressing national ruin, trauma, and despair, and the hope of redemption. What the solitary individual could not do, the nation could.

Bialik's use of autobiographical *aggadah* reaches an artistic peak in *Aftergrowth*, particularly the delightful chapters 9–15, written in 1918–19, at the end of World War I, after the Russian Revolution and the Balfour Declaration of 1917, as well as the emancipation of the Russian Jews, and during the Russian civil war of 1918–21.[37] *Aftergrowth* gives little sign of the turmoil in which it was written. It is a form of *kinnus*, a bringing together of fragments of the past, personal, and national:

> From the blurred letters of these dog-eared books – Chumash and Rashi and the rest of the Tanakh – which I studied in sporadic, disordered bits – rose in confused fragments long-forgotten generations and ages, peoples, lands and stories. I spoke with the ancients and took part in their lives and deeds. I did not need whole sections. I built myself their ruined world even out of verse fragments and shards of meaning.[38]

In *Aftergrowth*, Bialik creates a child's-eye view of Judaism in which the imagination is free to roam and the child becomes virtually a part of the *aggadic* world. In a Hebrew style of unique beauty, richness and style, he describes the village of Radi, his birthplace in Ukraine, as a mirror-image of this fantasy world, whose origin and guardian is God himself. Every detail of this landscape comes from the Bible and rabbinic literature: for example, a pit in a nearby field is none other than the pit where Joseph was cast by his brothers; the river Teterov is where Moses was hidden among the bulrushes; a sandy track is the wilderness crossed by the Israelites on their way to the Promised Land. *Aftergrowth* is not free of nightmare, isolation, and depression, yet for Jewish children in Eastern Europe, *aggadah* could be a limitless source of entertainment and pleasure, an inner world with a language of its own: Hodu and Cush, the giants Ahiman, Sheshai, and Talmai, the Zuzim, Nachbi ben Vafsi, the Gibeonites, Sambatyon, Og king of Bashan.

To Bialik, as to the Jews generally, memory is itself a form of territory in exile. Yet the landscape of memory, both personal and collective, is not Jerusalem or Galilee but, ironically, Ukraine. Not even Shevchenko described the Ukrainian landscape as lovingly as Bialik, though (like other Hebrew writers) Bialik tended to find in the hills, fields, and woods of his childhood biblical images of the land of Israel. Bialik followed Mendele in depicting the landscapes of Eastern European Jews in language deriving from biblical and talmudic literature. Whereas Mendele was an enlightened *maskil* critical of the narrow horizons of traditional Jewish education, Bialik, a cultural nationalist, saw *aggadah* as a precious national heritage. In *Aftergrowth*, he tells how as a boy in *heder*, he studied the Psalms in the open air, and the Ukrainian exile was transformed into the land of the Bible:

> The gate of understanding opened by itself. 'As a tree planted' [Psalms 1: 3] meant the tree in whose shadow we sat; 'by streams of water', the pool in the valley; 'The valley of the shadow' [Psalms 23: 4], the ruin where the evil spirits were found, which Rabbi Meir told us never to enter; 'Thou preparest a table before me' [Psalms 23: 5], the table where we sat studying the holy Torah.[39]

Bialik was inspired by Mendele and, in turn, inspired Agnon to capture the spiritual fervor of Judaism – particularly Hasidism – in new creative forms. Already as children, these writers learned to use *aggadah* to escape into a semi-idealized world of the past and, later, as a creative means of expressing and mastering early trauma. Seeking a form of healing and unity in ancient Jewish myth and legend, in the sacred language beloved to Jews from ancient to modern times, they gave eloquent voice to the longing of a broken people for national renewal.

Notes

1 See Aberbach (2006). On anti-Hebraism among German Jews, see pp. 2, 9–11.
2 On the uncertain state of vernacular Hebrew in early-20th century Jaffa, as Agnon knew it, see pp. 4–5.
3 'A Pleasant Story about my *Siddur*' (*Sippur na'eh al Siddur Tefilati*, 1932) in Agnon (CW ii 246–7).
4 On Agnon's Nobel speech, see p. 11.
5 On Agnon and the Haskalah literary genre of satire, see p. 33 note 26.
6 Agnon (CW ii 468).
7 Agnon (CW vii 189). This type of intense idealization is often shattered in Agnon's stories. See p. 36 note 42.
8 Agnon (CW ii 527–9).
9 *Ta'anit* 5a. In his stories, Agnon often contemplates his role as an author within a sacred tradition. In 'At the Outset of the Day', for example, the narrator finds that a scroll of his is included in the Holy Ark on Yom Kippur. See pp. 138–9.
10 Agnon (CW ii 531).
11 Fisch (1975: 94).
12 Agnon (CW vii 189).
13 In the story, 'Under the Tree' (*Tahat ha-Etz*), written shortly before the Arab Revolt of 1936, a prominent Arab praises the Jews for their efforts to reclaim the land, and asserts the rights of the Jews to fulfill their religious destiny in the land of Israel.
14 Agnon (1970: 224). Agnon hints at his satiric intent in the name of the 'benefactor' – 'Gedalia Klein' – with its 'greatness' (Gedalia might be translated 'God is great') and smallness ('Klein' in German = small).
15 Agnon (CW vi 259).
16 *Shlom Olamin* (Eternal Peace, 1942), Agnon (CW vi 267).
17 Janouch (1971: 120).
18 Agnon (CW vi 193-4).

19 On Agnon's relations with Bialik, see Be'er (1993) and Shamir (2017).
20 *Sanhedrin* 98a.
21 Agnon (CW ii 257).
22 Agnon (CW ii 258).
23 Agnon (1976: 26). Agnon drew on his own dreams for his stories, including (as in 'The Kerchief') dreams of the Messiah, such as the one he related to Schocken in Germany in July 1917: 'Leonardo is making a very high horse, and its head reached the heavens. On the horse rides the King, the Messiah, but as the horse was so high up I could not see the rider' (Agnon and Schocken 2003: 50). This dream, alluding to Jacob's dream of the ladder whose 'head reached the heavens' (Genesis 28: 12f.), suggests the lofty artistic ambitions encouraged by Schocken – comparable in Hebrew to Leonardo's pictorial genius.
24 *Berachot* 3b.
25 Mendele (1947: 282–3).
26 Mendele (1947: 287).
27 Mendele (1947: 295).
28 Poets who describe childhood trauma include: Burns, Solomos, Shevchenko, Byron, Kolcsey, Leopardi, Fikret, Prešeren, Pascoli, Shawqi, Bharati, and Neruda. See Aberbach (2015).
29 Aberbach (2015: 79).
30 On Pithom and Rameses, see Exodus 1: 11; also, see p. 98. Agnon, too, alludes to these midrashim. See p. 105–06.
31 *Bava Batra* 73b–74a. The biblical source is in Numbers 14. Tchernichowsky draws on the same talmudic source in the poem *Manginah li* (My Song, 1916).
32 *The Dead of the Wilderness* (*Mete Midbar*, 1902), Bialik (2004: 62).
33 Aberbach (2023: 119–120).
34 II Maccabees 1: 19f.; *Gittin* 57b. Among many *aggadot* retold by Agnon in *In the Heart of the Seas*, the story in *Gittin* 57b on the captive children is given much prominence (Agnon, CW ii 515–17); and Bialik's influence is clear. In comparing Bialik and Agnon's use of this *aggadah*, the reader may see Bialik's iconoclastic originality and Agnon's stylistic charm.
35 Aberbach (2023: 120). For biblical sources of the curse against the cruel nations which seek to destroy Israel, see Psalms 79: 6–7, Lamentations 3: 66. These are customarily recited at the Passover *seder*, at the end of the festive meal, when Elijah is ceremoniously 'welcomed' and 'drinks' from his wine glass (to the children's delight), before the recital of the Hallel (psalms and prayers of praise).
36 Bialik (1935: ii 26).
37 On 'screen memories' in Bialik and Freud, see Aberbach (1983).
38 *Aftergrowth*, ch. 9; Bialik (1975: 204).
39 *Aftergrowth*, ch. 8; Bialik (1975: 203). Heine, in *Prinzessin Sabbath*, describes the Sabbath transforming the Jew from a dog into a prince and transporting him to the Holy Land: '*Hör ich nicht den Jordan rauschen*?'

3 Beggars of love: Agnon and Flaubert

The influence of Gustav Flaubert (1821–1880) on Agnon appears in a variety of shared characteristics in their fiction: similar language, scenes, images, and psychological patterns and relationships. The extent of these parallels is considerably greater than has been observed by scholars.[1] Agnon, wary of admitting literary debts, was openly reverential toward Flaubert.[2] This chapter explores some of the similarities and discusses why they are central to an understanding of Agnon's artistic aims, both in style and in the realistic socio-psychological depiction of individuals in small towns. There are also significant differences between the two writers, and Agnon, as mentioned in the Introduction, read widely, particularly in German as well as Russian and Scandinavian literature, in German, Yiddish, or Hebrew translation.[3] Yet, Flaubert, as a model of the creative artist, inhabiting a fictional world of his own yet recognized internationally as a great writer, was a beacon to the ambitious young Agnon. Agnon's fiction can be understood more clearly with Flaubert in mind.

Clear signs of Agnon's debt to Flaubert are found in *A Simple Story*, set in a provincial town in Polish Galicia around 1905, thirty years before the book was first published. As we have seen, the deceptively simple story tells of Hirshl Horowitz, his scholarly father and manipulative mother, the little shop his parents own, his frustrated love for his orphaned cousin, Blume Nacht, his unhappy arranged marriage to Mina Tzimlich, and his breakdown and recovery. Lovelorn as a married man, Hirshl wanders through town finding himself repeatedly in Synagogue Street where Blume lives. Sunken in melancholy yearning, he gazes at the light in her window above.[4] In Flaubert's *Sentimental Education* (*Education Sentimentale*, 1869), Frédèric Moreau stands under Madame Arnoux's window in the Rue Paradis in Paris in a hopeless gesture of desire.[5] Frédèric lives with his suffering, even wallows in it, but Hirshl crosses the border into madness. Terrifying fantasies, particularly of being a cock about to be slaughtered, make him break down. Sent to an asylum in Lemberg (Lviv/Lvov), he sits quietly while his psychiatrist, inexplicably but with therapeutic effectiveness, spins stories about his own small town with its blind beggars. When Hirshl, apparently cured, leaves the asylum with his wife, the couple meet a blind beggar. Hirshl tosses him a coin: 'Had the beggar not been blind he would have marvelled. The coin was worth more than all the

DOI: 10.4324/9781003594802-4

coins he was usually given'.[6] Here again, Agnon borrows from Flaubert. Madame Bovary, tormented by her provincial marriage, failed love affairs, and mounting debts, visits Rouen in a desperate last attempt to raise cash. Passing a blind beggar, she impulsively throws him a coin worth far more than he is usually given. After Emma swallows arsenic in despair, the beggar reappears as she dies 'laughing, a ghastly, frantic desperate laugh, fancying she could see the hideous face of the beggar rising up like a nightmare amid the eternal darkness'.[7]

From early in his career, Agnon saw Flaubert as a literary master. In a letter from late 1916 to his friend and, later, publisher, Salman Schocken, Agnon wrote reverently of Flaubert as a 'poet who sacrificed his life to art'.[8] Agnon's love for Flaubert continued throughout his life; Flaubert was 'Agnon's major literary idol', perhaps the principal model for the 'moderate and controlled realism' to which he aspired.[9] Perfectionists both, Flaubert and Agnon were fanatically dedicated to art and identified with their fictional characters.[10] Flaubert's immersion in his art fascinated Agnon. Flaubert became an expert on the Punic wars for *Salammbo* (1862), on hunting for 'The Legend of St Julian Hospitator' (1876), and for a few brilliant, frenetic pages (consulted by historians to this day) in *Sentimental Education* (1867), on the 1848 revolution in Paris. Agnon, too, did his homework. He made himself a leading expert on rabbinic and hasidic literature, whose style he imitated; and in his years of labor on his last, unfinished novel, *Shira* (1971), he read widely on the crusades. The Flaubertian ideal of artistic perfection to which Agnon aspired recalls the total, selfless religious dedication to the study of Torah.

Flaubert and Agnon were committed monk-like to art, living for it, making everything else – including life itself – subservient to it. From Flaubert, Agnon apparently learned to identify himself with his characters, whether or not as autobiographical portraits. When asked about the origin of Emma, Flaubert famously declared: '*Madame Bovary, c'est moi*!' While writing *A Simple Heart* (*Un Cour Simple*) in 1876, he borrowed a stuffed parrot from the Rouen Museum to put on his desk to inspire his creation of Felicité's parrot and its metamorphosis into the Holy Ghost. Agnon, too, would 'live' his characters' lives. In the late 1920s, he startled a visitor to his Jerusalem home by appearing in his best suit, wearing a top hat and holding a glass of whisky, in celebration of the wedding of Reb Yudel's daughter in the closing scene of his novel *The Bridal Canopy*.

Flaubert and Agnon came from religious cultures in which novels – both writing and reading them – were looked upon as evil. Emma Bovary's mother-in-law tries in vain to wean her from her wicked novels.[11] Agnon's family hoped that he would become a rabbi; they were shocked when he announced that he intended to become – God forbid! – a writer.[12] His family was strictly Orthodox, and East European Orthodox Jews at the time discouraged men from reading secular literature, particularly fiction. Yet there was greater leniency with women, especially in bourgeois homes in which some secular education (e.g. reading German or playing the piano) was a status symbol, improving matrimonial prospects. Since Agnon's mother (confined to home with a heart ailment) and sisters had access to secular literature, Agnon did too, and this reading contributed to his decision as a teenager to become a writer. Agnon found in Flaubert's depiction of mid-19th-century rural

France significant parallels with the Galicia he knew a half-century later: in both worlds, secular learning replaces traditional religious faith which, nevertheless, has a powerful undertow.

The Jewish view of secular literature as a dangerous lure to a forbidden gentile world retarded the development of the Hebrew novel. Flaubert's *Madame Bovary*, one of the most sophisticated modern novels, appeared in 1857, just a few years after the first Hebrew novel, Abraham Mapu's *The Love of Zion* (*Ahavat tsiyon*, 1853), which, despite its historic and linguistic interest, has scant artistic merit. Hebrew and Yiddish writers feeling deficient in a Jewish tradition of fiction were drawn to European literary models: Mendele Mokher Sefarim, for example, to Turgenev, Sholom Aleichem to Dickens, Gnessin to Chekhov, Brenner to Dostoyevsky, and Agnon to Flaubert. These writers sought in mainstream European literature (increasingly available in Hebrew and Yiddish translation) their own voices as Jewish novelists writing about the contemporary world. Agnon was not content with internal Jewish criteria for success as a writer. He sought to compete with the best in European literature.

There was also, of course, the colossal achievement of Mendele, Agnon's main contemporary inspiration in Hebrew, a stylist of enormous invention and versatility, the master-creator of modern Hebrew (and Yiddish) fiction as art.[13] Yet Mendele, like other Haskalah writers, used his art as a tool for social change. Flaubert, in contrast, was closer and more congenial to Agnon's artistic instincts: he saw art as supremely valuable for its own sake. This dedication to art, to *le seul mot juste*, was part of Agnon's heresy, his break with Jewish tradition, seeking the beautiful almost, at times, as the Greeks did, while seeming to remain within Jewish tradition.[14] Flaubert taught Agnon more, how ordinary people – a housewife, doctor, chemist, laborer, psychiatrist, professor – could be elevated above more heroic figures. There is also Agnon's fascination with Flaubert's psychological realism, particularly his depiction of men and their relationships with women. The men tend to be introverted, malleable, and passively subservient to dominant women; they generally need caring for – at times they want to suffer illness for this purpose – and their relationships are often triangular, with hints of latent homosexuality, sadism, and incest, in a counterpoint of romantic idealism and cruel disillusionment.[15]

Flaubert and Agnon were drawn to the small town: Flaubert in France, Agnon in Poland. Agnon made East European Jewish provincial life, particularly in Galicia, his main literary territory. He admired Flaubert's accuracy – especially in *Madame Bovary* and perhaps also *Bouvard and Pecuchet* (1881) – in depicting small-town life, its pettiness, illusions, narrowness, frustrations, and stupidities. Agnon's satirical purposes, inspired perhaps most immediately by Mendele's fiction,[16] are apparent in his creation of the fictional *shtetl* (small town) of Shibush, a play on Buczacz, the name of his birthplace in Galicia, and meaning 'Muddle' or 'Distortion'.[17] There are striking parallel scenes and uses of imagery in Flaubert and Agnon – of flowers, dogs, and cannibals; of children who enter at moments of tension or crisis between grown men and women, as though to suggest childhood roots of their behavior; and of beggars who appear at critical junctures, evidently with symbolic meaning. There is also comparable existential agonizing and questioning of life's meaning amid unfulfilled dreams. Flaubert, confessing to an admirer his aim in writing *Sentimental Education*, did not seek to exalt popular illusions, but on the contrary: '[Flaubert] turned his big hands upside down and opened them as if to let his dreams fall into a bottomless pit'.[18]

Agnon's distinctiveness

Agnon's world in some respects has little in common with Flaubert's. In particular, Frédèric's Parisian social life in *Sentimental Education*, with its hard-up university students and powerful aristocrats, grand madams and courtesans, duels and races, revolutionary passions and brothels, is alien to Agnon, who is largely confined to *shtetl* life, with its types and customs, its religious piety, and unique valuation of study.[19] Flaubert's works are almost all set in early and mid-19th-century France and rooted in French society, while Agnon's fiction, as we have seen, is set in four main locations, corresponding with the main geographic upheavals of his life: from Galicia (1888–1908) to Ottoman Palestine (1908–1912) to Germany (1913–1924) to Palestine under the British Mandate and Israel, where he lived until his death. In a manner characteristic of diaspora Jewry until the modern period, Agnon's characters, mostly diaspora Jews, tend to see themselves as being in exile – and the non-Jews around them see them likewise. Born in Eastern Europe, they cannot regard themselves as Europeans, as do the assimilated West European Jews. Their only spiritual home is the Land of Israel.

The different backgrounds of the two writers are evident in their writings. The almost clinical picture Flaubert gives of his characters, his unflinching accounts of their suffering and darker motivations, remind us that he was a doctor's son, while Agnon's remarkable scholarship testifies to his upbringing by a father and grandfather steeped in Torah. Flaubert's relatively unambiguous, authoritative narrative voice clashes with Agnon's mock pietistic naiveté, slyly disguising and revealing endless subtleties and meanings. Against Flaubert's richly sensual style, with its musical and visual beauty, Agnon's style – though fascinating in its intellectual complexity and psychological penetration, rising to moments of tremendous emotional power – seems at times tone-deaf and color-blind. Also, in much of Agnon's work, especially *A Guest for the Night*, set in Poland after World War I, the owl of Minerva evidently has arrived in the dusk to give its judgment on a doomed world before the final cataclysm. French society in Flaubert's time faced no comparable crisis. The survival of French republicanism was threatened, but not the survival of France.

Triangles, sadomasochism, and incest

Differences aside, Agnon evidently felt a psychological affinity with Flaubert's art. Agnon's creations, like Flaubert's Frédèric in *Sentimental Education*, tend to be inhibited and immersed in their inner lives. They endure frustrating triangular relationships, often in a heady brew of romantic idealism and incestuous sadomasochism.[20] In his handling of triangles, which appear from 'Agunot' (1908), the first story signed 'Agnon', to *Shira*, his last, unfinished novel, Agnon might have learned from Flaubert. The sadistic scenes in *Salammbo*, which Agnon apparently knew,[21] foreshadow Charles' first encounter with Emma, the young, beautiful, headstrong, farmer's daughter from Les Bertaux, as he brushes against her and she hands him his whip.[22] Once married to Charles, Emma, bored and seeking romantic stimulus, has affairs with the dissolute aristocrat, Rodolphe, and the opportunistic young lawyer, Leon.

In *Sentimental Education*, likewise, Frédèric, though platonically attached throughout his adult life to Madame Arnoux, has affairs with various women, including Rosanette ('the Marshal') and Madame Dambreuse. He is also intermittently smitten with Louise Rocque, whom he has known since she was a child in Nogent, and nearly marries. Yet, his love for Madame Arnoux is constant. His idealization of her persists even in later years, when she becomes, in Rosanette's (admittedly biased) words, 'a dumpy, middleaged creature with a complexion like liquorice and eyes as big as manholes'.[23] Frédèric remembers every detail about her: the shape of her nails, the rustle of her dress, the scent of her handkerchief, her comb, gloves, rings, 'as important as works of art, almost endowed with lifelike human beings; they all took possession of his heart and strengthened his passion'.[24]

These fetishistic attachments have many parallels in Agnon,[25] whose characters, too, often idealize, even worship, women who, like Madame Arnoux, seem to be surrogate mothers.[26] Ben Uri adores Dinah in 'Agunot'; Raphael the scribe in 'The Legend of the Scribe' is totally devoted to his wife Miriam; Hirshl yearns hopelessly for Blume Nacht in *A Simple Story*; Gamzu in *Iddo and Enam* elevates Gemulah to the level of a virginal *Shekhinah* figure; Hemdat in 'The Hill of Sand' (*Giv'at ha-Hol*, 1931) describes himself as a 'sleeping prince whose love rouses him to dream again'.[27]

In Flaubert and Agnon, the hero yearns for an out-of-reach beloved with semi-religious feeling. Frédèric's desire for Madame Arnoux is held back by 'a sort of religious awe [*une sorte de crainte religieuse*]' for her,[28] as when he visits her home to gaze sadly at the light shining in her window above.[29] Agnon, adapting this scene in A *Simple Story*, characteristically dresses it with religious associations, of Jewish exile, yearning for the *deus absconditus* and messianic salvation, and of being 'at the handles of the lock' (*al kapot haman'ul*, the phrase from the Song of Songs, which recurs in his fiction and he used as the title of his love stories). Hirshl's beloved Blume is as much out of reach as Madame Arnoux to Frédèric. Hirshl's incessant romantic dreams make him a potential soulmate/victim of Emma Bovary. He gazes longingly up at the light in Blume's window as though praying on the Ninth of Av.[30]

The inner violence that compels this idealization and brings Hirshl to emotional breakdown also recalls Flaubert. Frédèric's lyrical vision of Madame Arnoux, for example, is broken constantly by frustration and violent fantasies. All women remind him of her, 'through some resemblance or some violent contrast'.[31] The sexual side of Frédèric's attraction to Madame Arnoux is diverted onto Rosanette (and, presumably, other women): 'If Madame Arnoux merely brushed him with her finger, his desire immediately conjured up the image of the other woman'.[32]

Frédèric's beloved is the eternally blessed virgin, uncontaminated by his lust: the same might be said of Agnon's longed-for women – for example, Dinah in 'Agunot', Blume in *A Simple Story* and Gemulah in *Iddo and Enam*.

In Flaubert and Agnon, sadomasochism is unleashed in nightmare. In one of Frédèric's fantasies in *Sentimental Education*, 'he thought he was harnessed side by side with [Jacques] Arnoux in the shifts of a cab, and the 'Marshal', sitting astride him, was tearing his belly open with her golden spurs'.[33] In Rosanette, Frédèric finds an outlet for emotions blocked by Madame Arnoux: not just lust but a craving to degrade sadistically. In his Paris home, he keeps a room for a never-to-be rendezvous with Madame Arnoux, and takes perverse satisfaction in bringing Rosanette there: '[A]s a refinement of hatred [*un raffinement de haine*], in order to degrade Madame Arnoux more completely in his mind, he took Rosanette to the house in the Rue Tronchet, and into the room prepared for the other woman'.[34] Towards Rosanette, similarly, Frédéric feels unspoken, unexpressed sadistic hatred: 'Sometimes he was so exasperated by her that he could have watched her die without feeling the slightest emotion'.[35] A similar split between the idealized woman and the hated woman appears in *A Simple Story*, between the virginal Blume, whom Hirshl idealizes, and Mina, his wife who, like Rosanette, becomes the object of his suppressed murderous rage.[36]

Incestuous undercurrents of Frédèric's relationships with women are psychologically linked to his father's death in a duel before his birth.[37] An only child, he is raised entirely by his mother, as Emma Bovary is raised by her widower father. Frédèric discovers his mother in other women, and recreates with them a pattern of filial dependence. Melancholic at school, he sees a woman's face shining in his poetic paradise, 'so that, the first time he had seen [Madame Arnoux], he had promptly recognized her'.[38] Though her name is Sophie, he calls her Marie,[39] with connotations of holiness and virginity. The psychological barrier to the consummation of his love for Madame Arnoux is clear in his final meeting with his beloved, when he is filled with 'a frenzied rabid lust such as he had never known before' together with 'a repugnance akin to a dread of committing incest [*comme l'effroi d'un inceste*]'.[40] As Madame Arnoux leaves him for the last time, 'she kissed him on the forehead like a mother'.[41] Frédèric's obsession has a suicidal side: 'If he had made [Madame Arnoux] his mistress, it had been out of despair, like somebody committing suicide'.[42]

Sado-masochistic triangular relationships in Agnon, too, recreate an infantile pattern of dominant mother and passive son. The maternal image inhibiting Frédèric's sexual feeling for Madame Arnoux in *Sentimental Education* has many parallels in Agnon, who often writes of ailing mothers who die young, leaving their sons withdrawn and troubled in their relationships with women.[43] Like Frédèric, the Agnon hero tends not to be jealous when he loses his 'beloved' to another man. *Yesteryear*, set in Jaffa and Jerusalem around 1910, tells of a young man, Yitzhak Kummer, recently arrived from Galicia. Yitzhak is curiously untroubled when Sonia, with whom he has a brief flirtation in Jaffa, turns to other men: 'Yitzhak knew that he should have been jealous, but he wasn't'.[44] In search of a replacement for his dead mother – '... he was certain there was no one on earth like his mother. Now she was dead, another woman, modest and kind as she, would take her place' – an orange Sonia gives him reminds Yitzhak of his mother. When he kisses Sonia, he thinks of the kiss he gave his mother on her deathbed.[45] Yitzhak tries to escape this incestuous dead end by becoming engaged to another woman, Shifra, daughter of a religious fanatic in Jerusalem. The prospect of marriage fills him with further anxiety and conflict. Shortly before the marriage, he dreams of the woman who has 'abandoned' him and the one whom he is about to marry. Shifra asks 'Do you love me?' He takes her in his arms and finds that he is embracing Sonia.[46] This psychological self-revelation recalls Flaubert in its cruel inadvertent truth.

Shira is the last in a long line of Agnon's stories of men in pursuit of an obscure object of maternal desire. The novel, set in 1930s Jerusalem, opens as Manfred Herbst, professor of ancient Greek history at the Hebrew University, begins an affair with Shira, a nurse in a local lepers' hospital, as his wife gives birth to their third child. This rendezvous coincides worryingly with the anniversary of his mother's death:[47] in fact, Shira's name is a variation of that of his mother, Sarah, after whom the newborn is named. Herbst's graphic fantasies of Shira are full of infantile murderous rage whose irrationality recall Frédèric's cruel impulses toward women in *Sentimental Education*.[48] No sadistic relationship in Agnon's earlier works is as explicit as in *Shira*, though there are hints in *A Simple Story*, for example, when Hirshl's wife accuses him of wanting her to die.[49] Sex, in Agnon as in Flaubert, is inseparable from death. The carriage in which Madame Bovary has a rendezvous with Leon is 'sealed tighter than a tomb';[50] and in 'Agunot', the Holy Ark carved by Ben Uri expresses his sexual longing for Dinah, but when she pushes it over in a fit of rage it resembles a coffin.[51]

Romance and reality

In Flaubert and Agnon, innocent romantic idealism cannot exist free of cynicism and harsh truth. Emma Bovary's adultery with Rodolphe begins at an animal show, in a subtly satiric counterpoint of romantic love, with its cruel, alluring linguistic legerdemain, and the direct, earthy language of the stable. Underneath Rodolphe's flowery language are his sly seduction and Emma's animal lust, unsatisfied and increasingly desperate:

> 'We, now, why did we meet? What turn of fate decreed it? Was it not that, like two rivers gradually converging across the intervening distance, our own natures propelled us towards one another?'
> He took her hand, and she did not withdraw it.
> 'General prize!' cried the Chairman.
> 'Just now, for instance, when I came to call on you …'
> 'Monsieur Bizet of Quincampoix.'
> '… how could I know that I should escort you here?'
> 'Seventy francs!'
> 'And I've stayed with you because I couldn't tear myself away, though I've tried a hundred times.'
> 'Manure!'[52]

Emma discovers the truth about Rodolphe when he aborts their elopement and abandons her. In the crisis before she takes her life, he refuses coldly to help her. Yet Emma, addicted to romance, remains open to seduction. For her, the language of love is not the coin of cliché, but burning reality. She cannot face the truth which, as Flaubert describes it, is as beautiful as it is cruel: to men such as Rodolphe, 'human speech is like a cracked kettle on which we strum out tunes to make a bear dance, when we would move the stars to pity'.[53] Nature herself hints at the betrayal and heartache that follow Rodolphe's empty protestations of his adoration for Emma: poplar branches cover the moon 'like a torn black curtain'.[54]

In *Sentimental Education*, too, romantic attachment – this time genuine and lifelong, that of Frédèric to Madame Arnoux – is played against the disgustingly vulgar. The wealthy, elegant (and conveniently widowed) Madame Dambreuse takes Frédèric to an auction of the possessions of Jacques Arnoux and his wife who, bankrupt, have vanished. The auction tolls the doom of Frédèric's creaky affair with Madame Dambreuse. She commits the unforgivable sin of denigrating Madame Arnoux's belongings, which he worships practically as holy relics. She bids successfully for the casket, linked with Frédèric's dearest memories, in which Madame Arnoux kept her love letters. Frédèric, overwhelmed by love for Madame Arnoux, is furious at Madame Dambreuse's desecration: as the auction ends, so does their affair.

Similar romantic yearnings punctured with vulgarity fill Agnon's fiction. In *A Simple Story*, Hirshl's engagement to Mina is foisted on him in an atmosphere of forced celebration. His strong-willed mother, driven by the allure of bourgeois respectability, wants him to marry Mina as her family is well-off and 'seemly' ('Tzimlich' is her family name). Yet, his cousin, the impoverished Blume Nacht, devoid of a family, obsesses him. Hirshl's frustration and uncertainty reach breaking point at a Hanukkah party given by a friend of Mina's, Sophia Gildenhorn. With psychological precision, Agnon sets out the process leading to Hirshl's unexpected and unwilling engagement to Mina, though Blume's idealized image is always in his thoughts. In his confusion and anger, Hirshl takes Mina's hand, whereupon one of the card-playing men comes to shake Hirshl's hand in mockery: '*Ich gratuliere*'[55] – 'congratulating' him for his unwitting engagement as though Hirshl has won at cards. This '*Ich gratuliere*' deflates Hirshl's romantic longings much as 'Manure' does Emma's at the animal show.

Latent homosexuality

Frustration with women inclines the characters in Flaubert and Agnon to homosexuality. They are often attracted to men, whether out of resemblance or because these men seem to have the forceful ambition and capability they lack. As mentioned earlier, in *Sentimental Education*, Frédèric evidently feels no jealousy toward his beloved's husband, Jacques Arnoux, though he becomes obsessed by Rosanette's former lovers. He is drawn to Arnoux, perhaps because of a 'hidden resemblance'.[56] Even greater is Frédèric's attraction to Deslauriers, his childhood friend. Precisely when Arnoux invites Frédèric to his home for the first time, Deslauriers appears, and his effect on Frédèric is to make him tremble 'like a guilty wife under her husband's gaze'.[57] Frédèric is also drawn to dominant masculine women such as Rosanette ('the Marshal'), toward whom he has fantasies of sado-masochistic encounters.[58]

In Agnon's fiction, too, there are coded signs of latent homosexuality,[59] a clear example of which is in *A Simple Story*. Hirshl, blocked in his sex life, is alarmed by his responsiveness to the touch of Yonah Toiber, the matchmaker who arranges his marriage to Mina: 'Isn't it a disgrace that when he takes my hand in his I want to kiss it? … How smooth are Yonah's hands'.[60] In Flaubert and Agnon, men are often attracted to the lover or husband of women who obsess them. In *Sentimental Education*, Frédèric becomes unbearably curious to know of Rosanette's former lovers. His sexual impulses are mixed with hatred and latent violence:

> He … went on trying to find out the names of her old lovers. She denied them all. A sort of jealousy took hold of him. He took exception to the presents she had been given in the past and was still receiving; and while her personality irritated him more and more, a sensual urge, bestial and violent, would still impel him towards her, producing a momentary illusion which always turned to hatred.[61]

In Agnon's 'The Doctor's Divorce', a doctor comes unhinged by thoughts of his wife's former lover, and his marriage breaks down.

Passivity

Gripped though they are with sado-masochistic fantasies, the male characters of Flaubert and Agnon are notably passive and inconsequential in their outward behavior. In contrast, the women to whom they are attracted are often strong-willed and dominate them. This pattern is especially clear in *Madame Bovary* and *A Simple Story*, in which a dominant, manipulative mother determines the psychology of the central male character. The opening of *Madame Bovary* gives the background to Emma's mismatch with Charles Bovary. As a child, emotionally damaged by his dissolute, drunken, philandering, often-absent father, Charles shuns his father's haphazard efforts to 'make a man' of him. He retreats into the arms of his lonely, doting mother who transfers her frustrated ambitions onto him. She guides him through medical school and arranges his first marriage, to a 45-year-old widow from Dieppe, who is similarly dominant: 'his wife was master'.[62] In *A Simple Story*, too, Hirshl is the victim of a match engineered by his mother. He goes through life convinced that 'everything is in the hands of the woman'.[63]

Madame Bovary opens not with Emma, but with the awkward, unloved 15-year-old Charles in boarding school in Rouen. Years later, Charles qualifies as a doctor, and his first wife dies of a stroke. Only then does Emma enter the story. So shy is Charles that he asks her father, not her, for her hand in marriage. Emma is drawn to the gawky widower to escape her suffocating life on the motherless farm. From the start, Charles is set in uxorious passivity toward her, which suits her. Just as

Charles fails in his medical ambitions (he risks a dangerous operation and, out of his depth, kills the patient), his marriage, too, becomes gangrenous with Emma's adulteries. Yet he tolerates Emma's self-destructiveness as his mother endured his father. He is blind to her betrayals.

In Flaubert and Agnon, the men wait for the women to make the moves. Emma is mannishly assertive in her affairs: with Rodolphe, she steps out squeezed into a waistcoat 'like a man',[64] puffing on a cigarette – a too-daring scene in a novel of 1857: Flaubert was tried for offending public morals with one of the first women in fiction to smoke. Her other lover, Leon, becomes her 'mistress'.[65] Similar sexual reversals are frequent in Agnon, signifying male submission to dominant females: in 'The Hill of Sand', for example, Hemdat has the hands and the laugh of a girl, while Sonia in *Yesteryear* is compared to a boy.[66]

In Flaubert as in Agnon, the unwhole or unconsummated attachment to women is paralleled by the unfinished deed. Despite his mother's 'lofty ambitions' for him, Frédèric has 'no ambition at all'.[67] At most, prodded by Madame Dambreuse, he contemplates becoming a government minister,[68] but in the end he achieves nothing in life. Frédèric's lack of drive emerges in his relations with women, and not only Madame Arnoux. When Madame Dambreuse tells him of her husband's hopes to get him into the Council of State, he thinks: 'So that was her wish. He obeyed'.[69] As for Rosanette, Frédèric is 'her property, her chattel'.[70] Frédèric never proposes marriage, but is proposed to, futilely, twice by Louise Roque and once by the widowed Madame Dambreuse.[71] When Louise first asks him to marry her, his response is: '"But …," replied Frédèric, searching for a reply, "probably … I should like nothing better"'[72] – presumably with emphasis on the conditional.

Agnon's characters share the subservience of Flaubert's characters and their wariness of attachments. In the story 'The Well of Miriam' (*Be'era shel Miryam*, 1909), Hemdat (a loose self-portrait of the young Agnon) drifts with no direction: 'Hemdat did not decide his actions. He was blown by every passing gust of wind.'[73] Hirshl's belief in *A Simple Story* that women control his life is generally shared by Agnon's men: 'A man cannot change himself. Mina and the others do with us as they please'.[74] In his deeper psychological workings, Herbst in *Shira* is an older version of Hirshl: 'By nature Herbst is a passive man, with no small measure of infantilism'.[75]

The clay of personality

Flaubert and Agnon use imagery of clay, wax, or dough to convey the malleability of their characters in the hands of women. In *Sentimental Education*, Frédèric visits Jacques Arnoux's dilapidated pottery factory near Paris, where his beloved shows him around. Amid the dust, noise, and junk, he declares his love – and a wish that he too might have become a potter, 'because then I could have lived close to you!'[76] In reply, Madame Arnoux takes balls of paste from failed repairs, flattens them into a cake and imprints her hand on it. Frédèric, filled with his usual veneration, asks to keep it, a memento of his malleability, for he himself might be described as a 'failed repair' in the hands of the 'eternal Potter' (as in the book of Jeremiah, ch.

18). Madame Arnoux can shape him as she wishes. It is her decision to keep her love for Frédèric platonic and remain a faithful wife, regardless of her husband's infidelities.

Agnon uses similar imagery, of dough or wax, to describe Hirshl's passivity in *A Simple Story*. Hirshl is 'not kneaded from the dough of men of action'.[77] Otherwise he would defy his mother and marry his beloved Blume. His mother ordinarily treats Hirshl coldly, and it is easy for her to manipulate him into marrying the more respectable Mina instead: 'his heart became soft as wax which can be shaped however one wants'.[78] Once married, Hirshl is driven to madness, starting in synagogue when he takes wax from a candle and kneads it: 'He hid his hand in his pocket so no one would see him kneading. The wax fell from his hand and he kneaded himself. Fear hit him that he was doing this without sensation – his fingers seemed to have lost the sense of touch. Perhaps he had died'.[79]

Illness

In Flaubert and Agnon, the hero often wants to be ill and cared for, recreating the maternal bond. In *Sentimental Education*, Frédèric 'longed for a dangerous illness, hoping that he might arouse [Madame Arnoux'] interest in this way'.[80] Agnon's Hemdat, in 'The Well of Miriam', longs to be cosseted with ambiguous maternal and sexual care. He hopes to waste away from tuberculosis to have the pleasure of being nursed.[81] In Agnon's 'Forevermore' (*Ad Olam*, 1954), originally part of *Shira,* the medieval scholar, Adiel Amzeh, voluntarily enters a lepers' hospital in a scene which recalls the end of Flaubert's 'The Legend of St Julian Hospitator': the formerly bloodthirsty prince, scourge of all living creatures, murderer of his own parents, completes his penitential saintly self-abnegation by warming a dying leper with his own body.[82] Perhaps Adiel, too, is a saint, but he comes to the lepers not to perform acts of selfless charity, but because they possess an ancient scroll that unlocks secrets that have baffled him for years. Like those willing to die for the Torah, he is ready to risk his life out of love for his 'scripture'.

Flowers, dogs, and cannibals

Flaubert and Agnon use flowers, dogs, and cannibals to give heightened intensity to the emotional troubles of their characters. Madame Arnoux in *Sentimental Education* throws out the flowers her husband has bought her, while Toni in Agnon's 'Metamorphosis' tosses away a bunch of flowers that her ex-husband, Hartmann, has bought her.[83] In both works, the discarding of flowers might symbolize a woman's rejection of a man much loved, whose self-centredness undermines the marriage.[84]

Dogs appear in Flaubert and Agnon in times of sexual conflict and guilt.[85] On the night before Madame Arnoux is to rendezvous with Frédèric at his Paris home, she dreams of a horrible barking dog and wakes to find her son seriously ill.[86] She interprets this as a heaven-sent warning to avoid adultery. The dog in her dream might represent both her animal instinct and guilty conscience. The dog in Agnon's

Yesteryear is a more complex symbolic creation reflecting, among other things, the hero Yitzhak Kummer's psychological sickness. Driven mad by rabies, the dog bites and infects Yitzhak a week after his marriage, though the marriage itself might be considered a fatal infection. Similarly, Frédèric's 'frenzied rabid lust' for Madame Arnoux is an outer sign of an incurable disease of the soul.[87] Men are consumed not only by their psychological failings, but also, at times, figuratively by women who dominate them. 'Poor darling, I could eat you!' says Rosanette to Frédèric.[88] In Agnon's 'The Lady and the Pedlar', a woman literally slaughters and eats her lovers.[89]

The child

In Flaubert and Agnon, children appear at critical moments. At the life-changing moment in *Sentimental Education* when Frédèric sees Madame Arnoux for the first time, and is overwhelmed as though in a mystical vision, 'A negress with a silk scarf appeared, holding a little girl by the hand'.[90] The little girl is Madame Arnoux's daughter, Marthe, and from the start of his chaste affair with Madame Arnoux, Frédèric is drawn to Marthe. As he rides at night through the Bois de Boulogne, with Marthe asleep on her mother's lap, her head supported by his leg, Frédèric feels that he is communicating with the mother through the child's body.[91] Later, Frédèric imagines having a daughter with his mistress, Rosanette: this daughter 'took after Madame Arnoux and a little after him'.[92] In his hometown of Nogent, Frédèric is attracted to a child, Louise Rocque, as she reminds him of Madame Arnoux, and Louise and Marthe are the same height. When he shows Louise his room, she stretches out on his bed pretending to be his wife.[93] Such a 'marriage' to a child seems less threatening to Frédèric than the prospect of marriage to an adult. Yet, Louise's love for Frédèric does not die. When years later she has become a young woman, he returns home from Paris and his feelings for her reawaken: 'For the first time in his life, Frédèric felt himself to be loved'.[94] He understands, perhaps for the first time, that neither his mother nor Madame Arnoux has ever loved him. Louise could fill the void in him and transform his life. Yet the pattern of unsatisfactory relationships is deeply ingrained. He abandons Louise for Paris and continues his bachelor existence for the rest of his life – like the unloved Agnon heroes, 'at the handles of the lock'.

Little girls appear repeatedly in Agnon's stories of relationships between men and women: for example, in 'The Legend of the Scribe', *A Guest for the Night*, 'Metamorphosis', 'The Doctor's Divorce', *Betrothed*, and *Shira*.[95] In *Betrothed,* Jacob Rechnitz, in his twenties, is reunited in pre-1914 Palestine with Susan, whom he has not seen since they were children in Vienna. A little girl, about the same age as Susan when he last saw her, approaches them and he lifts her up and swings her in the air: 'Darling, I'd love to carry you off'.[96] In *Shira*, a little girl appears the morning after Herbst first commits adultery with Shira. Riding on a tram, Herbst is offered a seat by a little girl, but another man sits down instead and he is left standing with the girl.[97] This pairing hints at Herbst's immaturity, exposed in his sado-masochistic relationship with Shira and his unsatisfied infantile craving for maternal love.

The beggar

Flaubert and Agnon repeatedly use beggars to incarnate a sense of inferiority, a life of emotional poverty. In *Madame Bovary*, the beggar marks the heroine's deterioration.[98] Emma Bovary might be described as a 'beggar of love', seeking fruitlessly in adultery what she lacks in marriage. Her tossing of a valuable coin to the beggar, like Hirshl's identical act in Agnon's *A Simple Story*, suggests a symbolic acknowledgment of inner poverty, an identification with a fellow beggar. Hemdat, in Agnon's 'The Hill of Sand', describes himself as 'a beggar of love who puts his love in a torn knapsack'.[99] Other Agnon protagonists are beggared by love to madness, as is Hirshl. In *Shira*, the beggar, as in *Madame Bovary*, is the ugly image of adulterous neediness. *Shira* opens with Herbst's fantasy at the time his wife is giving birth. Displaced from the marital bed, he is about to start his affair – unplanned, like his newborn child. A blind beggar singing a song with 'no beginning and no end' is swallowed by Shira,[100] a distorted reflection of an infantile wish, perhaps, to have the maternal figure all to himself, even if he is destroyed by it.[101]

The existential quest

The beggar, the cripple, or leper appear in the stories of Flaubert and Agnon to symbolize the purposelessness of their characters, troubled by feelings of emptiness, uselessness, coldness, numbness, and futility. Whatever ambitions they may have, come to dust. In *Sentimental Education*, Frédèric, torn all his life by hopeless idealization of a perfect maternal image sexually out of reach, and loveless lust for real but imperfect women, sums up the futility of his love life: 'Women's hearts were like those desks full of secret drawers fitting one inside another; you struggled with them, you broke your fingernails, and at the bottom you found a withered flower, a little dust, or nothing at all!'[102] The narrator of Agnon's novella *Thus Far*, convinced that his life is empty, tells a parable of a man's pursuit of meaning, ending with his discovery of a scroll addressing him as a fool on a futile quest.[103] The rabid dog in *Yesteryear* is given a conscious awareness of its suicidal misery – and that of the human characters in the novel:

> 'What are we and what is our life? Are all our sorrows and suffering worth the brief moments of pleasure which come our way? As for me, there is no pleasure at all but many troubles, each leading to greater ones.' [The dog] became depressed and wanted to die.[104]

Conclusion

Flaubert's influence on Agnon derived mainly from the example Flaubert set as an artist, his style and insight. Taken together, the similarities in the writings of Agnon and Flaubert indicate how much Flaubert meant to Agnon, as the highest exemplar of the fanatically dedicated artist and as a guide to the depiction of emotional and spiritual suffering. Their works might sometimes be interpreted as having social or religious significance: Madame Arnoux, for example, could be identified with the true and faithful ideals of revolutionary France, steadfast though betrayed and tempted to betray; while Agnon's idealized women, such as Blume, might be seen as symbols of the divine presence (the *Shekhinah*), wandering with and comforting the Jews in exile, always out of reach, yet rousing hope of messianic redemption. Yet the main parallels in their works are in the psychology of their characters and their relations with women. They are mostly ordinary flawed people – except for the authors' genius in bringing them vividly to life. Even when beggared by love, horrified by life's vagaries, and defeated by its cruelty, they do not stop dreaming.

Notes

1 For Agnon's acknowledgment of Flaubert's influence, see Agnon (1976: 245). Among scholars who have drawn attention to Agnon's debt to Flaubert are: Aberbach, Alter, Band, Hochman, Hoffman, Laor, Shaked, Werses, and Yaffe. Details are given in the notes to follow. There are also substantial differences between the two novelists. See p. 68. Agnon did not know French and read Flaubert in German and Hebrew translations. However, neither the scholarly sources nor the autobiographical and biographical writings on Agnon refer to specific translations he would have read in Hebrew and/or German. On the important role of translation in the development of modern Hebrew literature, particularly Agnon's works, see Miron (1992: 397–419).
2 On Agnon's reluctance to acknowledge literary influences, see p. 13.
3 On literary influences on Agnon, including that of Flaubert, see Band (1994: 36ff); Laor (1998: 109–10); and Werses (2000). Flaubert's possible influence on Agnon's love stories has, however, been neglected.
4 Agnon (CW iii 186).
5 Flaubert (1964: I v 86, III iii 352). As there are many Flaubert translations, chapter numbers of the French texts are given here as well as page numbers in the editions used.
6 Agnon (CW iii 268).
7 Flaubert (1977 iii 8: 337). On the symbolism of the beggar in Flaubert and Agnon, see Aberbach (1984) and Alter (1985).
8 Agnon and Schocken (2003: 36). The Hebrew reads: *Hameshorrer shehaya memit atzmo be'ohala shel hashira* (literally: the poet who would kill himself in the tent of poetry), alluding to a talmudic saying attributed to the early 3rd century CE rabbi, Resh Lakish: 'Where do we learn that Torah survives only through the one who kills himself for it? From the passage (Numbers 19:14): "This is the Torah: A man who dies in the tent…"' (*Berakhot* 43b). Agnon, then 28, was a patient in the Berlin Jewish Hospital, undergoing five months convalescence with kidney trouble (evidently self-inflicted through excessive smoking and sleep deprivation, to avoid conscription in World War I). Schocken had recently sent him Emile Zola's book on Flaubert. Agnon's autobiographical novella *Thus Far*, set in Germany during World War I, reflects his interest in Flaubert at this time: the narrator refers to the father of a friend of his as looking like Flaubert (Agnon, CW vii 52). Agnon's wartime convalescence in Berlin, when 'books were Agnon's entire world' (Laor 1998:109), seems to have been crucial in his education as a writer: 'While cannons roared at the front and privation began to gnaw at the civilian population, Agnon was cocooned in the heart of Berlin. Instead of the terror of combat and the misery behind the lines, Agnon spent his days and nights in a stirring encounter with the great European writers. At that fateful moment, they alone truly interested him' (Laor 1998: 110).

9 Shaked (1989: 41, 42). In 1962, Agnon spoke of his joy in reading Flaubert, among others (Agnon 1976: 245). One stylistic trick he might have learnt from Flaubert is the diffusion of unusually powerful emotions and conflicts with seemingly naïve throwaway endings. 'The Legend of St Julian Hospitator' ends: 'And that is the story of St Julian Hospitator, more or less as it is depicted on a stained-glass window in a church in my part of the world' (Flaubert 1961: 87). The end of Agnon's *A Simple Story* is similarly flat: 'And so ends the story of Hirshl and Mina, but not Blume's story. What happened to her is a story in its own right. And the same with Getzl Stein, whom we mentioned briefly; and as for other characters in the story, infinite pens and ink will be needed to get their stories down. God in heaven knows when' (Agnon, CW iii 252). These endings, uncharacteristically clumsy, throw into relief, and create aesthetic distance from, the shocking scenes preceding them, with which the stories actually end: Saint Julian lies down with the leper to keep the dying man warm; Hirshl, the psychiatric patient, just restored to his wife as his sickly firstborn son is sent away, psychologically takes the son's place in his wife's care. Dry and banal, the concluding words enhance the harsh credibility of the scenes preceding them.

10 Considered as a Gestalt, the similarities suggest a very strong influence of Flaubert on Agnon. Yet, as mentioned earlier (p. 13), Agnon was always cagey in acknowledging influence. Apart from Agnon's somewhat uncharacteristic admission of admiration for Flaubert, which falls short of confessing a literary debt, he gave no sign that any of the similarities between his work and Flaubert's were owing to direct influence.

11 Flaubert (1964 ii 8, 12: 138–9, 204).

12 Personal communication with the author, Emunah Yaron (Agnon's daughter).

13 On Mendele and his influence on Agnon, see pp. 8–9, 22–4, and Chapter 5.

14 An identification with Greek rather than rabbinic culture is a striking aspect of Agnon's story, *Betrothed*. See p. 92.

15 On these and other psychological attributes of Agnon's characters, see Aberbach (1984).

16 On Mendele's extraordinary degree of identification with his characters, which might have inspired Agnon, see Aberbach (1993: 30–1). Mendele had a good deal more influence on Agnon, both in style and content, than is generally realized. In particular, Agnon's account of Hirshl's breakdown in *A Simple Story* evidently owes much to Mendele's depiction of Israel's breakdown in *The Mare*. See Chapter 5.

17 Compare Saltykov-Shchedrin's Glupov or Dylan Thomas' Llareggub.

18 Baldick (1964: 13). A more immediate influence on Agnon for the depiction of disillusionment in Hebrew was Mendele. See pp. 23, 49 note 1.

19 Agnon's *shtetl* Jews are in some ways similar to those portrayed by Mendele, his chief literary model for this world, notably in the novella, *And the Crooked Shall be Made Straight*, his most ambitious pre-1914 work; but although Agnon and Mendele are both satirists, Mendele is more overtly a social critic and reformer. Mendele's Jews live a uniform, colorless life, defined by negatives – 'plain Jews, with beards and sidelocks, thin and poor, bent and broken… with all kinds of trouble and poverty': nothing exotic or extravagant, no pomegranates or roses, no heroism or magnificence, no kings and queens, no explorers or adventurers, no spectacle or romance, no bloody combat or love trysts. Introduction, *Of Bygone Days* (1894), (Mendele 1947: 259).

20 On love triangles in Agnon, see, among others, Barzel (1975); Aberbach (1984).

21 Agnon had read *Salammbo* by 1913 (Shaked 1989: 259 note 55). The sadomasochism in *Shira* and other works by Agnon might have been influenced by Flaubert – especially *Salammbo*.

22 Flaubert (1964 i 2: 29).

23 Flaubert (1977 III v: 404).
24 Flaubert (1977 I v 66).
25 Agnon's characters sometimes attach almost fetishistic importance to objects associated with the beloved: e.g. the prayer book in *The Outcast*, the asters in 'Metamorphosis' (1941), or seaweed in *Betrothed* (1943).
26 See Aberbach (1984: 52–6).
27 Agnon (CW iii 371). 'The Hill of Sand' (1931) is a revised version of Agnon's story, 'Tishre' (1911). For a comparison of the two versions, see Band (1968: 68f.). The story crops up also in *A Guest for the Night* (CW iv 74) and *Yesteryear* (CW v 369, 556), again in the context of unhappy love triangles.
28 Flaubert 1977: II iii 86.
29 Flaubert (1977: I v 202, III iii 352).
30 Agnon (CW iii 186).
31 Flaubert (1977: I v 78).
32 Flaubert (1977: II ii 149).
33 Flaubert (1977: II i 134).
34 Flaubert (1977: II vi 283).
35 Flaubert (1977: III iv 386).
36 Agnon (CW iii 172). On Hirshl's homicidal impulses toward his wife, see pp. 17–18 above and p. 99 below.
37 Flaubert (1977: I i 23).
38 Flaubert (1977: II vi 270).
39 Flaubert (1977: II iv 223, II iv 271).
40 Flaubert (1977: III vi 415). Similarly, in Agnon's *Yesteryear*, the moment of Yitzhak Kummer's greatest attraction to Sonia – repeatedly described as a mother figure to him (Agnon, CW v 90, 116, 127) – is the moment when he parts from her (185). Incestuous inhibition evidently contributes to Frédèric's difficulties with women. Flaubert's observation on Frédèric's passivity with women might apply to some of Agnon's characters as well: 'For some men, the stronger their desire, the more difficult it is for them to act [*L'action, pour certains hommes, est d'autant plus impracticable que le desir est plus fort*]' (Flaubert 1977: II iii 174).
41 Flaubert (1977: III vi 415). The pattern of attachment of men in Flaubert's stories to older women evidently had its life model in Flaubert's romantic passion for Elisa Schlesinger, who was 26 when he met her aged 14 in 1836. In *Madame Bovary*, Emma is several years older than her lover, Leon, and behaves 'like a virtuous mother [*comme une mère vertueuse*]' to him (Flaubert 1964: III vi 294).
42 Flaubert (1977: III iii 353).
43 On the dead mother in Agnon, see Aberbach (1982, 1984).
44 Agnon (CW v 239).
45 Agnon (CW v 90, 116, 127).
46 Agnon (CW v 90, 393).
47 Flaubert, too, associates change in the sexual life of his characters with bereavement: Charles Bovary marries Emma during the period of mourning for his dead first wife, and Emma's adultery with Leon coincides with the death of her father (Flaubert 1964: 33ff, 261).
48 Flaubert (1977: II vi 283).
49 Agnon (CW iii 172). See pp. 17–18. According to Robert Alter (1989: 575–6), 'Herbst, unlike Flaubert's Emma, does not "discover in adultery all the platitudes of married life" but, on the contrary, finds that a fleeting carnal encounter with an unlikely object of

desire opens up vertiginous new perspectives, makes bourgeois hearth and home unliveable for him, impels him in ways he is hardly conscious of to do something radically other with his life'. In fact, for Emma, too, adultery opens new perspectives – including the possibility of eloping overseas with her lover – and makes her home life ultimately unliveable: what she does that is 'radically other' is try to take control of her life through her adulteries and, when this fails, commits suicide. A death-wish or preoccupation evidently afflicts Herbst as well, as suggested in his morbid interest in burial customs in ancient Greece and his fantasies of contracting leprosy. Herbst's lack of productivity is comparable to that of Flaubert's *Bouvard and Pecuchet* (Hoffman 1991: 17).

50 Flaubert (1964 iii 1: 256).

51 Agnon (CW ii 209).

52 Flaubert (1964: I viii 161).

53 Flaubert (1964: II xii 203).

54 Flaubert (1964: 210). Similar imagery of torn cloth, symbolizing damaged relationships, recurs throughout Agnon, starting from the opening of 'Agunot'. See p. 43 above and pp. 133–4 below.

55 Agnon (CW iii 108).

56 Flaubert (1977: I v 79, II iii 176).

57 Flaubert (1977: I iv 54).

58 Flaubert (1977: II i 134).

59 On homosexual fantasies in Agnon, see below p. 102ff.

60 Agnon (CW iii 213).

61 Flaubert (1977: III iv 385–6).

62 Flaubert (1964: I i 24).

63 Agnon (CW iii 98).

64 Flaubert (1964: II xii 204). In Emma's first meeting with Charles Bovary, 'she carried a pair of tortoise-shell eye-glasses attached, in masculine fashion, to two buttonholes of her bodice' (1964: II xii 29).

65 Flaubert (1964: III v 289).

66 Agnon (CW iii 363, 405; v 94, 95, 116).

67 Flaubert (1977: I i 23, I v 93).

68 Flaubert (1977: I vi 107).

69 Flaubert (1977: II ii 160).

70 Flaubert (1977: III iii 350).

71 Flaubert (1977: III v 253, III ii 347, III iv 372).

72 Flaubert (1977: II v 253).

73 In Yaron et al. (1994: 13); originally in *Hapo'el hatsa'ir*, 21 May 1909.

74 Agnon (CW iii 98, 163).

75 Schocken (1978: 230). There seems to have been a strong autobiographical basis to the passivity of Agnon's characters. Like the narrator of Agnon's posthumous novella *In the Shop of Mr. Lublin*, who says 'I am not a man of deeds' (Agnon 1974: 12), Agnon said of himself 'I am not a man of deeds and, if given the opportunity by Heaven, I would almost certainly choose the spirit, not the deed' (Agnon 1976: 41). Yet, according to Dov Sadan, a Hebrew University professor who knew Agnon well for many years, Agnon actually 'hated passivity' and wanted badly to create strong and active characters, but found, however, that his work was too closely anchored to his own psychology (personal communication to the author, Dov Sadan). Similarly, Robert Baldick points out in the Introduction to *Sentimental Education* that Frédèric, including his passive temperament, 'is basically a self-portrait of the author' (1977: 8). Nevertheless, Flaubert and Agnon

shared a healthy egotistic self-regard for their own talents. Flaubert, for example, was deeply annoyed at being awarded the Legion d'Honneur with another writer whom he despised as a nonentity, while Agnon, awarded the Nobel Prize jointly with Nelly Sachs in 1966, lamented that in his old age he had been saddled with a 'concubine'.

76 Flaubert (1977: II iii 199).

77 Agnon (CW iii 80).

78 Agnon (CW iii 100).

79 Agnon (CW iii 214). Hirshl's breakdown has limited points of contact with Emma Bovary's. Both collapse when their futile romantic hopes prove to be illusory (when Emma is frustrated in her love for Rodolphe, and Hirshl in his love for Blume Nacht), both require several months convalescence, and neither tells their spouse the true reason for their unusual behavior.

80 Flaubert (1977: I v 79).

81 In Yaron et al. (1994: 21); originally in *Hapo'el hatsa'ir*, 3 June 1909.

82 'Forevermore' was originally part of Agnon's *Shira*, in which the leprosy motif is extended and, as Gavron (1997) observes, there is an admiring portrayal of Saul Adler (1895–1966), founder of the Institute of Microbiology at the Hebrew University, whom Agnon knew personally, who risked his life to conduct medical experiments. Adler's name might be alluded to in the title *Ad Olam* and in the first name of the scholar in this story, Adiel Amzeh, who enters the lepers' hospital and never leaves. On a personal note: my father, Moshe Aberbach, then 14, met Saul Adler's father, Sinai, after arriving in Leeds in a *Kindertransport* in 1938. Sinai Adler, a merchant and trustee of the Leeds Talmud Torah, helped save the lives of my grandparents, Joseph and Rachel Aberbach, whom he sponsored in their flight from Nazi-ruled Vienna in 1939.

83 Flaubert (1977: I v 94, II iii 190); Agnon (CW iii 463).

84 In Turgenev's *First Love* (1860), the young man Vladimir's disappointment in love is symbolized by trampled flowers. In contrast, when Herzog, at the end of Saul Bellow's novel, 'being thoughtful, being lovable', picks flowers for Ramona, his lover who is coming to dinner, he considers throwing them away – he has suffered much and caused much suffering in his two marriages – but he keeps the flowers for the coming rendezvous.

85 On similarities in descriptions of dogs in Flaubert and Agnon, see A.B. Yaffe (*Davar* 24/31 May, 1984). In both Flaubert and Agnon, dogs symbolize not just the animality of human nature, but also the folly of ambition. In a scene that Agnon might have had in mind in his portrait of the dog Balak in *Yesteryear*, Flaubert's *Bouvard and Pecuchet* decide to commit suicide (unsuccessfully) after seeing the corpse of a dog: 'The four legs were all dried up. The jaws grinned to reveal ivory fangs beneath bluish lips; in place of the belly was a muddy coloured mass, so swarming with vermin that it seemed to palpitate. It shook, struck by the sun, under the buzzing flies, in this intolerable stench, a savage and almost devouring stench' (Flaubert 1976: 218). Agnon's description of the death agonies of Yitzhak Kummer, who dies after being bitten by a rabid dog at the end of *Yesteryear*, might be compared to Flaubert's gruesome account of the protracted death of Emma Bovary. Sexual disgust in Flaubert might be attributed partly to the fact that the author contracted syphilis during his travels in the Middle East (1849–1851), and his early death at 58 was brought about by this disease.

86 Flaubert (1977: II vi 278–9).

87 Flaubert (1977: III vi 415).

88 Flaubert (1977: III iii 350).

89 At times, though, the woman is consumed: the auction of Madame Arnoux's clothes, suggesting to Frédèric crows tearing a woman's body to pieces (Flaubert 1977: III v

406), recalls the end of Agnon's 'The Lady and the Pedlar', when crows literally consume the lady's corpse. On 'The Lady and the Pedlar', see pp. 14–15.

90 Flaubert (1977: I i 18).
91 Flaubert (1977: I v 94–5).
92 Flaubert (1977: III iii 356). Frédèric's fantasy of having a child with some of his own traits is paralleled in an extreme form in Agnon's 'The Doctor's Divorce'. The doctor in Agnon's story also imagines having a child, but is driven insane with irrational jealousy. He is terrified at the idea that the child will look like his wife's former lover.
93 Flaubert (1977: I vi 103).
94 Flaubert (1977: II v 251).
95 On the appearance of children in moments of crisis in adult relationships in Agnon's stories, see Aberbach (1984: 66–9).
96 Agnon (CW vii 270).
97 Agnon (1971: 32).
98 Flaubert (1964: I ix 79, III vii 311, III viii 337).
99 Agnon (CW iii 371).
100 Agnon (1971: 8).
101 The phrase about songs 'with no beginning or end' recalls the beggars in *A Simple Story* (Agnon, CW iii: 233, 236).
102 Flaubert (1977: III iv 384).
103 Agnon (CW vii 51). For the full quote, see p. 26.
104 Agnon (CW v 575). The phrase, 'What are we and what is our life?', is taken from the introductory section of the Morning Prayers (*Shacharit*), which culminates however by denying the evident futility of existence in an assertion of faith.

4 Loss and creativity: Agnon and Lawrence

Agnon shares with a number of writers, such as Walt Whitman and D.H. Lawrence, the arrival of an artistic gift where little, or relatively little, had been evident before. A new maturity in Agnon's creative voice coincides with the period of grief following his separation from his mother and her death in 1909. Lawrence (1885–1930) underwent an even greater transformation after his mother's death in late-1910; and as Frank Kermode observes, 'The death of a parent often signifies mysterious upheaval and change in the personal life, but the totality of Lawrence's break with the past is very striking.'[1] Both were young men at the time, at the start of their careers, and not yet widely known.

The differences between the two novelists, in background, upbringing, and artistic aims, are considerable; yet they share the experience of overwhelming grief at the outset of their careers. Loss was a watershed in their creative lives, marking their departure from the small towns of their childhood – Agnon from Buczacz in Austro-Hungarian Galicia, Lawrence from Eastwood, Nottinghamshire – to the great urban centers of literary culture, Agnon to Berlin, Lawrence to London. Loss proved vital both as a motivating force in their writing and also in furnishing, directly or indirectly, much subject matter.[2] In general, it may be that art enlisted in the process of grief confronts and masters otherwise-unbearable emotions, especially those linked to difficulties in the relationship with a dead parent. We possess art, wrote Nietzsche, so that we shall not perish of truth.[3] Art can help palliate grief, perhaps also to distance the self from grief. The fiction of Agnon and Lawrence records the close attachment to the mother in life and the impact of her death for many years afterwards.

The death of Agnon's mother triggered a remarkable outpouring of creativity which, in some ways, continued until his own death, in 1970. In an insight suggesting a strong psychoanalytic influence (perhaps of Max Eitingon, his wife's analyst, or Freud himself), Agnon in 1948 linked his destiny of fame to his tearful longing for attention from the absent mother.[4] In Spring 1908, he left Europe for Jaffa. His mother was mortally ill with a heart condition and, as he put it in *A Guest for the Night*, 'a dark sadness crouched over our heads'.[5] Her precarious health must have stirred up his guilt at leaving her.[6] As the eldest of five children, Agnon had a special place in his mother's affections. They were drawn even more closely

DOI: 10.4324/9781003594802-5

together by the frequent absences of her husband on business (he was a furrier) and by her infirmity. She spurred her son's literary ambitions, introducing him to the classics in world literature, stimulating him to become an artist.

Agnon had written a great deal in Buczacz, mostly in Yiddish, but after landing in Jaffa, he underwent an artistic metamorphosis; at this time, he adopted the name 'Agnon'. His story '*Agunot*', written a few months after his arrival, is stamped with his distinct Hebrew style, filled with delicate shades of feeling and music, a triumph for a man barely into his twenties. Some credit for Agnon's blossoming as an artist must go to the cultural milieu of his new home, where Hebrew, however imperfectly used, was a living and inspiring language. But can the change in environment alone explain Agnon's artistic leap forward?

Agnon wrote a series of stories during his mother's final illness and after her death, of which '*Agunot*' stands out. Written before the mother's death, and evidently in anticipation of it, this story reflects Agnon's grief over separation from her and fear that he would not see her again. Even so, '*Agunot*' is not simply disguised autobiography. Agnon was clearly aware of the need for artistic distance: he portrays a woman, not a man, bereaved of her mother; but a man – the artist, Ben Uri – is afflicted with grief, remorse, and guilt, as if he were the one bereaved.[7] Set in the 19th century in the ancient community of Jewish Jerusalem, the story quivers with the melancholy of unrequited love. The wealthy Ahiezer betrothes his daughter, Dinah, to Ezekiel, a promising young rabbi and scholar in Poland whom he has never seen, and for whom he builds a house of prayer and study. While awaiting Ezekiel's arrival, he hires a local artist, Ben Uri, to carve the Holy Ark, without which the building would be soulless. Ahiezer's plans begin to unravel as Ben Uri secretly falls in love with Dinah, and she with him, but so absorbed is he in his art that he forgets her; unknown to him Dinah is filled with jealousy at being supplanted by a work of art. When he finishes the Ark, it is as though he has suffered a great loss: he feels like 'an empty vessel', and he weeps in misery.[8]

The dead mother is not vital to the plot; she enters the story after Dinah, enraged at Ben Uri's devotion to his work, goes to his workroom at night and pushes his Ark over, into the garden outside. In tainting herself with this heretical act, she feels bitter remorse, she is no longer the pure image of her mother:

> On her couch at night Dinah lies, her heart beating mercilessly with remorse. Her wickedness is great, her sin unendurable, in shame she buries her head in the pillow… Dinah leaped from the bed, lit a taper – and saw the large mirror on the wall. She saw her mother's face, but it no longer had her goodness. It was the face of a sinner, a rebel… 'Mother, mother!' her heart cried out – but she found no one.[9]

Dinah's guilty feeling of being judged, and her contrition, though brought on by the act of violence against the Ark, resembles emotions often felt by the bereaved toward the dead; and her anger, too, is a characteristic reaction to loss.

From '*Agunot*' onwards, the Agnon hero cannot fully detach the memory of his dead mother from other women to whom he becomes attached. This is a fundamental point of similarity between Agnon and Lawrence: both grapple with a similar emotional torment. 'The Well of Miriam' (1909), written shortly after the death of Agnon's mother, contains three stories, each of which tells of an artist whose beloved is ill and dies before her time, and whose grief is expressed in art. In one of these stories, a young writer, Hemdat (based on Agnon), mourns his beloved Zohara and writes the story 'Luz' in her memory; in another (the seed of the later story, 'The Legend of the Scribe'), Raphael the scribe writes a scroll in memory of his wife 'who passed away in the prime of her days'; and in the frame story, Hemdat describes the imminent death of his mother. Hemdat's guilt at leaving Zohara is transparently Agnon's: 'The day you leave, she'll surely die.' Zohara dies, blood streaming from her mouth over Hemdat's picture and the verses he has written for her; and he is left vulnerable, his soul turned to 'bits of rags' by her death. It might be said that the stain of the mother's death is indelibly present in all Agnon's later writing.

An early poem, 'I am the cup of dreams', used as the epigraph for one of the stories Agnon wrote in the wake of his mother's death, '*Tishre*', recalls Lawrence's confession of being shattered by grief for his mother:

> She lifted the cup to her lips,
> and swallowed my dreams.
> My cup shattered, her teeth plundered the pieces,
> only a part miraculously survived.[10]

Lawrence uses similar imagery of the shattered cup and of being swallowed when he wrote to Louie Burrows in Eastwood proposing marriage a few days before his mother's death in 1910 (by coincidence, approximately the same time that Agnon wrote his poem):

> Then when you think of my mother: if you've ever put your hand round the bowl of a champagne glass and squeezed it and wondered how near it is to crushing – the wine glass going through your fingers – that's how my heart feels – like the champagne glass... Nobody can have the soul of me. My mother has had it, and nobody can have it again. Nobody can come into my very self again, and breathe me like an atmosphere. Don't say I am hasty this time – I know, Louie – whom I wish I could marry the day after the funeral – she would never demand to drink me up and have me.[11]

Agnon's grief, like Lawrence's, was evidently never fully overcome, and enters his later, more sophisticated works. 'The Outcast' (*Ha-Nidakh*, 1919), which Agnon began at the time he wrote '*Agunot*' and 'The Well of Miriam', tells of a young man, Gershom, in a 19th century East European town. His mother's premature death drives him to an infantilism preventing him from separating her memory from the image of his fiancée: 'He was overcome by childishness, like a baby by his mother's side. Sleep enveloped him sweetened with passages from the Song of Songs and the image of his betrothed.'[12] Objects belonging to his mother are charged with meaning for him: her prayerbook becomes almost an extension of her, an object of semi-erotic veneration and longing: 'How he desired to embrace and kiss his mother's prayerbook. When she, of blessed memory, had prayed, her hands would embrace the covers as the hands of Moses had grasped the two Tablets of the Law.'[13] After the mother dies, her shrouds call up in Gershom the terror of desertion. His grief breaks his heart, and he dies. In 'The Sister' (*Ahot*, 1910), Na'aman, a young man in Jaffa recently bereaved of his mother, is struck by the resemblance between her and his sister who sits, as their mother did, by the window, her trembling shoulders, bent head, and the halo of sadness around her, all recalling the mother, as does the novel she is reading, which had belonged to the mother and, like her, leaves it unfinished. Overcome by these memories, Na'aman kisses his sister passionately.[14]

In other works, too, the same preoccupation with an ailing or deceased mother is found. The stories, *In the Prime of Her Life* and *A Simple Story* both start with the death of a mother, a trauma that determines the events that follow. In *Iddo and Enam*, the mood of loss and searching prevails, but in ethereal form, as if the hurt has shrunk, leaving a mist of grief, a scar hidden at the center. Yet, it is in the early stories that Agnon expresses most forcefully the shock and despair of bereavement and the intricate process of grief. Crude as these stories are in some respects – they are, after all, the work of a very young man struggling to create his own artistic voice – they are impressive in emotional conviction and, at times, in stylistic beauty. Agnon's separation from his mother, her final illness and death, were among the chief catalysts in his rapid growth to artistic maturity, bringing to the surface conflicts and obsessions which haunted him to the end of his life.

Lawrence and the lost mother

D.H. Lawrence belonged to the same generation as Agnon – he was two years older – and he came to artistic maturity at about the same time, also during the emotional crisis of his mother's death from cancer in December 1910. Unlike Agnon, he was at home, in Eastwood, at the time, and he nursed his mother as she lay dying. His response to this, the greatest blow of his life, was to explore his grief, confronting it again and again until he emerged from it some two years later. He recorded his shock and despair as he sat by her bed, in the first draft of *Sons and Lovers* and in poems such as 'The Inheritance', in which the dying mother bequeaths her son the 'gift of tongues', the power of his art.

The years 1910–1912, from his mother's death until Lawrence's elopement with Frieda Weekley, saw an extraordinary outburst of creativity: most of the poems in *Amores, Love Poems*, *New Poems*, the novel *The Trespasser*, drafts of most of the stories in *The Prussian Officer*, including 'The Vicar's Daughter', and Lawrence's crowning semi-biographical achievement, the novel *Sons and Lovers*. As in Agnon's case, Lawrence's style changed in the process of his grief, from the awkward, imprecise romanticism of his youth to a more mature and distinctive style, sharper and freer, and more realistic emotionally.

In the period after his mother's death, Lawrence's physical health declined, and serious illness began, partly under the burden of grief. In a cancelled passage in the 1928 preface to his *Collected Poems*, Lawrence wrote of his 'sick year', when:

> For me, everything collapsed, save the mystery of death, and the haunting of death in life. I was twenty-five and from the death of my mother, the world began to dissolve around me, beautiful, iridescent, but passing away substanceless. Till I almost dissolved away myself, and was very ill.[15]

In some poems (e.g. 'Bereavement' and 'Loss'), he describes his grief as physical pain and a heavy pressure across his chest. Lawrence declared that 'many of the poems are so personal that, in their fragmentary fashion, they make up a biography of an emotional and inner life.'[16] His relentless obsession with his loss at this time may be gauged by the titles of these poems and others, such as 'My Mother Dead' (later changed to 'The End'), and 'My Love, My Mother' (later 'The Virgin Mother');[17] and the openings of some of these poems – 'Since you did depart' ('The Inheritance'), 'Since I lost you…' ('Silence') – declare the depth of the poet's grief.

The content of these poems later found its way into *Sons and Lovers* and other works: the main difference between the poetry and the prose is that the poetry is often an immediate creative reaction to grief, perhaps even written down at the time, whereas the prose explores this grief, amplifying and adapting it in the dynamic context of family bonds, focusing particularly in the end on the mother's illness and death. From the poems alone, the reader would hardly have an inkling of the abnormal attachment and conflict between mother and son, created by the mother's troubled marriage, by the father's distance from the family as he was a rough, uneducated miner, by the older brother's death when Lawrence was sixteen, and by his own weak constitution. All this brought him firmly under his mother's control, and together with his consequent struggle for self-realization, is central in the novel, in which the account of the Morel family is essentially that of Lawrence's own family.

In *Sons and Lovers*, Gertrude Morel, trapped in marriage, becomes abnormally attached to her sons, first William, then with William's death, to Paul, who responds to her grief with a near-fatal illness. Their bond is sealed by the love with which she rescues him, and this helps to account for the extremity of Paul's grief when she dies:

> 'I s'll die, mother!' he cried, heaving for breath on the pillow.
> She lifted him up, crying in a small voice:
> 'Oh, my son – my son!'
> That brought him to. He realized her. His whole will rose up and arrested him. He put his head on her breast, and took ease of her for love.
> 'For some things,' said his aunt, 'it was a good thing Paul was ill that Christmas. I believe it saved his mother.'
> Paul was in bed for seven weeks. He got up white and fragile. His father had brought him a pot of scarlet and gold tulips. They used to flame in the window

> in the March sunshine as he sat on the sofa chattering to his mother. The two knitted together in perfect intimacy. Mrs. Morel's life now rooted itself in Paul (ch. 6).[18]

This family background is mostly absent in the poetry, though the elements of grief for the mother are virtually identical in the poetry and in the prose: for example, the mother as dead bride appears in the poem 'The Bride' and is repeated in *Sons and Lovers*. Both poetry and prose convey an absence of feeling, familiar in grief. Lawrence's confession on December 12, 1910, three days after his mother's death, that 'I have died, a bit of me…'[19] is repeated in 'The End': 'some of me is dead tonight'; and in *Sons and Lovers*, this numbness is associated with Paul's sense of meaninglessness when spring comes: 'The first snowdrops came. He saw the tiny drop-pearls among the grey. They would have given him the liveliest emotion at one time. Now they were there, but they did not seem to mean anything' (ch. 15).[20] In a letter dated five days after his mother's death, Lawrence writes that he cannot get his mother out of his thoughts, and images of her, for example of her grey hairs, intrude persistently;[21] and this image is translated beautifully in 'Sorrow', where the poet contemplates the disturbing sight of the smoke from his cigarette, reminding him of how in her final illness he would carry his mother gaily downstairs at Eastwood and find, in somber reprimand,

> a few long grey hairs
> On the breast of my coat; and one by one
> I watched them float up the dark chimney.

The poetry is echoed, again, in *Sons and Lovers*:

> He [Paul] sat in the kitchen, smoking. Then he tried to brush some grey ash off his coat. He looked again. It was one of his mother's grey hairs. It was so long! He held it up, and it drifted into the chimney. He let go. The long grey hair floated and was gone in the blackness of the chimney (ch. 13).

Lawrence conveys a desperate searching, and the mother's presence is felt constantly in the poetry – 'I see each shadow start/ With recognition' ('The Inheritance'); 'I feel your silence touch my words as I talk' ('Listening') – and in *Sons and Lovers*, too, 'his soul could not leave her, wherever she was. Now she was gone abroad into the night, and he was with her still. They were together' (ch. 15). The poet seeks to incorporate her into himself – 'If I could have wrapped you in myself' ('The End') – a wish linked in *Sons and Lovers* with Paul's death-wish and the consolation, frequently felt by the bereaved, that the dead live on in them:

> 'She's dead. What was it all for – her struggle?'
> That was his despair wanting to go after her.
> 'You're alive.'
> 'She's not.'

> 'She is – in you.'
> Suddenly he felt tired with the burden of it.
> 'You've got to keep alive for her sake,' said his will in him (ch. 15).

In the poetry, the wish for death is at times unambiguous. In 'Trouble and Shame', the poet likens his body to a useless piece of lumber which he would like to cast off, and in 'Call into Death' he longs for reunion in death, like a bird ascending from a cathedral dome, lost in the haze of the sky. In the sense of emotional depletion, of being small and helpless in a cruel, despairing world, Lawrence found new assurance and power of expression. In 'Blue', the poet's sense of detachment from life –

> I who am substance of shadow, I all compact
> Of the stuff of the night, finding myself all wrongly
> Among the crowds of things in the sunshine
>   jostled and racked –

is shared by Paul Morel, tormented by the barrier between himself and the world after his mother's death:

> He saw the face of the barmaid, the gabbling drinkers, his own glass on the slopped, mahogany board, in the distance. There was something between him and them. He could not get in touch (ch. 15).[22]

Paul no longer knows where he belongs in the world, amid 'the vastness and terror of the immense night… Where was he? – one tiny upright speck of flesh, less than an ear of wheat lost in the field.'[23] In the poem, 'The Chief Mystery', again, the poet stands in the dark of night contemplating the grass, the wind and clouds about him, asks, 'But I, where among them am I?'

Finally, in poetry and prose alike, a movement toward recovery is felt, in poems such as 'Brother and Sister' – 'let us here forget, let us take the sheer/ Unknown that lies before us…' – expressed with finality in the concluding lines of *Sons and Lovers*:

> She was the only thing that held him up, himself, amid all this. And she was gone, intermingled herself. He wanted her to touch him, have him alongside with her.
>
> But no, he would not give in. Turning sharply, he walked towards the city's gold phosphorescence. His fists were shut, his mouth set fast. He would not take that direction, to the darkness, to follow her. He walked towards the faintly humming, glowing town, quickly.

Lawrence greatly admired, and was influenced by, Walt Whitman who, likewise, wrote *Leaves of Grass* (1855) at a time of grief for a lost parent. In 'As I Ebb'd With the Ocean of Life', Whitman describes a sense of union with a parental natural world which he is a part of but can never understand, in imagery of lines of drift and debris – 'The rim, the sediment that stands for all the water and all the land of the globe…/ These little shreds standing for you and me and all' – on the seaward side of Long Island (Paumanok), where the poet was born in 1819:

> Chaff, straw, splinters of wood, weeds and the sea-gluten,
> Scum, scales from shining rocks, leaves of salt-lettuce, left by the tide…

Amid this detritus, the poet finds the source of his poetry, in the ebb and flow of life, and in death and union with the lost beloved. Union with nature is for the poet union with the eternal father on the shores of his birthplace:

> I too Paumanok,
> I too have bubbled up, floated the measureless float, and been
> wash'd on your shores,
> I too am but a trail of drift and debris,
> I too leave little wrecks upon you, you fish-shaped island.
>
> I throw myself upon your breast my father,
> I cling to you so that you cannot unloose me,
> I hold you so firm till you answer me something.
>
> Kiss me my father,
> Touch me with your lips as I touch those I love,
> Breathe to me while I hold you close the secret of the murmuring I envy.

Lawrence, in 'New Heaven and Earth' (1917), has imagery reminiscent of (and possibly influenced by) Whitman:

> I am thrown upon the shore.
> I am covering myself with the sand.
> I am filling my mouth with the earth.
> I am burrowing my body into the soil.
> The unknown, the new world!

Lawrence's final poems, written shortly before his own death in 1930, are filled with sharp emotion, as in 'Shadows', with its rhythmic portrayal of the slow fall of leaves amid the shadows and silence of autumn, connecting the poet with 'the deep oblivion of earth's lapse and renewal'.

Agnon and Lawrence: the failure to escape

Any sense of an ending, of reconciliation, with the dead mother in Agnon and Lawrence is undermined and rejected in their later fiction. In the semi-biographical novel, *A Guest for the Night* (1939), Agnon describes a writer, also named Samuel, returning to his Galician hometown, intending to visit his mother's grave. Shortly before the visit, he meets her nurse, the ancient, embittered Freida Kaisar, who complains, to the narrator's discomfiture, that her son has left her, and she has no use for life without him: 'Wouldn't it have been better if he had cut my throat?'[24] When Samuel turns to go to his mother's grave, his eyes are filled with tears of guilt.[25]

The mother's grave appears also in the story, 'Metamorphosis' (*Panim Aherot*), where Toni, just divorced from Hartmann, has planted asters on a mound over her mother's grave; through these asters the mound, from which Hartmann recalls falling as a child into a ditch, is associated with the mother's grave and with Toni herself, for in a fantasy of his, Toni holds a bunch of asters to her face and 'the asters spread, covering the mound' – like the asters over the mother's grave.[26] Toni, in this subtle way, is identified with her dead mother much as Susan is in *Betrothed* (*Shevu'at Emunim*). Hartmann's fantasies, like those of Jacob Rechnitz in *Betrothed*, point to a strong attachment, typical in Agnon, to the dead mother.

Set in Jaffa c. 1900, *Betrothed* tells of Jacob, a marine botanist trained at Vienna University, who devotes himself to the study of seaweed in the eastern Mediterranean. Though Rechnitz works as a schoolteacher in Jaffa, real education for him lies in the living world of the sea. He revels in having the seaweed to himself almost as a child might rejoice at having a loved mother to himself.[27] Rechnitz's love of the sea, influenced by Homer, and expertise in the natural sciences, are a living example of Haskalah ideals. Here is a young man devoted to science amid the growing and dynamic Hebrew-speaking environment of the second *aliyah* in the land of Israel. Each day, when he hires a boat to fish for seaweed, he feels himself transported to the origins of human life, 'where Adam's ancestors lived'.

> With a kind of net and iron tools, he pulled in seaweed that did not reach the shore. His heart beat hard like a hunter after the prey. He never was seasick; no, these underwater mysteries, miracles of creation, gave him strength, as they grew in the sea like flower gardens, like tangled shrubs, like a forest in the shadowy waters, their eyes like yellow brimstone, like crimson, like live flesh, like clear pearls, like olives, like coral, like peacock feathers, clinging to reef and rock. Lovingly, he called the sea and its plants 'My orchard! My vineyard!'[28]

Though absorbed in his work, Jacob remains bound to Susan, his childhood fiancée, and to her mother, who died prematurely.[29] Both the childhood oath and his grief are reawakened when Susan and her father re-enter Jacob's life in Jaffa.

Lawrence, too, was magnetized by the effects of traumatic early relationships. In stories written over a decade after his mother's death and collected in *Three Novellas* (1923), Lawrence explores the obsessional fear of dependence and inner rage, as Agnon does in his fiction – particularly *A Simple Story* – in which love and marriage are, likewise, associated with entrapment.[30] 'The Captain's Doll' is blunt in rejecting love – 'If a woman loves you, she'll make a doll of you'; the vice of mother-love threatens the human race with crippling dependence. Women should not be assertive but passive – and unmaternal. At the end of the story, 'The Fox', seaweed imagery describes the way the murderer, Henry, wants March, the woman for whom he has committed murder:

> No, she had to be passive, to acquiesce, and to be submerged under the surface of love. She had to be like the sea-weeds she saw as she peered down from the boat, swaying forever delicately under water, with all their delicate fibrils put tenderly out on the flood, sensitive, utterly sensitive and receptive within the shadowy sea, and never, never rising and looking forth above water while they lived.

A prime attraction of work of all kinds to the Agnon hero, including Jacob's work with seaweed in *Betrothed*, is that the objects of work are passive and controllable: relationships are not. In 'The Fox', Henry, like Jacob, is plagued by dependence upon dominant women: 'He chafed, feeling he hadn't got his own life. He would never have it till she yielded and slept in him' – i.e. before he can live with March, her masculinity must be put to sleep. Jacob, for his part, is never so happy as when Susan is asleep and her dominance dormant, passive as seaweed. March, ominously though, struggles against sleep: '… she was so tired, so tired, like a child that wants to go to sleep, but which fights against sleep as if sleep were death… she would not sleep: no, never.' And indeed, the maternal shadow neither slumbers nor sleeps, to the end of the authors' lives, to Mrs. Bolton in *Lady Chatterley's Lover* and Agnon's Shira.

Notes

1 Kermode (1973: 34).
2 This chapter is concerned mainly with the effects of the loss of the mother on the writings of Agnon and Lawrence, but there are other significant points of comparison: both came from small towns where they were unusually well educated; for both, the experience of World War I was transformative in their art; both married women from prominent German families; both are concerned with the breakdown of their respective societies in World War I; both depict the decline of orthodox religious tradition (though Agnon, like T.S. Eliot, returned to it); and in their writings both change from a settled world of pre-1914 Romanticism to harsher post-1918 realities.
3 Nietzsche (1968: 435).
4 'When my mother was with me I was at peace and did not raise my voice. When she left briefly, I would burst into tears. And that's how I was destined to be famous' (Agnon 1976: 37).
5 Agnon (CW iv 172).
6 The recurrent theme of guilt toward the dead mother evidently reflects the author's own guilt toward her, in particular for leaving her when she was ill. Perhaps for this reason he would sometimes give the late Spring of 1909 – i.e. after her death – as his date of arrival in Jaffa; in fact, he had arrived a year beforehand, see Aberbach (1982: 52–3). In *Yesteryear*, Agnon perpetuates the myth he created about himself by having his semi-biographical hero, Yitzhak Kummer, lose his mother a year and a half *before* he leaves for Palestine (CW v 515). My Hebrew article in *Moznayim* on the lost mother in Agnon is included as Appendix 1.
7 Over thirty years later, in *Betrothed* (1943), Agnon tells once again of a young man affected by the death of a mother not his own (Agnon, CW vi 224–5). Jacob Rechnitz, a university student in early-20th century Vienna, is a childhood friend of Susan Ehrlich,

daughter of a well-to-do consul; when her mother, Gertrud, dies, he is affected inexplicably, almost as though she were his own mother.

8 Agnon (CW ii 408). Agnon revised the original 1908 version of '*Agunot*' twice, but retained the portrayal of extreme grief in all the versions. In the depiction of loss and grief, as well as guilt, Bialik's poetry, notably *The Scroll of Fire* (*Megillat ha-Esh*, 1905) was evidently a significant influence. Bialik's use of mystical imagery such as the *Shekhinah* is stamped on Agnon's portrayals of idealized women. (Bialik also had a decisive influence on Gershom Scholem in his scholarship on Kabbalah.) Bialik's poem *Ayekh*? (Where are you? 1906) echoes the famous Hasidic song, '*A Dudele*', by Levi Yitzhak of Berdichev: 'Where will I find you, and where will I not find you—you, you, you, you…'

All day long, between letters of the Talmud,
in a shaft of light, a bright cloud,
in my prayers and my purest thought,
in my bitter suffering –
I searched only for you,
only you, you, you…

9 Agnon (CW ii 409).
10 Epigraph to 'Tishre' Ha-Poel Ha-Tzair 22 October 1911, p. 9. Transl. David Aberbach (1984: 165).
11 Moore (1965: i 70).
12 Agnon (CW ii 37).
13 Agnon (CW ii 32). Gershom 'seems to be eaten by a guilt towards his mother whom he feels he has betrayed. The guilt is exacerbated by his interest in his betrothed which implies, to him, a further betrayal of his mother and by the fact that he himself is so similar to his mother' (Band 1968: 99).
14 Agnon (CW iii 406).
15 Lawrence (1972: 851).
16 Lawrence (1972: 27).
17 It may be that Lawrence changed the titles as the obsession appeared to be too glaring.
18 Lawrence (1976: 175). Both Lawrence and Agnon choose the name Gertrude for the beloved mother lost to illness, in *Sons and Lovers* and *Betrothed*, respectively. Freud's archetypal example of the Oedipus complex, in *The Interpretation of Dreams*, is Hamlet, whose mother, Gertrude, is the alleged source of his inability to 'take arms against a sea of troubles'. For Agnon, whose first reader was his wife, Esther, there might also have been private implications: Esther's mother was named Gertrud and she, like his own mother, had died before her time. For biographical details, see Laor (1998) and Falk (2018).
19 Lawrence (1979: 199).
20 Lawrence (1976: 498). Compare Coleridge's 'Dejection Ode' in which the poet is numb to the sky, clouds, moon, and stars: 'I see, not feel, how beautiful they are!'
21 Lawrence (1979: 202).
22 Lawrence (1976: 501).
23 Lawrence (1976: 510).
24 Agnon (CW iv 79).
25 Similarly, in the dream-like 'The Face and the Image', the narrator (again a writer) is sorely disturbed by his failure to visit his ailing mother who, for all he knows, might already be dead. Hartmann's fall and the unexpected bliss he feels amid the pain, recalls Vladimir's leap from a high wall in Turgenev's *First Love* (1860), with its suicidal

implications – he is in love, futilely, with Zinaida – and the bliss he feels when Zinaida comforts him, which he never again experiences. Agnon, in a letter to Schocken in late-1924, experienced a similar suicidal bliss on his journey to Palestine, when a storm at sea shook him from despondency: 'In the sweetness of my joy, I wanted to jump into the sea' (Agnon and Schocken 2003: 167). On *First Love* and Agnon's *Betrothed*, see note 29.

26 Agnon (CW iii 468). Agnon links this scene to the life of Samuel, the author/narrator in *A Guest for the Night* (CW iv 384), significantly in a chapter in which Hartmann (as well as the mad doctor in 'The Doctor's Divorce') is mentioned. Agnon's practice of including in his stories characters from previous stories recalls Balzac; on Agnon and Balzac, see Agnon (1976: 245) and Agnon (1983: 118). On the interconnection of Agnon's stories, their characters, and repeated imagery, which can be read as one whole, see Sadan (1978).

27 Agnon (CW vii 273).

28 Agnon (CW vii 218–19).

29 As a story about first love, there are parallels between *Betrothed* and Turgenev's *First Love* (1860); among these is that both Susan and Zinaida, the objects of obsessional first love, are depicted as capricious, dominant creatures and their lovers, Jacob and Vladimir respectively, are passive and easily led by them. Vladimir might, in fact, be counted among the '*agunot*' in Agnon's fiction: a soul in search of a true mate whom he never finds. On *First Love* and Agnon's 'Metamorphosis', see pp. 94–5 note 25.

30 On the ungovernable rage felt toward women in Agnon's stories, see pp. 17–18, 29, 99–101.

5 Fantasies of deviance: Agnon and Mendele

Mendele's writings were a major influence on Agnon, as on Hebrew and Yiddish writers generally in the early 20th century.[1] This influence is universally acknowledged with regard to the growth of a highly expressive modern Hebrew prose style. Mendele was the chief model of stylistic excellence to all early 20th-century Hebrew writers of fiction, including Agnon. Less commonly recognized is that in psychological subtlety and complexity too, Mendele left a deep mark on Hebrew (as on Yiddish) fiction, again including Agnon. Agnon follows Mendele in creating characters persistently troubled by deviant fantasies. These characters are, for various reasons and to varying degrees, deflected from the social norms of their time and place. Yet, they seem to mirror in some ways the distortions and breakdown in the societies in which they live.

Repeated psychological elements in their works, taken together, point to inner malaise: most strikingly, dreams and fantasies in which sex roles are confused and identities reversed; the constant search for a strong man, or successful lover, as a model for identification and emulation; and more generally, their emotional immaturity, fear of women and difficulties with them, the men being rather weak and passive in contrast with dominant, at times, cruel women, leading to frequent expressions of sexual inferiority, frustration, and unwholeness.

Agnon and Mendele were both, at least nominally, Orthodox Jews who wrote in a still largely puritan age. Homosexuality was against the law both in religious and many secular societies. Neither writer could deal openly with sexual deviance *per se*: Mendele injects it with elements of ribald, even grotesque, fun, notably in *The Travels of Benjamin the Third*, while Agnon's treatment of it is often characterized by a mocking, recoiling allusiveness.

Agnon and Mendele: different worlds

There are notable differences between Mendele and Agnon, in biographical and historical background, and in the nature of their art. Mendele's world was the 19th-century Pale of Settlement, where the Russian Jews were confined by law, subject to anti-Semitic restrictions and violence, and increasingly numerous

DOI: 10.4324/9781003594802-6

and impoverished under Tsarist autocratic rule. Agnon, a half-century younger than Mendele, was born into a society of late-19th-century emancipated Jews – Austro-Hungarian Jews were emancipated in 1867, when the kingdoms were unified; and he lived in Germany in the early years of the Weimar Republic where unconventional sexual behavior, including homosexuality, was tolerated.[2] He was more familiar than Mendele with Western European culture and behavior, and led a relatively privileged and protected life, while Mendele lived much of his life among the indigent poor, for whom Jewish religious norms did not always apply.

As headmaster of a Jewish school in Odessa, Mendele was in close contact with the poor and their children, to whom as a leading educator he was devoted; Agnon, unusually free of the need to take a job and able to write full-time, moved in academic circles and knew all too well the narrowness and pettiness of academia. Agnon, close to Flaubert and modernists such as Kafka, is more the self-absorbed artist. He turns away more completely than Mendele from the open didacticism of the Haskalah. Mendele's anti-traditionalism and social realism often clash with Agnon's neo-Romanticism and his adherence to tradition. To Mendele, the rabbinic world and the Hasidic movement in particular were the benighted enemies of progress; to Agnon, the great Eastern European rabbis and Hasidism were a repository of a rich folk literature, of authentic Jewish tradition and culture. Mendele's influences included Dickens and Turgenev, and his main overall concern was the abject condition of Jews under Tsarist rule. He shared with Russian writers the disquiet at seeking cultural advancement for people who do not have enough to eat.[3] Mendele in his passion for social justice is closer to the Jewish ideal than Agnon in his passion for artistic perfection.[4] One sees more fully in Mendele the pressures driving Zionism, the humiliations and violence of anti-Semitism, the weaknesses and failing of the ancient rabbinic tradition in the face of overwhelming crisis, the desperate Jewish struggle for existence, and the pride in having an ancient religious civilization with a language rich in possibilities for the creation of a better world. Mendele invented a Hebrew style intensely alive in sensory awareness and emotional resonance, drawing masterfully, with immense erudition, on all strata of Hebrew in its long history.

Though both Mendele and Agnon portray the world of Eastern European Orthodoxy, Agnon's writings reflect the changes brought by emancipation in the Austro-Hungarian empire, while the Jews in Mendele's Tsarist Russia were never emancipated; and their 'emancipation' after the 1917 revolution led to the almost total destruction of Jewish life in Russia. For Mendele, then, the only 'free country' – apart from the memory of Zion – was the bath-house:

> The bath-house for the Jew is a motherland, a free country. Great and small alike can air their views there. Anyone can rise to the highest position and take courage in his misery, cast off his worries and troubles, and find rest – an hour of peace of mind.[5]

Breakdown in Mendele's The Mare

Yet, Mendele's influence on Agnon is detectable not just in Agnon's style and technique in recreating and memorializing Eastern European life, but also, to an extent, in psychological characterization. Parallels in the motifs of sexual deviance and homoeroticism in their writings are particularly clear in Mendele's *The Mare* and Agnon's *A Simple Story*.[6] As Mendele provided Agnon's chief artistic model in Hebrew prose, it is inconceivable that Agnon was not influenced by *The Mare*, a landmark in both Yiddish and Hebrew literature. Both novels have striking portrayals of weak family structures: in *The Mare*, the father has died, leaving the anxious, indulgent mother to raise her only son; and in *A Simple Story*, a strong-willed, manipulative mother and a weak father. Both young men go through emotional crises in which they are troubled by homoerotic fantasies.

The central struggle in *The Mare*, as stated in the title of its opening chapter ('Israel tries to be a man'), is the creation and assertion of masculine identity. Israel, an orphan raised by his mother in the Russian Pale of Settlement during the reign of Alexander II, is in his twenties and still unmarried. Ostracized by his society as a *maskil*, he fails to enter university. Trapped and frustrated, he projects his yearning for manhood into the mare. The mare, a figment of his imagination in madness, is herself an allegorical representation of the Jews as a people in search of masculine identity, lost when uprooted from their ancestral homeland. Once a noble prince, the mare has been unsexed in exile, she confesses to Israel:

> In those days there lived a wise, good prince. This prince, while still a boy, would wander far from home, to see what went on in the world, and he became famous among the nations. The king of Egypt, a land defiled with the idols of magicians, sorcerers, and wizards, got angry with the prince, who had come as a visitor to live in his country. He consulted his retinue and said: Let us find a good way of destroying him. The magicians used their sorcery to turn the prince into a mare and made him do the hardest work, building Pithom and Rameses with bricks and straw.[7]

Israel's longing 'to be a man' runs parallel with the mare's dream of becoming a prince again. His jumbled feelings for the mare betray his unconscious self-perception. At one point, he weeps for the mare and is even ready to sacrifice his life for her,[8] but she enrages him with her passive humiliation. When she groans and kicks he approves, for she has not given up the struggle to regain her former nobility.[9]

In wildly discordant fantasies, Israel reflects on the mare's sex change in relation to his own sexual insecurities. He thinks, for example, 'If the mare is a prince, I, a male, in contrast, am a princess'.[10] He imagines himself as Queen of Sheba in a former incarnation. But he also wishes, or suspects, that he was Judah Maccabeus.[11] Considering Israel's abject condition, this image of masculinity is so fantastically exaggerated that it suggests a desperate need on his part to compensate for weakness in his male identity. Later, his fear-ridden temptation by the Devil and the sexual abandon which this entails might express that side of him which seeks a perverse, distorted masculine identity at the expense of others, by abandoning moral scruples. The night after he fails his university examination at the hands of anti-Semitic examiners, Israel has continual nightmares of being a sacrificial cock. The slaughtered cock is a symbol of his social and emotional sense of emasculation:

> Eyes watched me in reproach and anger, and the game began, a terrifying game! The players took their parts: some as donkeys, oxen, or humans, and I was the rooster, bound at their mercy, a sacrifice for the Day of Atonement.[12]

As a sacrifice on the altar of the twisted world in which he lives, Israel is ripe for demonic possession. In breakdown, his distorted social and sexual identity merges with his role as symbol of the Jewish people. Breakdown is the gateway to enlightenment, and Israel confronts the truth of his predicament and recovers his sanity. In the end though, appropriately for a work first published in Tsarist Russia in 1873 – Mendele's Hebrew version appeared in 1911 – Israel's problems, like those of the Russian Jews, remain unsolved.

Influence of The Mare *on* A Simple Story

As a study of madness and latent deviance, *The Mare* is directly linked to Agnon's *A Simple Story*. The latter work, published in 1935, lacks the overall social impact of *The Mare*, but is distinguished by its subtle and controlled character study. Agnon's only novel of a youth growing up at home, *A Simple Story* is also, on one level, a study of emasculation and madness, with undertones of latent deviance. It, too, is set in an Eastern European *shtetl*; and it depicts an unstable family in a time of social upheaval producing a son vulnerable to breakdown. The madness of Hirshl Horowitz, like that of Israel in *The Mare*, erupts out of his suppressed, inturned anger, starkly exposed in his nightmare of being a sacrificial rooster. Hirshl's murderous rage at his wife, Mina, is linked to his tortured bond with his mother, who has engineered this loveless marriage. Hirshl has no way of disposing of this anger other than by turning it in on himself. He develops an insane fear of slaughtering roosters and of being a slaughtered rooster. We are told by the narrator that Hirshl hides his knife at night to protect himself from his sado-masochistic impulses:

> An angry man is not in control. In an impulse, he could kill every rooster on earth. Hirshl was right to hide his knife at night.[13]

Like Israel, Hirshl in madness feels himself to be disembodied and out of control. His sexual identity, too, appears distorted. Hirshl deliriously addresses trees, as Israel does animals, as superior beings. When found raving in the fields, Hirshl pleads, 'Don't slaughter me, I'm not a rooster.'[14] The Hebrew for 'rooster', *gever*, is the same as for 'man'; and the terror at being a sacrificial cock shared by Israel and Hirshl might symbolize fear of emasculation or the sense of having been emasculated, robbed of the power to act forcefully. For both Israel and Hirshl, the sense of emasculation, sexual frustration, and suppressed rage at women appear to bring out deviant impulses. In madness, both are tainted with unmanly weakness and ineffectuality. Israel bows to a rooster, addressing it as *gever*, a man of valor; and Hirshl is alarmed by his responsiveness to the touch of Yonah Toiber, the matchmaker who arranges his ill-fated marriage. Whatever Toiber's true character, Hirshl sees him in contrast with himself, as one who knows how to manage his life. Toiber's touch, implicitly 'feminine' as his first name and surname suggest – Yonah in Hebrew and Toiber in Yiddish are feminine and mean 'dove' – is similar to that of Blume,[15] Hirshl's cousin for whom Hirshl longs from a distance; and Yonah's touch also recalls, with similar perversity, that of Hirshl's mother.[16] Even after he marries Mina, Hirshl remains guiltily attracted to Toiber's touch: 'Isn't it a disgrace that when he takes my hand in his I want to kiss it… How smooth are Yonah's hands.'[17] When Hirshl breaks down and undergoes psychiatric treatment in Lemberg (Lviv), the hand of his psychiatrist, Dr. Langsam, takes over: 'The strong hand that casually held his when he arrived and left was not soft like Toiber's, and he felt no wish to kiss it.'[18]

Deviance in Agnon

Agnon goes more deeply into his exploration of troubled sexual relations and identity in later works, notably *Yesteryear*, set in Ottoman Palestine in the early-20th century, and *Shira*, set in British Palestine in the 1930s. The central characters in each, Yitzhak Kummer and Manfred Herbst, suffer from fantasies of deviance reflecting broader social breakdown. In *Yesteryear*, Yitzhak Kummer brings to the land of Israel a youthful pioneer idealism but gets bogged down in his life in Jaffa and Jerusalem. In Jaffa, he is drawn to the worldly Sonia who rejects him. In the end, he marries Shifra, daughter of an ultra-Orthodox zealot in Jerusalem. In the surreal last quarter of the novel, his story merges with that of Balak, a rabid dog who can be understood on one level as an embodiment of Yitzhak's tortured emotional life. In an act which appears to destroy the initial idealistic spirit of the novel, the dog bites him: he catches rabies and dies in agony. His delirium before death exposes his fantasies of troubled sexual identities. The taxidermist, Arzaf, the hermit, Sweetooth, and his friend, Rabinowitz, enter his consciousness as fortunate beings who, unlike himself, either have satisfying lives with women or live happily alone; in fantasy, Rabinowitz appears in women's clothes, and Arzaf speaks to a male dog as though he were female, using the word '*ati*' and coddling him like a bitch. The fatal poison from the dog-bite evidently reflects the 'poison' in Yitzhak's inner life, killing him as surely, emotionally, in his personal relations.

Fantasies of transvestism and confused sexual identity appear also in *Shira*, Agnon's last, unfinished novel, whose central theme is Herbst's obsession with Shira, a nurse in the local lepers' hospital in Jerusalem in the 1930s. In his violent fantasies against women, filled with lust, frustration, and rage, Herbst is an older Hirshl Horowitz. In one such fantasy, Herbst craves for Shira to become a man:

> He opened his mouth, the rows of chattering teeth stuck out, and he screamed: 'Live, if that's what you want, but turn into a man!'[19]

Agnon had in Mendele significant antecedents to these fantasies of sexual confusion, most obviously perhaps in the 'marriage' of two men in Mendele's *The Travels of Benjamin the Third*, portrayed, however, less with modernist Angst than in the spirit of a Purimspiel. The story opens in the fictional *shtetl* of Batlon ('Idlersville'), with the pious luftmensch Benjamin, a married man with children, undergoing a crisis of identity not unlike that of Israel in *The Mare*. Benjamin, like Israel, withdraws from his family. Intent, likewise, on proving himself a man, belatedly, by making the hard trek to the land of Israel, he adopts an ideal of tough masculinity, the opposite of his real self. Alexander the Great becomes his model of identification – much as Judah Maccabeus does to Israel in *The Mare*. Benjamin sets out to fight his natural temerity:

> He decided to act bravely, to suppress his nature, to root out all fear from his heart. He forced himself to walk out alone at night… to go beyond the town limits, even though it exhausted and terrified him.[20]

Next, he finds himself an ideal 'wife': Senderl the Woman (called such as his wife puts him to work around the house, and he often does women's chores), malleable and ludicrous, henpecked, beaten, and effectively emasculated by his wife, careless of his indignities to the point of masochism, ultimately warmhearted and loveable. Senderl is Benjamin's 'helpmeet' (*ezer ke-negdo*),[21] as Eve is to Adam; and the biblical and rabbinic language of sexual desire and union – *teshukah, zivug, hityahadut* – heightens the ribald farce: 'My blood boils and I long for you', *ve-elekha teshukati,* exclaims Benjamin to Senderl in his proposal that they 'elope'.[22] Senderl's agreement raises Benjamin's ecstasy to new heights in a parody of romantic love not unworthy of Groucho Marx: 'My soul, the air I breathe, let me kiss you!' When Senderl 'finances' the journey, pulling from his pocket a bundle of coins, his life savings, Benjamin's joy is unbounded as he embraces Senderl: 'you deserve a kiss on every limb', *kol ever me-evre gufkha.*[23] On the morning of their departure from Batlon, Senderl appears disguised as a woman, and once Benjamin ascertains that the bustling figure in skirts and kerchief is not his wife in hot pursuit, he brightens up and gazes at Senderl like a groom at his beautiful bride, *ke-khala na'ah be-eyne doda.*[24] They fairly sail along until Senderl tires as women do according to the Talmud, *tash kocho ki-nekevah.*[25] To his everlasting credit, Senderl had busied himself like a 'woman of valor', *eshet chayil,*[26] to prepare food for the way, unlike Benjamin whose preoccupations are masculine and spiritual – until he gets hungry. Each declares his inexorable attraction to the other, Senderl revealing that he was drawn to Benjamin 'like a blind person… like a calf after the cow'; and Benjamin, 'Our marriage was made in heaven, you and I are body and soul.'[27] When they reach the town of Kesalon, they parade like a honeymoon couple, 'like bride and groom in the seven days of feasting after marriage, alone together, strolling in the gardens, enjoying one another's every word and glance.'[28]

This parody of marriage reaches its climax when the 'newlyweds' unwittingly fall into the hands of *khappers*, this being Russia during the Crimean war of 1854–56, when Jews were legally empowered to seize other Jews without valid papers and, in return for payment, present them for recruitment in the Russian army. Unconsciously aware of the danger, they have complementary nightmares: Benjamin, clasping the hand of his hero, Alexander the Great – echoed perhaps in the fascination of Hirshl with the hands of Yonah Toiber in *A Simple Story* – wakes instead to find that he is holding a crushed flea; but Senderl, more dramatically, suffers labor pains in giving birth![29]

In the Hebrew story, *Bi-Yme ha-Ra'ash* (Earthquake Days, 1894), Mendele portrays yet another mock marriage in which, again, a pair of men, Mendele the Bookpeddler and Reb Leib, abandon their families in order to journey to the Promised Land: 'We made a covenant to live together and neither would abandon his mate.'[30] Leib, like Senderl, is the 'female' partner, and when the bedraggled travellers visit the Zionist representative (based on Leon Pinsker) in Odessa to ask about emigration – the story is set in 1881, after the outbreak of the pogroms – Leib 'bent and curtsied and twisted up his face as women do'.[31] Later, when Leib looks in the mirror, Mendele imagines him to be a narcissistic female, and ugly to boot: 'Putting on their makeup in front of the mirror, they tell themselves they are beautiful and unrivalled'.[32] There then follows a parody of homosexual competitiveness as Mendele is sorely distressed to see Leib with a young women who, it turns out, wants him not as a lover but as a Hebrew teacher. Leib is suspected of betraying not just his wife but also Mendele, to whom he is 'married' and who assumes the worst when Leib, dressed in his Sabbath best, disappears with the woman: 'Leib's everyday coat [*kapote*] hung sadly on the wall, her sleeves crusted with mud like the sleeves of a woman's dress on Sabbath eve.'[33] Leib returns from his rendezvous spouting Hebrew (the only time, incidentally, in the author's entire *oeuvre* when a character speaks Hebrew), full of excitement at being in demand as a Hebrew teacher. As in *The Travels*, this climax comes with a 'pregnancy': 'Reb Leib looked like a woman in labor struggling to give birth'[34] – revealing Mendele's disdain for the newfangled Russian-Jewish vogue for Hebrew conversation, a painful exercise for speaker and listener alike. Still, Leib is cleared of adulterous blame and, now that he has work, the 'marriage' with Mendele is dissolved.

Alongside the 'marriages', the 'matchmaking' done by Reb Alter, Mendele's fellow bookseller in *The Beggar-Book* (*Sefer ha-Kabbtzanim,* 1909) seems to fit into a pattern.[35] Alter, dreaming of a hefty matchmaker's fee at the Yarmolinsk fair, hatches a match with excessive dispatch – to find that he has paired two grooms! This little tale, spiced with interjections of comic disgust, is crucial in the structure of the novel: it triggers the story of Fishke the Lame, his disastrous marriage and his love for Beila the Hunchback (Alter's daughter, it turns out). As elsewhere in Mendele's fiction, women in *The Beggar-Book* are either cruelly dominant and manipulative or fruitlessly yearned for; divorce is common. Male bonds, such as those of Mendele and Alter, and, in the end, of Mendele and Fishke, are stronger and more stable. Mendele's initial amusement and pity for Fishke change to empathy and admiration once Fishke tells what it feels like to be in love, a state which Mendele has sadly never known.

This nose-in-the-candyshop mentality in sexual matters is shared by Agnon's creations. For this reason, Agnon chose the expression *al kapot ha-manul*, 'at the handles of the lock', from the Song of Songs (where it is the woman, not the man, who is in search of her beloved), as the title for his love stories. These are, more precisely, stories about men obsessed by women out of reach and, at times, by the lover, or former lover, of the beloved.[36] At times, this obsession is clearly pathological. In 'The Doctor's Divorce', a doctor is besieged by thoughts of his wife's ex-lover, to the point that his marriage falls apart. In the gruesome climax, the lover becomes by chance his patient. He treats the man, whom he hates, with exemplary care, suggesting an unconscious attraction to and identification with him.[37]

A comparably irrational hatred, of the brilliant Talmudic scholar, Moshe Pinchas, for another outstanding scholar, Reb Shlomo, appears in Agnon's later story, 'Two Torah Scholars in Our Town' (*Shne Talmide Hakhamim she-Hayu be-Irenu*, 1946), set in the late-19th century. Moshe Pinchas' humble background contrasts with Reb Shlomo's *yichus*, his wealthy, distinguished family. Yet, the difference in social standing, though significant, does not account for Moshe Pinchas' resentment towards Reb Shlomo.[38] Reb Shlomo, with the exception of one unfortunate remark which troubles him for the rest of his life, treats him with the respect and admiration due to a great Torah scholar. He tries to obtain for Moshe Pinchas a good rabbinic position, to free him from poverty and care. Moshe Pinchas refuses his help. To his mother, he admits in effect that it is not Reb Shlomo's insult that so troubles him, for his behavior is totally irrational and incomprehensible, even to himself:

> 'The man I hate wants to help me.'
> 'If so, why do you hate him?'
> 'I hate him for stirring up this contemptible hatred in me.'
> 'I don't understand what you're talking about.'
> 'I too don't understand it.'[39]

The obsession in this story in some ways recalls obsessions in some of Agnon's earlier stories, particularly 'The Doctor's Divorce': the doctor in this story, driven mad by his obsession with his wife's former lover, is similarly aware of the irrationality of his feelings. He recognizes his guilt in abusing his wife, a woman of upstanding character. He knows he is lucky she married him. Yet, he reveals with chilling casualness, he chose to remain childless for fear that his children would look like the former lover. Divorce is unavoidable. The evident fear of women and sex, and the childlike dependence brought home in the final sentence – the doctor sits up in bed and calls to his former wife as a child to its mother.

Echoes of this pathological jealousy are found elsewhere in Agnon's writings, to the very end, the unfinished *Shira*. Nurse Shira recounts to the adulterous Hebrew University professor, Manfred Herbst, her violent, tragic life. He is unresponsive, except to think: which men did she know?[40] In *A Guest for the Night,* Samuel, clearly an autobiographical figure, becomes obsessed with the lover of Rachel, a girl to whom he is attracted. Yeruham Hofshi is everything Samuel would evidently like to be: tough and manly, capable of hard physical work, sexually uninhibited, and living for the present. Samuel, in contrast, cannot break from the past, his one-time ambition to work the land in the land of Israel has come to nothing, and he lives alone infatuated with Rachel from a distance. He is drawn physically to Yeruham, to his body, his eyes and hair, and his earthy fragrance.[41]

In *Yesteryear*, too, the main character, Yitzhak Kummer, is attracted to Rabinowitz, another out-of-reach model of male success unhampered by inhibition, particularly in practical business affairs and with women. Rabinowitz, former lover of a girl whom Yitzhak desires from a distance, confides in Kummer his 'secret' – constantly to create new desires and lusts, however superficial, and satisfy them with money and action: in doing so, 'you build yourself up, and the land grows with you.'[42] Kummer's own lusts are evidently stifled, as are Hirshl's in *A Simple Story*, by unresolved family conflicts and imbalances. His vulnerability to deviance emerges strikingly in the delirious fantasies after being bitten by the rabid dog, Balak, following his marriage.

Agnon's characters are often drawn to older men who, in contrast with themselves, have succeeded in masculine forms of self-assertion, especially in business or public affairs. The most extraordinary relationship of this sort is that of the unnamed narrator and his 'special acquaintance', Mr. Gressler, in the story 'A Whole Loaf' (*Pat Shlema*, 1933), who 'has taken the trouble to show me all kinds of pleasures'.[43] The narrator speaks of Gressler (whose name suggests forbidden appetites) almost like a young women flattered by the attentions of an older man. Hunger and heat pervade the story, set in interwar Jerusalem, suggesting the sexual craving of a man living apart from his wife.[44] The story begins with the narrator as part of a crowd then going his own wayward way. Gressler takes the narrator in his horse-drawn carriage which takes a wrong turn and crashes, throwing both men together into the street. Gressler 'rolled with me, laughing as though it amused him to roll about with me in the muck.'[45] In this surreal context, the narrator's longing for a 'whole' loaf recalls the longing for wholeness associated particularly with unhappy homosexuals:

> Heterosexual lovers habitually report that the partner with whom they are in love seems to fulfill their lives, to complete them, to make them whole. Homosexual lovers less often repeat such phrases because, inevitably, their lives lack this quality of wholeness.[46]

Indeed, by the end of 'A Whole Loaf', the narrator appears to give up on ever obtaining 'a whole loaf'. In a restaurant, waiting futilely for his supper, he spies a boy munching bread similar to that which his mother baked when he was a boy. He would give everything, he thinks, for a mouthful. Confronted, if only symbolically, with his inner hunger, he yearns for childhood innocence. This is one of many such scenes in Agnon's stories, when in moments of heightened tension, children appear.[47] Hearing Gressler pass by in his carriage, he calls out to him. At this moment, Agnon echoes the passage in Song of Songs telling of the unrequited lover at the handles of the lock: is the narrator similarly lovelorn?

Agnon's stories contain many other strange states and encounters, dreams and fantasies, equally suggestive of a sense of unwholeness. The story 'Friendship' (*Yedidut*, 1932) is set just after the narrator's wife returns home after a long absence. On his way to see her, he forgets where they live. He meets an acquaintance, Dr. Rischel, who drags him into a streetcar going in the wrong direction: 'I remembered I had dreamed of Rischel wrestling with me. I jumped off the streetcar and left.'[48] On the one scrap of paper with his address, which he has torn up and thrown away, the narrator has written that the real trial in the book of Job was God's, for putting an upright man in Satan's power. A satanic impulse reminiscent of *The Mare* appears in the narrator's behavior and dreams: he seems to be avoiding his newly returned wife, he denies hysterically having had any contact with women in her absence, and he rides perversely away from home with Rischel who, wrestling partner that he is in dream, hints at latent homosexuality.

Similarly suggestive fantasies appear also in *Betrothed*, after Susan, a young woman with whom Jacob Rechnitz played as a child in pre-1914 Vienna, re-enters his life in Jaffa. When she reminds him of their childhood oath to marry, his fantasy life takes over. As in 'Friendship', he rides in a streetcar:

> Two young fellows got in and one sat on the other's knees. He heard them talking about Otto Weininger and his *Sex and Character*. They travelled this way for an hour. And then, how strange, Jacob was again sitting with Susan, and it was not eleven o'clock though he had left Susan's house at ten and she had accompanied him halfway, and he had spent an hour in the tram.[49]

Agnon weaves a fantasy of immaturity and retarded time, regression or fixation, involving inhibition of Jacob's feelings for Susan as being virtually incestuous, his being a 'womanly man' – this was Weininger's characterization of the Jewish people as a whole in *Sex and Character* (suggested also in the figure of the mare in Mendele's story, and found also in Joyce's *Ulysses apropos* Leopold Bloom)[50] – and the homoerotic suggestion in the scene where the one boy sits on the other's knees; this matrix of fantasy is linked ultimately to Jacob's persistent association of Susan with her dead mother, whom he regards virtually as his own mother.[51]

In *Thus Far*, too, fantasy points to emotional blockage. The story, set in Germany during the 1914–18 war, again presents the narrator alone, separated from his family. His nightmares reveal both his inner state and the tortured conditions of the European Jews during the war, for though they fought patriotically for the fatherland, they were still subjected to anti-Semitic suspicions and calumny. One of his nightmares alludes, with sinister implications, to the midrash on Exodus 2: 24 accusing the Egyptians of using Israelite babies in the mortar to build their cities:

> One night as I lay in bed, Pharaoh's executioners came and fixed me in the walls of a brick house. I cried out from the walls, and the Holy One, blessed be He, took me out and put me to bed. And still the executioners choked me, but in

> my struggle they all fell away except the tax official who lived in the opposite room: he came into my room by mistake, got into my bed and lay on top of me.[52]

Agnon left no full biographical account which could explain his repeated concern with fantasies of deviance, though his fiction might itself be seen to a large extent as disguised autobiography. Mendele, however, in his memoir *Of Bygone Days*, gives a clear biographical background to the problems addressed in his fiction: his father's death when he was in his early teens, his mother's inability to support him and her remarriage, his consequent departure from home for life in a yeshiva, a prelude to his later life among beggars in the Russian Pale of Settlement. His indiscriminate hunger for friendship and love presages the male bonds he portrays in his fiction:

> The essence of Shloymele's soul was a mixture of love, eternal longing, affection and friendship. Like a flame to the wick, he reached out to catch hold, indiscriminately, to everyone, and to live with him in love and friendship as with his own soul.[53]

Yet, the boy came to see this world as a moral swamp in which he was sinking and becoming fouled. Escaping, he joined a band of beggars. This experience permeated Mendele's later life and writings as no comparable experience did in Agnon's life. Still, Agnon follows Mendele in his lifelong use of beggar imagery to portray characters such as Hemdat, Menashe Haim, Reb Yudel, Hirshl Horowitz, and Herbst.[54] Both writers might have had similar reasons: beggars, being out of society's pale, can in theory live freely and, if they wish, in accordance with their deviances. Their economic state is, in a sense, an externalization of the emotional condition in which they are trapped, welling up from traumatic experiences in early life.

Conclusion

Emotional poverty and breakdown pervade the writings of Agnon and Mendele, notably in Mendele's *The Mare* and Agnon's *A Simple Story*. As we have seen, the problems of the young protagonists of these stories are reflected in their emotional immaturity, their feelings of sexual inferiority and emasculation, and fear of women, symbolized in the nightmares both have of being a slaughtered cock. They are, furthermore, drawn to various types of ideal masculinity (though not of the Charles Atlas variety), whether successful *hommes d'affaires* or men who succeed with women where they themselves fail; or in madness, with exaggerated or distorted images of masculinity; and with their strange dreams and fantasies of sex change or of men on top of one another, with their homoerotic implications. It is remarkable how much Agnon appears to have learned from Mendele, not just in imitation of the naïve and pious narrator who is, in fact, a sophisticated artist, but also in the psychological depiction of characters and their inner life, their fantasies and nightmares, as well as in the use of images of sexual immaturity and distortion as oblique counterparts to sickness and breakdown in the societies which they describe.

Notes

1 On Mendele's influence on Agnon, see pp. 8–9, 22–4.
2 Agnon's novel *Shira* (1971) is his only one whose central character is German rather than Eastern European. *Shira* most fully and freely, without judgment or condemnation, explores sexual deviation, involving adultery, emotional cruelty, incest, dependence, sado-masochism, and murderous rage. Manfred Herbst, a Hebrew University professor in the 1930s, has an adulterous affair with Shira, a nurse in a leper hospital. The most powerful emotion he feels for her is hatred, which overwhelms and bewilders him. His murderous impulses toward her recall Hirshl in *A Simple Story*, who perversely hides his knife to prevent himself from murdering his wife, Mina. In Herbst's fantasies, Shira is run over by a car, she contracts an incurable disease, she is whipped, raped, and dismembered; and in his nightmares he is constantly punished, attacked and injured, arrested, and eventually hanged for murder.
3 On Mendele's questioning of the value of art in a world of extreme poverty, a concern he shared with Russian writers such as Turgenev and Tolstoy, see Aberbach (1993).
4 On Flaubert's influence on Agnon, see Chapter 3.
5 In *The Travels of Benjamin the Third* (Mendele 1947: 83). On the influence of this classic work on Agnon, particularly on *The Bridal Canopy*, see pp. 8–9, 22–3.
6 *The Mare* (*Di Kliatsche*) was first written in Yiddish in 1872, in Odessa, in reaction to the Odessa pogrom in 1871, and published in 1873. Later Yiddish drafts appeared in 1888 and 1911. Encouraged by Bialik, Mendele rewrote *The Mare* in Hebrew, under the title *Susati* (1911). Agnon would have known both the Yiddish and Hebrew versions long before he wrote *A Simple Story* (1935). Quotes from Mendele's *The Mare* in the present chapter are from the Hebrew version of *The Mare* in the 1-volume 1947 *Collected Works* (1947); and quotes from Agnon's *A Simple Story* are from volume 3 of Agnon's *Collected Works* (1953–1962).
7 Mendele (1947: 212). The distorted self-image to which secularly educated Jews were particularly vulnerable is evident in the frequency with which Jewish writers in the 19th and early 20th century allude to the Jewish condition in animal fables. An allegorical line can be traced from Heine to Agnon: for Heine in 'Princess Sabbath', the Jew is a dog; for Mendele in *The Mare*, a broken mare; for Kafka in 'A Report to an Academy', an ape; for Agnon in *Yesteryear*, again a dog. For Kafka, too, in 'Metamorphosis', the Jew could be represented by a cockroach. Kafka describes the unwillingness of Jews to leave in the face of anti-Semitic violence as 'heroism of the cockroach' (Kafka 1983: 170).
8 Mendele (1947: 313).
9 Mendele (1947: 313, 322).
10 Mendele (1947: 315).
11 The satiric element in Mendele's allusion to the Maccabees is echoed in Bialik's *City of Slaughter*, written after the Kishinev pogrom in 1903, in which the poet (one of Mendele's most admiring and influential disciples) castigates the allegedly cowardly Jews at Kishinev for betraying the memory of the Maccabees, scurrying to hide like mice. Mendele's influence on Agnon is clearest in his early writings, particularly the novellas, *And the Crooked Shall be Made Straight* (*Ve-Haya he-Akov le-Mishor*, 1913),

and *With Young and Old Together* (*Bi-Ne'arenu uviZkenenu*, 1920), a satire on early-20th century Galician Jewish politics.

12 Mendele (1947: 320).

13 Agnon (CW iii 201).

14 Agnon (CW iii 218). Hirshl's madness, ironically, does not bring about a family stigma and his ostracism as a lunatic; on the contrary, he is viewed with approval for having hoodwinked the army authorities into thinking him unfit for conscription (CW iii 224–5). There may be a subtle allusion to Agnon's friend, Scholem, who was in Berlin during the 1914–18 war when he reached conscription age, and did precisely this (he actually showed me how, when I met him at his home in Jerusalem), having mugged up on schizophrenia from a German psychiatric textbook, he pretended to be mad, so convincingly that he persuaded the Berlin army board to exclude him from service; when his father, a loyal German patriot, found out, he angrily kicked Scholem out. Agnon himself tried to make himself physically ill to avoid conscription and succeeded so well that he damaged his health and had to spend several months recuperating in hospital. See p. 78 note 8.

15 Agnon (CW iii 82–3).

16 Agnon (CW iii 100).

17 Agnon (CW iii 213).

18 Agnon (CW iii 227).

19 Agnon (1971: 64).

20 Mendele (1947: 60).

21 Mendele (1947: 62).

22 Mendele (1947: 63).

23 Mendele (1947: 64).

24 Mendele (1947: 65).

25 Mendele (1947: 66).

26 Mendele (1947: 67).

27 Mendele (1947: 67).

28 Mendele (1947: 80).

29 Mendele (1947: 81, 82).

30 Mendele (1947: 407).

31 Mendele (1947: 410).

32 Mendele (1947: 413).

33 Mendele (1947: 415).

34 Mendele (1947: 415).

35 The Hebrew version of *The Beggar-Book* appeared in 1909. Yiddish drafts under the title *Fishke der Krummer* (Fishke the Lame) appeared in 1869 and 1888. The Hebrew version of *The Beggar Book* in included in the 1-volume edition of Mendele's *Collected Works* (1947).

36 Though Mendele and Agnon are comparable in their exploration of homoerotic relationships and fantasies, there are also significant differences (see pp. 96–7): above all, Mendele is more the social satirist while Agnon goes deeper into the intricacies of psychopathology. It is noteworthy that Agnon's picaresque novel, *The Bridal Canopy*, though clearly influenced by Mendele (see Band 1968: 130), avoids defining the relationship between the two men on the road, Reb Yudel and Nuta, as a mock marriage.

37 On the parallel between 'The Doctor's Divorce' and Hawthorne's *The Scarlet Letter*, see p. 29.

38 On the puncturing of illusion in *Two Torah Scholars*, reminiscent of Flaubert, see pp. 35–6 note 42.
39 Agnon (CW vi 23).
40 Agnon (1971: 25).
41 Agnon (CW iv 84, 421).
42 Agnon (CW v 454).
43 Agnon (1970: 86).
44 Agnon's letters to his wife from Jerusalem in periods when they lived apart indicate clearly the biographical basis for 'A Whole Loaf' (Agnon 1983).
45 Agnon (1983: 88–9).
46 Storr (1977: 89).
47 Aberbach (1984: 66–9).
48 Agnon (1970: 76). The name 'Rischel', like the name 'Shira', could be an anagram of Agnon's own name.
49 Agnon (CW vii 255–6).
50 Otto Weininger (1880–1903): Austrian-Jewish philosopher, notorious for his book *Geschlecht und Charakter* (Sex and Character), published in 1903 shortly before his suicide. Weininger's negative view of Judaism was later praised by the Nazis.
51 On the persistent motif of the dead mother in Agnon, see Aberbach (1982, 1984).
52 Agnon (CW vii 68).
53 Mendele (1947: 304).
54 In Mendele's satiric breakdown of the many species of Jewish beggar in *The Beggar-Book*, Agnon's Menashe Haim in *And the Crooked Shall be Made Straight* falls in the category of a *kabtazan de-nayde* (wandering beggar), and Reb Yudel in *The Bridal Canopy*, a *kabtazn mashmia al hakhnasat kalla* (a dowry-seeking beggar) (Mendele 1947: 113, 114). Some of Agnon's modern characters, too, recall a species of beggar portrayed by Mendele, the 'beggar of love', notably Fishke the Lame, the central figure of *The Beggar-Book*.

6 Foreshadowings of catastrophe: Agnon and German-Jewish literature

Agnon established himself as a leading Hebrew writer in Ottoman Palestine, lived in Germany from 1913–1924, after which he returned to Jerusalem, this time under British rule, where he lived until his death. Agnon's years in Germany, mostly in the spa town, Bad Homburg, were pivotal in his life and career.[1] In Germany, he gained recognition as the leading Hebrew writer of fiction, his writings were translated into German and were read with admiration and subjected to serious critical study; and he married into a prominent German-Jewish family – notwithstanding the opposition of his in-laws to an '*Ostjude*'.

Though German Jews such as Arthur Ruppin, Martin Buber, and Gershom Scholem were among his most ardent supporters, Agnon was highly critical of German Jews generally. This chapter explores Agnon's view of German Jews in the context of European literature of the early 20th century, by Stefan Zweig, Martin Buber, Arthur Schnitzler, Joseph Roth, and Franz Werfel, among others. Though as German writers they present a variety of viewpoints, subject matter, and style, they shared Agnon's anxiety about German society and the isolation of Jews, though highly assimilated and patriotic, within German society. These writers, like Agnon, frequently draw on imagery of unrequited love. As anti-Semitism spread, Agnon's stories of *agunot*, 'at the handles of the lock', struck a chord among a small but growing group of German Zionists in search of roots in Eastern European Jewish religious culture.

Ruppin, a sociologist who was the Hibbat Zion representative in Jaffa and befriended Agnon there, observed prior to World War I that popular Jew-hatred in Germany and Austria had led almost to the 'social ostracism' of the Jews.[2] Yet, recognizing Agnon's gift, Ruppin, encouraged the young writer to go to Germany to be immersed in an environment rich in culture – unlike Ottoman Palestine.[3] In wartime Germany, Agnon entered a world alive with creative ferment – and rife with Jew-hatred. To his astonishment, the German Jews, though hated, were totally loyal to the Fatherland.[4] Large numbers served at the front. He, not sharing their desire to sacrifice themselves for an anti-Semitic Fatherland, did everything he could to evade the draft, as he had done when he lived in Galicia. His self-harm had effect but landed him in hospital for several months. His closest German friend at the time was Scholem, another draft-dodger convinced that Jewish patriotism for

DOI: 10.4324/9781003594802-7

an anti-Semitic country was a grave error, and that the Jews in anti-Semitic Europe should seek refuge in their ancestral homeland.[5] In Agnon, Scholem found an image of Jewish authenticity lacking in his own highly-assimilated and secularized life; and in Scholem, Agnon found a young Jewish scholar of immense promise, with the insight and courage to proclaim the blindness of his community.

Agnon portrays East European Jews such as himself as skeptical about the patriotism of German Jews, seeing them as 'God's stepchildren'.[6] He shared Scholem's view that Jewish patriotic attachment to Germany was a one-sided love affair.[7] In his semi-biographical novella, *Thus Far* (1952), set during World War I, Agnon recalled the friction between patriotic German Jews and East European Jews: 'Throughout the time I lived in Germany I avoided Jewish landlords, as the German Jews were German patriots and they didn't like us [East European Jews] advertizing our Jewishness, which led to quarrels'.[8] In *Thus Far*, Agnon describes a wartime Jewish society so thoroughly Germanized that its sense of Jewishness came mainly from non-Jews. The narrator recalls a visit to a proud Jewish couple in Leipzig the day their son volunteered for the German army, 'and how the mother's eyes shone with joy at having a son with the good fortune and the readiness to defend the homeland'. The young man is killed in battle; the narrator remarks ironically, 'he paid for the right of his patriotism with his life'.[9] Agnon notes ruefully the patriotic sacrifice of German Jews during World War I and their realization that the loss of loved ones in battle failed to reduce anti-Semitic prejudice or bond them to their fellow Germans. Practically every German Jew the narrator meets has lost a loved one, yet they remain socially and psychologically segregated. The narrator's relative, Malka, for example, is 'one Jewess among many gentiles who see her as a stranger, though her son and husband risk their lives for Germany'.[10]

The one-sided love affair

The one-sided love affair is a prominent theme in German-Jewish literature from the early 19th century until the Hitler era, not only among writers in Germany or originating in Germany and writing in German – such as Heine, Rathenau, Toller, Wassermann, Lasker-Schüler, and Zuckmayer, but also those in the Austro-Hungarian empire, including Stefan Zweig, Kafka, Joseph Roth, Werfel, Buber, and Schnitzler, among others. Unrequited love figures in Jewish literature outside the German *Kulturkreis*, for example, in France, Italy, Poland, and Hungary, but is exceptionally pronounced in predominantly German-speaking countries.[11] Jewish writers responded to anti-Semitism with stories and poems of disappointed love, at times openly referring to Jewish patriotic love for the Fatherland and its unhappy consequences.[12] Among works exploring this theme, directly or otherwise, are Stefan Zweig's *Letter from an Unknown Woman* (*Brief einer Unbekannten*, 1922), Buber's *I and Thou* (*Ich und Du*, 1923), Schnitzler's *Dream Story* (*Traumnovelle*, 1926), Roth's *The Radetzky March*, (*Radetzkymarsch*, 1932) and Werfel's *The Forty Days of Musa Dagh* (*Die Vierzig Tage des Musa Dagh*, 1933). In exploring the struggle to be accepted and loved, German-Jewish literature is unexpectedly linked to other works depicting assimilated Jews in Europe, such as Joyce's *Ulysses*

(1922) – uniquely sympathetic to Jews at a time when Jews in European literature were often targeted with prejudice and scorn – and Hemingway's *The Sun Also Rises* (1926).

Growth of a dangerous passion

Hebrew literature had had relatively little influence on German Jews prior to 1914, though the Haskalah (Jewish Enlightenment) and its efforts to modernize Hebrew had begun in Germany in the 18th century. Emancipation and consequent assimilation after 1789 had made the Haskalah largely superfluous. By 1800, most German Jews spoke German. As emancipation brought the European Jews unprecedented blessings – legal equality, rights, tolerance, religious liberty, secular education, progress, modernity, professional training and advancement, and upward social mobility – it is not surprising that they often declared fervent patriotic loyalty to the munificent countries of their newly granted citizenship, or hoped-for citizenship. They became attached to the languages and newly developing cultures, secular and generally nationalistic, of their countries of citizenship. Their Hebrew and Jewish heritage tended to fall by the wayside.[13]

Full emancipation in German lands came with the creation of the Austro-Hungarian Empire in 1867 and the unification of Germany in 1871. As in other countries where Jews were emancipated, German Jews now avidly took part in German culture. Jews whose families had for centuries spoken Yiddish as their daily language were now from infancy immersed in German and other languages. These cultures weakened or replaced entirely their traditional ties to Judaism and the Jewish community. In some languages, Jews became leading writers. Particularly in German literature, Jews confronted the virulent contempt felt towards them by those they loved, or wanted to love and be loved by. Some, infected with self-hate, converted to Christianity, in search of the cold star of Christian love. Yet persistent Church anti-Judaism fuelled their growing sense of betrayal, of being a lover abandoned by the beloved. A parallel sense in Agnon's stories of *agunot*, men and women disillusioned in love and abandoned, struck a chord among young German Jews during and after World War I.

Unrequited love is commonplace in literature[14] but has especial poignancy among assimilated German-Jewish writers from Heine to Zuckmayer, with deep love for German culture, whose Jewish identity came to haunt them as European Jewish life came increasingly under threat. Patriotism in European countries, especially Germany, was itself often anti-Semitic in its xenophobic appeal to tribal distinctiveness, purity and 'blood'. In Germany, unlike France, the national model was based on organic, inherited factors. Consequently, Jewish love for Germany (or Austria) and for German *Kultur* tended to be one-sided. Despite initial optimism, Jewish patriotism often openly represented defeated hopes for acceptance. An entire Jewish literature argued the natural kinship of Jews and Germans, and the unity or compatibility of *Deutschtum* and *Judentum*. The Jewish longing for acceptance came up against anti-Semitic literature pervading Europe, which 'proved scientifically' that Jews were different, disloyal, and inferior.

Jews attracted at first to the 'spirit of love' professed by Christian supporters of emancipation, such as Christian Wilhelm von Dohm (1751–1820),[15] found that these liberals usually saw Jews as a degenerate people. Like many German Jews, Heine loved what was German more than anything in the world.[16] He converted to facilitate his acceptance among Germans, yet he found that many Germans refused to accept this 'entrance ticket'. They hated him as a Jew and denied his centrality in German literature. Heine's poetry, though quintessentially German, betrays his skepticism about Germany:

> Ich hatte einst ein schönes Vaterland
> Der Eichenbaum
> Wuchs dort so hoch, die Veilchen nickten sanft.
> Es war ein Traum.
>
> Das küsste mich auf deutsch und sprach auf deutsch
> (Man glaubt es kaum,/
> Wie gut es klang) das Wort: 'Ich liebe dich!'
> Es war ein Traum.'[17]
>
> [I once had a fine Fatherland/ where the oak grew tall/ and violets soft./A dream.// It kissed me in German, said in German/ (You'd hardly believe/ how good the sound) '*Ich liebe dich*!'/ A dream.]

Heine was forced into exile from Germany, and his works were banned in Germany. Even so, his love of and identification with the idea of Germany remained undiminished.

The failure of symbiosis

From 1871, when German unification brought full Jewish emancipation until the Nazis came to power in 1933, Jews increasingly had reason to doubt the rationality of their attachment to Germany. For many German Jews, World War I was a chance to show semi-sacred patriotic love for the Fatherland, but the war also exposed weaknesses of emancipation and Jewish vulnerability. The outbreak of war in 1914 triggered a massive Continent-wide outpouring of militant patriotism, particularly among German Jews, including Zionists. Statistics showed German Jews went out of their way to prove loyalty to the Fatherland in World War I: large numbers volunteered to fight in the front line. About 100,000 German Jews, or one in six, served in the German army, of whom 80,000 were front-line soldiers, 12,000 were killed in action, and 31,500 were awarded the Iron Cross. Despite this, the Jews were widely suspected of malingering. A deeply offensive survey of Jewish involvement in the war was carried out during the war, the so-called *Judenzählung*, with the aim of 'proving' Jewish disloyalty to Germany.

Agnon's impact on young German Jews during and after the war should be understood in the context of their profound disillusionment with wartime Germany. In the 1914–1918 war, German Jews made immense sacrifices for the Fatherland.

Yet, as Agnon observes in stories set in Germany at the time, the loss of loved ones in battle failed to reduce anti-Semitic prejudice or bond them to their fellow Germans. In his novella, *Thus Far*, Agnon observes the paradox of the German-Jewish ambition to gain acceptance by an anti-Semitic society: 'There's no difference between a Jew and a German except that one sometimes shows up at the Reform Temple while the other is suspected of anti-Semitism'.[18] In 1916, the German army suffered unprecedented casualties, an estimated 800,000 in that year alone. The Jewish industrialist and statesman, Walther Rathenau (1867–1922), chief administrator of Germany's war effort, was accused of profiteering. Privately, he confessed how deeply hurt he was: 'As more Jews are killed [in action] in this war, their enemies will prove with all the more stubbornness that they all sat behind the front and dealt in war speculation (*Kriegswucher*)'.[19] The *Judenzählung* results were suppressed by the War Ministry. They were reportedly too offensive to Jews to be made public. At the end of the war, 'results' were leaked 'proving' that the Jews were shirkers. They were blamed for the military stalemate, food shortages and bureaucratic chaos, immoral business practices, malingering and defeatism; and for 'the stab in the back' that led to Germany's defeat.

Rathenau did not renounce his German patriotism; and indeed, according to the German-Jewish philosopher, Hermann Cohen, Jewish ideals infused the German spirit; Judaeophobia gave urgency to the proud assertion of Jewish roots in 'native lands', an ancient shared history and culture, and perhaps (as in Poland) of suffering, sacrifice, and martyrdom.[20] This sense of the union of Jews and Germany, Jews and France, Jews and Poland, Jews and almost any country with sizable Jewish communities, was generally not shared by non-Jews – even those raised to believe that they were the 'new Israel'. The more Jews identified with such xenophobic states as Germany, the harder they found it to escape the maliciously defiled image of themselves as Jews, thinking at last the disfigured image must be true. It is striking how Jewish writers allude to (or hint at) the distortion of self-image among Jews in animal fables: Heine in 'Princess Sabbath'; Mendele in *The Mare*; Kafka in 'Metamorphosis' and 'A Report to an Academy'; Agnon in *Yesteryear*. Jewish patriotism was sometimes accompanied by self-hate, abdication of Jewish identity, betrayal of Jewish solidarity, and unconditional devotion to countries that did not, for the most part, want them.

Rathenau, uncompromisingly loyal to anti-Semitic Germany, exemplified the self-immolation of Jewish patriotism. Rathenau had no illusions about his inferior place and that of all Jews in German society. At the time of the *Judenzählung* in 1916, he wrote to Frau von Hindenburg, wife of the army head, that as a Jew he was a second-class citizen (*als Jude Bürger zweiter Klasse*).[21] This status he believed was a shared source of anguish among all German Jews from childhood, and which nothing could change. Yet, Rathenau described the Jews as 'a branch of the German nation' (*ein deutscher Stamm*) and he wrote love poetry to Germany: 'Country, my Country, my Love' (*Land, mein Land, du meine Liebe*).[22]

Rathenau believed he was so completely German that, even if he were forcibly exiled, he would remain German. As a patriotic German, he accepted the post of Foreign Minister in 1922, though warned that this appointment was a provocation to anti-Semites.[23] He was assassinated shortly afterwards. Stefan Zweig expressed at the time – without referring to anti-Semitism – the unfolding tragedy of German-speaking Jews in Europe, in his celebrated story, *Letter from an Unknown Woman*. An unnamed woman conceives an inexplicable, futile lifelong love for the famous novelist R. The novelist is totally blind to her existence, even after he (unknowingly) fathers a child by her. The German Jews, whose devotion to the Fatherland was similarly intimate yet *unbekannt*, might have expressed their bitterness as she does:

> You did not recognize me. You have never recognized me, never, never… this non-recognition, familiar as it had become, was a torture to me.[24]

Other German-Jewish writers came to similar conclusions. Ernst Toller, who in 1914 delighted in the opportunity to risk his life for Germany and served loyally throughout the war, felt his extreme patriotism wane as anti-Semitism grew. In an autobiography responding to the rise of postwar anti-Semitism, Toller looked back with rueful irony on his youthful love for Germany: 'Didn't I love Germany with all my heart?... And wasn't the German language my language, the language in which I felt and thought and spoke, a part of my very being…?'[25] Similarly, in his autobiography (revealingly entitled *Mein Weg als Deutscher und Jude*), the novelist Jakob Wassermann confesses that as a young man he felt it was better for Jews to be killed or exiled than to abandon their mission and destiny as Germans, but the war cured him of this foolishness. Weimar Jewish patriotism was no antidote to the poison of German anti-Semitism. Yet Wassermann's greatest sorrow was not for the Jews but for the Germans, loved by assimilated Jews with passionate futility.[26]

Other Jewish writers felt in different ways the falsity of the German-Jewish 'marriage'. In *The Castle* (*Das Schloss*, 1926), written after the anti-Semitic riots in Prague in 1920, Kafka evidently alludes, among other things, to the postwar alienation of European Jews such as himself. Joseph K has inflated hopes that marriage will enable him to enter the castle and gain acceptance. He rapidly becomes engaged to Frieda, a barmaid, and the engagement ends with equal rapidity: 'There will be no marriage [*Es wird keine Hochzeit geben*]'.[27]

At the same time, Agnon's close friend Martin Buber completed *I and Thou* (1923), rejecting the German patriotism he had controversially espoused at the start of World War I. Buber had reason to regret his Hanukkah lecture in Berlin on December 19, 1914, in which he compared Germany with the ancient Maccabees.[28] By 1916, the Jews were commonly blamed for the German failures in the war. In the following year, Buber published a bitter attack on German anti-Semitism and nationalism. He insisted now that 'the German Jews' primary identification had to be with the Jewish people'. Germany, Buber saw, was 'the antithesis of everything he stood for'.[29] The exacerbation of anti-Semitism after the war and the clear failure of German-Jewish assimilation underlie several key passages in *I and Thou* in which public and private life are interconnected: love of man and wife, or man and God, are models for love of nation. The collapse of an I–Thou relationship in marriage or faith is emblematic of social and national failure – including, by implication, that of the German Jews. Nationalism brings disillusionment, writes Buber with an unmistakeable allusion to the German Jews, gripped by futile hope of a 'loving community' (*Liebesgemeinde*) with fellow Germans:

> When the automatized state yokes together totally uncongenial citizens without creating or promoting any fellowship, it is supposed to be replaced by a loving community. And this loving community is supposed to come into being when people come together, prompted by free, exuberant feeling, and want to live together. But that is not how things are…[30]

Buber alludes to the chaotic conditions in post-World War I Europe, in which *Liebesgemeinde* is impossible:

> Modern developments have expunged almost every trace of a life in which human beings confront each other and have meaningful relationships.[31]

Nationalism, far from being an instrument of noble action and being, is, instead, a form of idolatry, a tool of selfishness, conquest, and suppression. Yet, as in the case of the unrequited lover blinded by love, the evil of nationalism is not always easy to see:

> If the nation is for [a man] an idol to which he desires to subjugate everything because in its image he extols his own – do you fancy that you only have to spoil the nation for him and he will then see the truth?[32]

One sees in passages such as these in *I and Thou* the basis for the close intellectual bond between Buber and Agnon, which lasted until Buber's death in 1965. Both found in Hasidic and mystical literature the imagery of personal, national, and universal fragmentation; both sought to heal the lovelorn, the '*agunot*' of the world.

Joyce and Svevo

The Jew as betrayed lover, untrusted nationalist and victim of nationalism, isolated and persecuted, is at the heart of James Joyce's *Ulysses* (1922). Much of *Ulysses* was written in Austro-Hungarian Trieste, with its strong irredentist movement. Joyce was acutely aware of the explosive nature of national conflict and the effects of anti-Semitism. Three quarters of Trieste's population was Italian and its language was an Italian dialect. In reaction against Austrian anti-Semitism, Trieste's Jews sought union with Italy, which was relatively free of anti-Semitism. The leader of the Italian nationalists was Teodoro Mayer, a Hungarian Jew who founded *Il Piccolo della Sera*, the main newspaper in Trieste, whose editor, Roberto Presioso, was a pupil of Joyce's.[33] Leopold Bloom was thus a creation of the hothouse of the Austro-Hungarian Empire, its surface tolerance hiding deep-rooted national and racial conflicts. Bloom's marriage on one level reflects these conflicts, particularly the broader failure of Jews to find secure mooring in the cultures they espoused and the societies where they sought acceptance. In a world in which national barriers were going up and passports, especially for Jews, increasingly hard to get, it is in the unbordered realm of the imagination – described by Schnitzler as *der Weg ins Freie*, and by Proust as *la patrie inconnue* – that Bloom, through Molly's rich unfading memory of his courtship, secures his 'passport to eternity'.[34]

Joyce strongly identified with the Jews, unusually so among early 20th century writers. He was fond of discussing alleged similarities between the Jews and the Irish. Though *Ulysses* is set in Dublin on June 16, 1904, its main character, Leopold Bloom, is based mainly on Jews whom Joyce knew in Trieste, where the book germinated (1905–15). A particular influence was the then-neglected Italian Jewish novelist Italo Svevo, pseudonym of Ettore Schmitz (1861–1928), one of Joyce's pupils, whose writings struck a chord with Joyce, an Irish exile in a foreign land – *terra di nessuna*, as Umberto Saba (1883–1957), another Jewish writer in Trieste, describes it in the poem 'Ulisse'. Svevo's novels *Una Vita* (1892) and *Senilità* (1898), with their failures in love involving seduction, betrayal, and suicide, but with sympathy for his characters and the complexities of their relations, greatly impressed Joyce. Joyce knew by heart the end of *Senilità*, the transformation of female betrayal into universal epiphany, and might have drawn on it for the portrayal of Molly Bloom at the end of *Ulysses*:

> Her figure even became a symbol. It was always looking in the same direction, towards the horizon, the future from which came those glowing rays, reflected in rose and amber and white upon her face. She was waiting![35]

Svevo was Joyce's chief model for Leopold Bloom (both converts, Hungarian in origin, and with non-Jewish wives) and one of his main sources for the Jewish lore in *Ulysses*, and for Zionism, Trieste being a port of departure for Jews going to the Land of Israel. Svevo's writings give little sign of his Jewish origin and education. His pseudonym declares his wish to assimilate and to be seen as a European writer; by 1910, about a fifth of the Trieste Jews had renounced their faith.[36] Svevo evidently transferred both his learning and sympathy for Judaism to Joyce. For the assimilated Svevo to introduce Jewish motifs into his writing might have seemed like special pleading, detracting from his universalist aims. Joyce had no such inhibitions. Svevo might have given Joyce the talmudic comparison (applicable also to the Irish) between the Jews and olives (*Menahot* 53b): like olives, the Jews gave their best when crushed.[37] Bloom is both quintessentially Jewish and Irish ('jewgreek'), and neither, a no-man ('nemo' in the 'Cyclops' episode), a modern Ulysses with no country: 'my Ulysses born anew/ In Dublin as an Irish jew'.[38] Though comic, Bloom in his marital disappointments – the death of his son in 1894 has ended his sex life with Molly, who has taken a lover – mirrors broader alienation within an anti-Semitic society, both in Dublin and in Europe generally.

A self-exile, Joyce observed with empathy as Europe betrayed its Jews, even in Ireland, an island off an island, with practically no visible Jews. In the 'Nestor' section of *Ulysses*, Stephen Dedalus, Joyce's self-portrait as a young man, encounters anti-Semitism as part of what is wrong with Ireland. Mr. Deasy, head of the school where Stephen has taught, claims that Ireland never persecuted the

Jews as Jews were never allowed in, yet is himself gripped by anti-Semitic prejudice: 'England is in the hands of the jews. In all the highest places: her finance, her press. And they are the signs of a nation's decay'.[39] Bloom's assimilation in Irish society is undermined doubly, by being Jew and cuckold. The confusion in Bloom's identity – his desire to belong among those who betray him – emerges particularly in the 'Cyclops' episode in *Ulysses*, set in a pub in which he is surrounded by a group of anti-Semites who – in a scene reminiscent of the solitary Bloch set upon by anti-Semitic Parisian aristocrats in Proust's *À la Recherche du Temps Perdu*[40] – insult him and challenge his nationality:

> Ireland, says Bloom. I was born here. Ireland. [...] And after all, says John Wyse, why can't a jew love his country like the next fellow? – Why not? Says J.J., when he's quite sure which country it is.[41]

The generally even-tempered Bloom is provoked into a remarkable outburst against national hatred and persecution, in which the bitterness of the failure of his love-life is also apparent, for he, a man devoted to family, seems fated to be reminded constantly, at times comically, of his wife's infidelity:

> Persecution, says he, all the history of the world is full of it. Perpetuating national hatred among nations. [...] And I belong to a race too, says Bloom, that is hated and persecuted. Also now. This very moment. This very instant... Robbed, says he, Plundered. Insulted. Persecuted. [...] That's not life for men and women, insult and hatred. And everybody knows that it's the very opposite of that that is really life. [...] Love, says Bloom, I mean the opposite of hatred...[42]

Schnitzler: 'mortal enemies' in bed

Whereas Joyce was an accidental sojourner in the Austrian-Hungarian empire, Schnitzler was in many ways the grandmaster of its sordid truths, including anti-Semitism and the convolutions of sexual relations. Schnitzler's deep concern with the Jewish Question is clear in works such as *The Road to the Open* (*Der Weg ins Freie*, 1908) and *Professor Bernhardi* (1912). In these works, the gulf between Jews and non-Jews often seems unbridgeable. In *The Road to the Open*, Schnitzler suggests that despite inevitable anti-Semitic persecution and betrayal, the inner life offered a form of freedom. If '*Der Weg ins Freie*' cannot be found within the hostile external world it can be found within oneself.[43] In his novella, *Dream Story* (1926), Schnitzler calls even inner freedom into question. The inner life, too, is subjected to social and psychological trauma, servitude, and terror.

Dream Story is a story of Vienna c. 1900 published there after years of mass anti-Semitic demonstrations starting from 1918 when Austria was losing the war and there were serious shortages of food, fuel, and housing. Schnitzler, who lived in Vienna all his life, would have witnessed the *völkisch* demonstrations at the time of the Fourteenth World Zionist Congress in August 1925, in which several thousand marched, and Jews were verbally abused and physically attacked on the

Ringstrasse.[44] *Dream Story* portrays a troubled marriage in which the gulf between husband and wife often seems unbridgeable. It has practically no open reference to Jews or anti-Semitism but can be read as an allegory of persistent European Jewish alienation. In this respect, it is close to Agnon whose portrayals of disharmony in sexual relations, of masks and nightmares, often appear to allude to wider social breakdown.[45] Narrated almost like episodes in a dream (and with Freud's *The Interpretation of Dreams* looming over it),[46] *Dream Story* reveals the truth of the marriage, stripping away its masks. Fridolin, a Viennese doctor (like Schnitzler), moves through a series of worlds to which he has entrée but does not belong, beginning and ending with his home and wife: the apartment of a dead court counsellor, a cafe, a prostitute's room, a costume shop where he buys a mask, an exclusive and dangerous erotic club, a morgue. These scenes range through all classes and strata of Viennese society. The climax is in the secret club, which Fridolin risks his life to enter, as a non-member. He is drawn to this club as a forbidden world: '*ich kann nicht zurück, dachte er bei sich. Weiter meinen Weg, und wär's mein Tod.*' ['I can't go back, he thought to himself. My way lies forward, even were it to my death.'].[47] He ignores warnings that his life is in danger and that there is time to flee, hoping that his mask and costume (as a monk) will protect him. The lust for acceptance, Schnitzler implies, can be fatal. Fridolin is unmasked when he cannot give the password when challenged: '*Sie gehören nicht hierher... du bist erkannt*'. ['You don't belong here... You've been recognized'].[48] Lucky to get out alive, Fridolin finds no protection at home: in marriage, too, he wears a mask – in fact, the costume mask appears on the marital bed – and his entire life appears to be a tissue of lies and illusions. His wife dreams of affairs with other men and of Fridolin crucified, his fate preordained, '*jede Flucht unmöglich war*' ['any escape impossible'].[49] He is gripped by lust for revenge. Though he and his wife lie side by side, a sword lies between them: they are '*wie Todfeinde*' ['like mortal enemies']. In comparison with his other encounters, his wife is '*die Schlimmste von allen. Ich werde mich von ihr trennen.*' ['the worst of them all. We'll have to part.'].[50]

Hemingway's **The Sun Also Rises***: the Jew as unrequited lover*

Dream Story shares with Hemingway's *The Sun Also Rises* – both published in 1926 – the theme of sexual alienation, a sense of otherness as anti-Semitism grew in the 1920s. Since 1921, Hemingway had lived in France and Spain, where the novel is set. Hemingway's German-Jewish acquaintances, including Gertrude Stein and Harold Loeb, influenced the novel as did the King James Bible, whose spare narrative style with its 'iceberg' effect forces the reader to imagine and interpret what is beneath the surface. Yet, little is submerged in Hemingway's portrait of Robert Cohn (based partly on Loeb, who came from a prominent German-Jewish family) in *The Sun Also Rises*. American anti-Semitism in this novel, set in the 1920s, is similar to much European anti-Semitism, though without the violence and the racism. *The Sun Also Rises* was written at a time of American anti-immigration legislation (1924), mainly aimed to stop Jewish refugees, desperate to escape persecution, from entering the United States. There were widespread American anti-Jewish restrictions in the professions, residential neighborhoods, societies and clubs, as well as quotas in universities. Jake Barnes, the narrator of *The Sun Also Rises* does not generally condemn the frequent anti-Jewish slurs he hears in his circle, though at times he disapproves of them. As a product of its time, the book is anti-Semitic. Barnes, Cohn's friend, is disgusted by his own failure to defend Cohn. He admits his malicious pleasure at hearing Cohn maligned. Only Lady Brett Ashley, an English aristocrat with a tragic past in the war, objects to 'that sort of rot' coming from her drunken fiancé, Mike Campbell. Even she succumbs at times to the common discourse, referring to Cohn as a 'damned Jew'. Hemingway describes anti-Semitism realistically, as acceptable behavior in its time, though he also makes unusually clear the psychopathology of this prejudice, linking it to the weaknesses and failings of his characters. As Cohn is thoroughly assimilated, his defences against anti-Semitism are atrophied. At Princeton, he was a champion boxer, as many Jews in German university had learned to duel, to defend himself against anti-Semites; but in the end Cohn boxes himself into a corner, exposing his outsider status. He is not helped by his German origin at a time when Germany was still viewed with suspicion and hatred by many ex-combatants.

Cohn, the only Jew in a group of American expatriates, seeks acceptance in a society in which anti-Semitism is the norm, as it was in American and European society and literature of the period. Cohn's life as a would-be bohemian writer can be seen as part of his struggle to assimilate and break out of traditional anti-Jewish prejudices. He is stung constantly by familiar anti-Semitic taunts: of being an alien 'kike', pitiful and superior, stingy, usurious and stubborn, of mixing where he is not wanted, doomed to hell. He is pinned down by his name. Cohn is trapped, as were many German Jews, by his desperate need for acceptance among non-Jews whose psychopathological tendencies seek an outlet in his victimization. Among people scarred by the war, Cohn stands out in not having served, though over a million Jews, including about a quarter-million American Jews, served in the war. Cohn is out of place among Americans seeking escape from post-traumatic stress in drink, promiscuity, gambling, racing, fighting, fishing, and the heroic dignity of the bullfight – a recreation, in controlled form, of their own proximity to death on the front line. Cohn cannot share their barracks-room camaraderie, nor can he hold his drink as they can. He has the sobriety of a *yekke*, the traditional Jewish repulsion by drink, blood-sports, the arena.

In love, too, Cohn is an outsider. In a world made cynical by war, he conceives of the Circe-like Brett, serially unfaithful to her men, as a romantic ideal. Cohn the romantic is not unlike Jay Gatsby in Fitzgerald's *The Great Gatsby* (1925), published the year before, which Hemingway had read and admired. Yet, Gatsby's hopeless love for Daisy is poignant and tragic. Cohn's devotion to Brett is sneered at with anti-Semitic jibes. When Brett leaves him for the bullfighter, Romero, Cohn snaps: he pursues Romero and beats him to a pulp. Cohn is less remarkable as a target of anti-Semites than as a fighting Jew who up to a point is accepted by non-Jews, even for his failings – his 'arrested development', as an acquaintance puts it. A writer and editor, he thinks of Jake as his best friend and is proud of his affair with Brett. Yet Cohn's anxiety to assimilate, to be accepted, blinds him to the reality of his friendship and love affair. Jake, himself in love with Brett, but blocked from sex with her because of a war wound, secretly smoulders with jealousy of Cohn. He gets perverse satisfaction when Mike Campbell and Bill Gorton, like a couple of amateur bullfighters, goad Cohn and hurt him with their anti-Semitic barbs: a lapsed Catholic, obsessed by honorable behavior, Jake is tainted by Catholic anti-Semitism. His betrayal of Cohn could even be seen as a foreshadowing of the larger betrayal of the Catholic Church: in 1933 the Church made a pact with Germany and refused to speak out in defence of the persecuted Jews. Like a bull in the ring, Cohn becomes the sacrifice. Yet, Cohn colludes as a victim, in his anxiety for acceptance by non-Jews. He does not reject them as the drunken Jew-haters they are. He refuses to see Brett as the promiscuous drunk she is, who has slept with him as she sleeps with many men. He cannot believe their relationship has no meaning, no future. Romantic gallantry to Cohn is contemptible Jewish intrusion to Mike. Cohn's entrapment in his own blindness is disturbingly familiar in interwar German-Jewish literature, such as Zweig's *Letter from an Unknown Woman*. In this wider context, Cohn's unrequited love for Brett suggests the outsider status of Jews which, far from driving them away in despair, made them redouble their efforts to be accepted, bringing further opprobrium upon their heads.

Love and alienation

Alienation from society and dissociation from the self, described by Schnitzler in *Dream Story* and Hemingway in *The Sun Also Rises*, characterized the so-called 'lost generation' of the postwar years. Assimilated Jews strongly attached to their countries were doubly alienated, by the stresses of the age and by being made increasing aware that as Jews they were unwanted. In a story about her father, *Arthur Aronymus* (1932), Else Lasker-Schüler explores the possibility of love between Germans and Jews in the centuries-long panorama of German-Jewish history. She concludes with a fantasy in which Christians overcome their hatred and sit down with Jews to celebrate the Passover.[51] In the following year, beaten by Nazis, she escaped, bleeding and bruised, without suitcase or money, to Switzerland. Even the more hard-headed Hannah Arendt, who came to Zionism in 1933 convinced that 'When one is attacked as a Jew, one must defend oneself as a Jew',[52] was in the 1920s a typical assimilationist who believed in the unity of *Deutschtum* and *Judentum*, and whose affair with her professor, Martin Heidegger, seemed to seal this union, before Heidegger ditched her. Her doctoral thesis at Heidelberg University was on love in St. Augustine (1929). In her thesis Arendt searched for a universal or transcendent principle to unite Jewish and German elements in the protective power of a universalist German culture. She overlooked the fact that philosophy 'can be dangerously blind to history'.[53] Heidegger's behavior exemplified the increasing feeling of divorce from Germany among Jews: he welcomed Hitler, joined the Nazi Party, and distanced himself from Jews.

Yet love did not die easily, even under the Nazis. Carl Zuckmayer called his last story before he was forced out of Germany 'A Love Story' (*Eine Liebesgeschichte*, 1934). Set in 18th-century Prussia, it conveys Zuckmayer's despair at contemporary

Germany: an army officer, rejected by a world in which he is torn between love and his code of honor, commits suicide. Life imitated art. Under Nazi rule about 10,000 German Jews or part-Jews, or nearly 2 per cent of the total German-Jewish population, committed suicide.[54] Many who left remained attached to Germany. After escaping Germany in 1938, Jewish journalist and socialite Bella Fromm wrote of her love for 'old Germany', its culture and landscape: 'I was rooted deeply in its soul and in its history and in its language'.[55]

Austrian Jews clung similarly to Austria: some retained patriotism and loyalty to the memory of the emperor Franz Joseph, who died in 1916. In this respect, they were not unlike others whose world had collapsed with the war and tried to adapt with outmoded pre-war reflexes. The pre-war Jewish attachment to the Empire is epitomized in Robert Musil's novel, *The Man Without Qualities* (*Der Mann ohne Eigenschaften*, 1930–43): Leo Fischel, a Jewish banker, hopes Austrian Jews like himself will continue to assimilate in Austrian society, a hope undermined by Austrian anti-Semitism. Vienna's most famous Jewish citizen, Sigmund Freud, expressed love for the so-called 'prison' of his Austrian homeland.[56] The novelist Joseph Roth, too, remained a loyal Austrian patriot, who loved with almost religious awe the remnants of the Empire.[57] In *The Radetzky March* (1932), set in the last years of the Austrian-Hungarian Empire, Roth depicts the relationship between a Jewish army doctor, Max Demant, and his Christian wife as a tragedy of unrequited love: '*Ich vermisse dich nie*!' '*Du liebst mich also nicht*?' *Nein*!' ['I never miss you' … 'you don't love me?' 'No!'].[58]

Werfel and The Forty Days of Musa Dagh

Franz Werfel's novel, *The Forty Days of Musa Dagh* (1933), written as Hitler came to power but set against the Armenian genocide by the Ottoman Turks in 1915, presents a love triangle as an oblique reference to the failure of European Jewish assimilation. Gabriel Bagradian, based partly on Werfel himself, is a wealthy Westernized Armenian who has spent much of his life in Paris; his wife is Juliette, an elegant, beautiful Parisienne (based partly on Alma Mahler, to whom Werfel was married at the time); they have a fourteen-year-old son, Stephan. Gabriel's changing sense of identity and *Weltanschauung* are not unlike those of many early 20th-century assimilated Jews. Gabriel at first supports the Young Turk revolution in 1908, believing that the modernization of the Ottoman empire would lead to greater integration and acceptance of the Armenian minority. In the Balkan War of 1912, he volunteers from Paris and fights patriotically for Turkey, as German Jews fight for Germany in World War I. By 1913, however, he questions his loyalty to the Ottoman Empire as Armenians are subjected to massacres no less vicious than those in the 1890s: '*Diese meine alten Freunde sind nun meine Todfeinde?*' ['Can such old friends be my mortal enemies?'][59]

The death of an older brother in late 1913 brings Gabriel and his family to the family home in Syria, where he claims his inheritance on Musa Dagh ('Mountain of Moses'), a mountain region on the Syrian coast. The family is caught there when war breaks out in August 1914: Turkey is at war with France, and the family cannot return to Paris. Turkey, defeated in early battles of the war, suspects the Armenians as a fifth column. In early 1915, the Turks begin deportations of hundreds of thousands of Armenians from their villages into the desert.[60] Most of them die. A few, including the director of an Armenian orphanage, Aram Tomasian, his wife Hovsannah, and sister Iskuhi, who is attacked and crippled, make their way to Musa Dagh where they tell their story. There is a belief that Europe cannot allow such atrocities (*Europa wird es nicht dulden*).[61] Gabriel, aware of the fate awaiting the Armenians living in the villages of Musa Dagh, makes a plan of resistance. At an open meeting of several thousand villagers, addressed by their spiritual leader, Ter Haiguson, Gabriel persuades them to fight. All this is based on a true story, in which Armenians in 1915 held out for weeks against far superior Turkish forces.

However, the triangle that Werfel goes on to describe, between Gabriel, Juliette, and Iskuhi, comes entirely from the novelist's imagination and is least credible in a traditional Armenian setting.[62] Gabriel, initially alienated from Armenia, rediscovers his roots, as did many Jews with the rise of European anti-Semitism in the late-19th and early-20th century. From the start, Gabriel knows his marriage will be under strain and suggests divorce (*Wir sollten uns scheiden lassen*).[63] Though Juliette loves and is loyal to him and Stephan, and is no coward, Gabriel realizes that she cannot understand the suffering of his people: 'It's in my bones. My ancestors in me, who suffered incredible things, can feel it. My whole body feels it. No, Juliette, you can't understand! Nobody could understand who hasn't been hated because of his race' ('*Wer niemals um seiner Rasse willen gehasst worden ist, kann das nicht begreifen.*')[64]

Indeed, Juliette cannot take the Armenian plight seriously. She claims to have experienced nothing but Turkish friendship and civility (*nur Freundlichkeit und Galanterie*) and actually blames the Armenians for being unjust to the Turks.[65] She seems to have no conception that the Armenians have 'no protection, no help, no hope' (*kein Schutz, keine Hilfe, keine Hoffnung*).[66] She is even insulting about the lack of an Armenian high culture, claiming that the Armenians have never had a Racine or a Voltaire.[67] In her attitude to Iskuhi, Juliette echoes the racial condescension that educated Europeans often expressed to individual Jews, that they were exceptions. Juliette contrasts Iskuhi with other Orientals as she looks and behaves like a Western woman.[68] Iskuhi, though, preserves her innocence. She has experienced at first hand the sufferings of her people and has no illusions about the Turks. She has survived a forced march, and her arm has been crippled by her Turkish assailant.

As the battles rage on Musa Dagh between the Turks and the beleaguered Armenians, the triangle of Gabriel–Juliette–Iskuhi emerges. Gabriel, immersed in directing the Armenian struggle, is increasingly estranged from Juliette and turns to the devoted Iskuhi. Juliette has little commitment to the Armenian cause. Amid the privations of Musa Dagh, she is disoriented and unbalanced. She misses the comforts of Paris. Turning to a Greek journalist, Gonzague Maris, for comfort, she is reviled as an adulteress. As weeks pass with no hope of salvation, she sickens and loses her sanity. Iskuhi nurses her faithfully, out of love for Gabriel. When Stephan is murdered by the Turks, Iskuhi comforts Gabriel; Juliette is too delirious to be told. Finally, the Armenian survivors are rescued by a French warship. By then it is clear that, at least in the imagination, Gabriel and Iskuhi are a true Armenian soul couple. In the final scene, Gabriel leaves the rescue ship and climbs Musa Dagh alone. As he climbs to the scene of his greatest devotion to the Armenian cause, he seems to hear Iskuhi's footsteps, and is shot dead by a Turkish sniper.

According to Meyer Weisgal, Werfel referred to the Armenians in his novel as '*meine Ersatzjuden*'.[69] The triangle he depicts is comparable to those in some of Agnon's stories, in highlighting inner conflicts of European Jews, particularly the dilemma of emancipated Westernized Jews who, like Gabriel, encountered hatred rather than acceptance. Jews, like Armenians, had tried and failed to assimilate and to prove their patriotism, especially in wartime. Gabriel is torn between Juliette, representing the brilliant allure of the West, and Iskuhi, who embodies the soul of Armenian identity and culture. The sophisticated Juliette is superficial by comparison. She never overcomes her French susceptibility to *haute couture*.[70] Iskuhi, in contrast, is rough and direct but naturally beautiful, with a love for Armenian poetry and song. She sings to the children during the forced march and, on Musa Dagh, finds that Stephan loves her songs as if he were a native Armenian.[71] Love for one's own cultural heritage is always, by implication, requited.

Vogel and Agnon: lovers and vampires

As relations between European Jews and Christians worsened in the interwar years, David Vogel's Hebrew novel, *Married Life* (*Haye nisu'im*, 1929–30), written in Paris, warned that anti-Semitism threatened the future of European Jews. The novel is a uniquely gritty picture of inter-war Vienna, its population reeling from the 1914–18 war, the collapse of a seemingly stable social and political order, and ten thousand per cent inflation. A young, impecunious Jewish writer, Rudolf Gurdweill, meets a baroness of the Habsburg nobility, Thea von Takow, in a café. Within twenty-four hours, she virtually proposes, 'You'll marry me, won't you, Rudolfus?'[72] She becomes an instant convert to Judaism, an act ominously unaccompanied by repudiation of the racist anti-Semitism of her environment. Thea and Gurdweill marry two weeks later. Thea turns out to be cruel, rapacious, and leech-like: 'From the day she met Gurdweill she had had an urge to hurt him, to make him miserable in any way she could'.[73] She delights in the prospect of tormenting Gurdweill: 'I'll torment him to death… because it gives me pleasure'.[74] Gurdweill does not lack initiative and courage. Though poor, he is an intellectual aristocrat, and a fighter with a suppressed violent streak. Drawn to the spell of Thea's domineering, Gurdweill finds perverse pleasure in the pain she inflicts. He becomes almost zombie-like: 'he was enslaved to this woman forever'.[75] His friends cannot save him. Gurdweill's hopes rise when Thea becomes pregnant, but she torments him with threats of abortion. After the baby is born, she hurts him further by neglecting the boy. She taunts Gurdweill, claiming he is not the father and that she will sleep with whomever she wants, including all Gurdweill's friends. Immensely self-centred, she has a Nietzschean belief in the strong and the elect, in passion, boldness, and force, while Gurdweill longs for an ordered family life and, unlike Thea, is delighted by being a parent. When the baby dies, Thea is coldly indifferent; Gurdweill is shattered.

Like many assimilated Jews, Gurdweill has radically broken with his family background: he is a descendant of the great 17th-century rabbi, the Maharal of Prague, yet little about him – apart, perhaps, from a strong moral conscience – is Jewish. As a child growing up in Galicia, he felt strongly the separation between Jews and Gentiles: 'People seemed to be divided into two species, utterly different from each other, as different as cats and dogs'.[76] In Vienna, he changed and came to feel that the old barriers had broken down, but his marriage seems to argue that the divisions were as dangerous as ever. It can be seen as a mirror of failure of Jewish-Christian relations. The sado-masochism of wife and husband recalls the entire history of Christian cruelty to Jews who are 'married' to the countries where they live.[77]

Vogel's novel might have influenced Agnon's earlier-mentioned allegory of sado-masochistic Christian-Jewish relations, 'The Lady and the Pedlar' (1943), a chilling vampire horror story written during the Holocaust.[78] That the 'marriage' between Jew and murderess alludes to the failure of Jewish assimilation in Europe is brutally clear. The story was published in 1943 amid daily reports in the Hebrew press of mass killings of Jews. Up to a point, the partnership of the lady and the pedlar is rational: the lady offers food and shelter and the pedlar does odd jobs for her. He first makes his home in the barn and ends up in her bed. Yet the illusion of intimacy blinds him to her murderous nature. Nor does he see how important is the Jewish faith he has abandoned: it helps him survive. The pedlar thinks he is accepted, the very image of a middle-class landowner. His loyalty to the murderess parallels the loyalty of European Jews toward anti-Semitic countries. His blindness to his impending fate has many analogues in Jewish history, though Agnon probably had Germany mainly in mind. The pedlar's suicidal attachment to the murderess even after her wicked plan is laid bare reflects Agnon's repugnance for European Jewish patriotism towards countries which made no secret of their murderous hatred of Jews.

Conclusion

Agnon's portrayal of German Jews as blinded by their love for their anti-Semitic homeland has many parallels in interwar literature, particularly in the motif of unrequited love. The notion of writers as antennae of society is borne out among those who, like Agnon, responded to the crisis of European Jewry struggling for acceptance amid rising anti-Semitism, warning that the loyalty of assimilated European Jews to the state and its culture made them vulnerable to persecution and ultimate extermination. Agnon's Galician friend, the Hebrew poet, Uri Zvi Greenberg, having risked his life fighting for anti-Semitic Austria-Hungary as an officer in World War I, was driven to Palestine, and back to the love of Zion and of the Jewish God – he confesses this in the poem 'With My God, the Blacksmith' (*Im Eli hanapah*):[79]

Like a woman who knows I've fallen
for her charms, my God mocks me: escape if you can!
But I can't.
For when I flee raging in despair
and like a hissing coal I swear
'I'll never see him again!'
I come back
and knock at his door
like a tormented lover.
As if he'd written me a love letter.

Notes

1 Agnon's main works with a German background are *Thus Far* and *In the Shop of Mr. Lublin*; and among his outstanding shorter works, 'Metamorphosis', 'The Doctor's Divorce' and 'Fernheim'. On Agnon's years in Germany, see Laor (1998); for a collection of studies on German influences on Agnon's writings, see Becker and Weiss (2010).

2 Ruppin (1913: 198–9). Agnon was Ruppin's Hebrew teacher in a relationship significant in the social integration of East European Jews among German Zionists (and often a valuable source of income): in Germany, Agnon taught, among others, his future wife, Esther Marx; his future publisher, Salman Schocken; and Martin Buber's son, Raphael. Assimilated German Jews were often hostile to East European Jews, referring to them contemptuously as *Ostjuden*; and the *Centralverein deutscher Staatsbürger jüdischen Glaubens* (CV), the most important German Jewish organization, 'dissociated itself from any political form of cooperation with Jewish communities outside Germany', even declaring in its 1893 charter that 'We have no other common interests with the Jews in other lands' (Margaliot 1988: 101–2). Maximilian Horwitz, first president of the CV, infamously summed up the position of the German Jews: 'Stepchildren must behave themselves' (*Stiefkinder müssen artig sein*) (Reinharz 1975: 67). Agnon gravitated particularly to German Zionists who rejected German Jewish patriotism and, despite immersion in German *Kultur*, sought renewal in Jewish culture, in its poetry, folklore, legends, and mysticism, which they regarded as equal if not superior to German literature. Among Agnon's supporters in Germany were some, such as Gershon Schocken, who recognized Agnon's vast superiority in the mastery of Hebrew and rabbinic culture; they greatly admired his Hebrew fiction and translated his main works into German; and they sought to promote him as a unique literary genius and guide him from the provincial backwater of Eastern Europe to the mainstream of *Weltliteratur*.

3 For Brenner's view of Ottoman Palestine as a cultural backwater in 'Nerves', see pp. 4–5.

4 During World War I, even Zionists were divided by national loyalties. Shortly after the war began, and the Ottoman empire which ruled Palestine was allied with Germany against Britain and France, Ruppin wrote to the German consul in Jaffa of 'our highly developed sense of duty to Germany' displayed by Palestinian Jews who volunteered to fight for Germany: 'We can all say with pride that this brave Zionist troop marched in the front line' (Zechlin 1969: 90, n. 34). That such fervent declarations of loyalty to Germany came from committed Zionists was not extraordinary and continued up to and even during the Hitler era (Aberbach 2009a, 2013). Some German Zionists returned to Germany from Palestine to fight for the fatherland (Reinharz 1975: 223). One of these wrote at the time: 'We came [back to Germany] joyfully, not just out of duty but, above

all, love for the land of our birth … '; and some regarded their Jewish nationalism as an enhancement of their German patriotic loyalty and volunteered 'because we were Zionists (*dass wir in den Krieg zogen, weil wir Zionisten waren*)' (Zechlin 1969: 90, n. 34; 94). Agnon felt the German Jews had effectively created a fiction of their assimilation, while in his fiction he was telling the truth: that their love for Germany was unrequited.

5 Scholem once described to me – acted out, in fact – how, like Homer's Ulysses who feigned madness to avoid conscription, he had pretended to be mentally unhinged and physically sick to evade German army service in World War I. Agnon's portrait of madness and resistance to army service in *A Simple Story* might involve an in-joke with Scholem: Hirshl's madness and institutional treatment would normally have been a stigma in his small home town, as it was for his mad uncle, but he is able to resume life as a respectable citizen as everyone assumes his madness was not real but a rational and effective trick by means of which he succeeded in evading conscription (Agnon, CW iii 224–5, 243–4). Agnon's draft-dodging was common among Eastern European Jews, whereas Scholem's was unusual among German Jews who (like Scholem's father, who kicked him out of the family home) were fiercely patriotic.

6 Agnon (CW vii 63). Agnon is echoing, critically, a familiar description of European Jews, particularly in Germany, as essentially unwanted: in France (Marrus 1980: 156), in Austria (Wistrich 1990: 300), in Poland (Meirtchak 2004: 294), in England (Macaulay 1963: 122), and in Germany (Reinharz 1975: 67). See p. 126 note 2.

7 Scholem (1976: 86).

8 Agnon (CW vii 90)

9 Agnon (CW vii 95). On statistics of Jewish service in the German army, see p. 113. Agnon's *A Guest for the Night* is similarly critical of Jewish patriotism and sacrifice in World War I, with its harrowing portrait of Frieda Kaiser – her very name reflects the popularity of the emperor among Austro-Hungarian Jews – who has lost most of her children in the Great War and in pogroms; and *In the Shop of Mr. Lublin*, too, reflects Jewish revulsion at the militant patriotism for anti-Semitic countries, which drew many assimilated Jews to Zionism in the interwar years.

10 Agnon (CW vii 57).

11 Aberbach (2013: 208–223).

12 On various ways in which literature anticipates the Holocaust, see Aberbach (2009). Although Agnon's interest in German *Kultur* was primarily literary, there are also occasional shadowings of German cinema in his stories, for example the sleepwalkers in *The Cabinet of Doctor Caligari* and *Iddo and Enam*; the young man tormented by murderous impulses in *M* and *A Simple Story*; and the professor obsessed with a dominant woman who humiliates him in *The Blue Angel* and *Shira*.

13 On the status of Hebrew in German lands in the 19th century, see pp. 2, 9–11.

14 Love unrequited is a frequent motif in Romantic literature, especially in Germany, in Goethe's *The Sorrows of Young Werther*, for example. The use of relations between the sexes to represent broader social and political issues goes back to the Bible, the prophets (for example, Hosea and Jeremiah) in particular.

15 See, for example, Mendes-Flohr and Reinharz (1995: 34).

16 Prawer (1983: 209). The German-Jewish journalist and writer, Ludwig Börne (1786–1837) declared that, as a Jew with no Fatherland, he loved the German Fatherland more than other Germans (Mendes-Flohr and Reinharz 1995: 260).

17 *In Exile* (*In der Fremde*, 1827) in Heine (1961–1964).

18 Agnon (CW vii 102).

19 Rathenau (2006: 1552). The accusation came from the anti-Semite, Houston Stewart Chamberlain. Rathenau replied by sending Chamberlain a balance sheet of his finances,

with affidavits from the War Minister, the Deputy War Minister, and the Chancellor to prove his innocence (Field 1981: 392).

20 Mendelsohn (1993: 10–13).

21 Rathenau (2006: 1818).

22 Quoted by Joll (1960: 61, 66).

23 When in 1922, the Russian-born Chaim Weizmann, president of the World Zionist Organization, met Walther Rathenau, then the German Foreign Minister, shortly before Rathenau's assassination, he had the impression that Rathenau was typical of many patriotic German Jews: 'they seemed to have no idea that they were sitting on a volcano' (Weizmann 1949: 289). To observers of the ferocity of German anti-Semitism during and after World War I, Rathenau's murder came as no surprise.

24 Zweig (1934: 86–7).

25 Toller (1934: 281).

26 'Leidet man nicht immer am meisten dort, wo man am tiefsten liebt, wenn auch am vergeblichsten?' Wassermann (1921: 124).

27 Kafka (1994: 318); (1926: 472). Kafka was critical of Jewish loyalty to the newly created Czechoslovakian state at a time of intense anti-Semitism after World War I. After witnessing anti-Semitic riots in the streets of Prague in November 1920, Kafka asked why the Jews did not emigrate: failure to leave was 'heroism of the cockroach' (Kafka 1983: 170). *The Castle*, written during this period, on one level reflects the futility of Jewish longing for acceptance in a hostile world.

28 Horwitz (1988: 240).

29 Friedman (1981: i 214, 224).

30 Buber (1970: 94).

31 Buber (1970: 97).

32 Buber (1970: 154).

33 Ellmann (1983: 196–7). In their language teaching, Joyce and Agnon made valuable contacts: Joyce with Italo Svevo, a model for Leopold Bloom; Agnon with Ruppin, the leading German Zionist in early 20th century Palestine, and with Salman Schocken, his patron and publisher. Else (Esther) Marx was Agnon's pupil before she became his wife.

34 Ellmann (1983: 501).

35 Svevo (1965: 224). Svevo's writings contrast with Agnon's, being singularly devoid of Jewish content; yet his characters are not unlike Agnon's *agunot*, 'at the handles of the lock'.

36 McCourt (2000: 223).

37 Ellmann (1983: 446).

38 Ellmann (1983: 416).

39 Joyce (1993: 33).

40 The anti-Semitism mocked by Joyce and Proust, in Ireland and France respectively, in the two great experimental novels of the early 20th century, was a growing phenomenon in Europe at the time of the Dreyfus case and after; and the unconventionality of both novels includes the rejection of anti-Semitism.

41 Joyce (1993: 323).

42 Joyce (1993: 317, 318, 319).

43 As a leading Viennese author, Schnitzler was vulnerable to attacks that as a Jew he was incapable either of depicting accurately the German-speaking world or of understanding German literature: 'He, the lover and discriminating connoisseur of German literature, had to endure being told by a Germanophile Austrian writer that he, Schnitzler, could not hope to understand a German classic like Goethe' (Gay 2001: 116).

44 Pauley (1992: 108–116).
45 On Agnon's admiration for Schnitzler, see Agnon (1976: 113).
46 On Freud's German patriotism and disillusionment as reflected in his dreams, see Aberbach (2013: 178–9).
47 Schnitzler (2001: 40; 1999: 43). On anti-Semitism in Austrian private clubs, see Pauley (1992: 117–120).
48 Schnitzler (2001: 41, 431; 1999: 45, 47).
49 Schnitzler (2001, 60; 1999: 67, 69).
50 Schnitzler (2001: 66; 1999: 75). After the traumatic night of *Traumnovelle* a new perhaps hopeful dawn breaks: which is the more real, the day or the night? Yet, in his posthumous story, 'The Second' (*Der Sekundant*, 1932), Schnitzler appears to resume in allegorical form the darker implications of *Traumnovelle*: regardless of how assimilated the Jews are, they remain outsiders.
51 '... mit einem bisschen Liebe geht's schon, dass Jude und Christ ihr Brot gemeinsam in Eintracht brechen' (Lasker-Schüler 2001: 4.1, 266)
52 Young-Bruehl (1982: 109).
53 Young-Bruehl (1982: 499). Elias Canetti's novel *The Deception*, or *Blinding* (*Die Blendung*, 1935) – in English, *Auto-da-fé* – describes a Viennese intellectual who lives (somewhat like Prospero in *The Tempest*) entirely in his books, in his 'world in the head,' blind to the outer world and the malice of those closest to him, including his wife.
54 Vital (1999: 826).
55 Fromm (1942: 1).
56 Jones (1957: iii 245).
57 Roth (1970: 240). Continued love for Hungary among Hungarian Jews, despite growing alienation, is conveyed in the fiction of Baron Lajos Hatvany (1880–1961) (Patai 1996: 376).
58 Roth (2002: 92); Roth (1975–76: ii 89).
59 Werfel (2012: 89; 1947: i 97). On historical and biographical elements in *The Forty Days of Musa Dagh*, see Jungk (1990: 137–147).
60 Werfel (2012: 68; 1947: i 75). In German, 'arme Menschen' plays on 'arme' (poor, unfortunate) and 'Armenian'.
61 Werfel (2012: 83; 1947: i 91).
62 Jungk (1990: 147). The allegorical triangle in *The Forty Days of Musa Dagh* recalls the triangle in Agnon's *Iddo and Enam*, in which rivals in love represent rival ideas and ways of life. On Agnon's acquaintanceship with Werfel, see Agnon (1983: 65).
63 Werfel (2012: 68; 1947: i 77).
64 The Turks justify the genocide in much the same way as the Nazis rationalized their treatment of the Jews, as a hygienic measure against internal enemies (*innere Feinde*): 'Zwischen dem Menschen und dem Pestbazillus gibt es keinen Frieden.' (Werfel 2012, 155; 1947 i 163). The Armenians, too, are 'innere Feinde' (1947 i 157).
65 Werfel (2012: 70; 1947: i 78).
66 Werfel (2012: 101; 1947: i 109).
67 Werfel (2012: 187; 1947: i 197).
68 '*Ma chère*, do you know, as a rule I detest Oriental women, their laziness, their languid movements? I can't even bear brunettes at home. But you're not an Oriental, Iskuhi. Right now, sitting there against the light, your eyes look quite blue' (Werfel 2012: 185; 1947: i 195).
69 Weisgal (1971: 120).

70 On being rescued from the siege by a French warship, Juliette's first concern is that she looks a mess and is not dressed for the occasion: '*Die Franzosen sind da, die Franzosen sind da... Was soll ich anziehen...*' (Werfel 2012: 861; 1947: ii 455).
71 Werfel (2012: 108, 188-90; 1947: 117, 198–200). In Agnon's *Iddo and Enam*, Gemulah's love for her native land is expressed similarly in song.
72 Vogel (1986: 37).
73 Vogel (1986: 147).
74 Vogel (1986: 177).
75 Vogel (1986: 159).
76 Vogel (1986: 149).
77 In its treatment of the unrequited love of a Jewish man for an unfaithful Christian woman, Vogel's novel unexpectedly recalls Hemingway's *The Sun Also Rises*, also set in the immediate postwar years and published about four years earlier, in 1926. Vogel and Hemingway were in Paris in the early 1920s, but neither knew of the other's existence.
78 On 'The Lady and the Pedlar' see pp. 14–15.
79 Greenberg (1990, i 1240), translated by David Aberbach (2003a: 17).

7 Agnon and psychoanalysis: the quest for wholeness

The cultural milieu in which Agnon came to maturity as an artist was one in which psychoanalysis began to have profound influence on the arts, and on culture and society generally, in the understanding of human nature, of childhood, inner reality, and relationships. Most psychoanalysts in Agnon's time, including Freud, were a generation or two removed from the East European Jewish Orthodoxy portrayed by Agnon. That psychoanalysis touched Agnon's circle there is no doubt: Agnon's wife, a cousin of the psychoanalyst, Frieda Fromm-Reichman (herself married to the psychoanalyst, Erich Fromm), was a patient of Freud's disciple, Max Eitingon; Agnon's friend, Gershom Scholem, was in contact with Carl Gustav Jung and took part in Jungian conferences in Switzerland; and a children's book by Agnon was illustrated by Freud's niece, Tom Freud.[1]

Psychoanalysis in the interwar years, when Freud was still alive, is of particular interest in the study of Agnon's fiction, much of which was written at this time, when psychoanalysis began to enter popular consciousness. Significant points of contact between Freud and Agnon are many: for example, a shared background among the Eastern European rabbinic elite; family roots in small Galician towns, an upbringing in the Austro-Hungarian empire, in which Jews were emancipated in 1867; both first-born favorites to young, intelligent mothers who, however, suffered from long-term physical illness – Freud's mother, her lungs, Agnon's mother, her heart – which affected the bond with their children; both rebels against Orthodoxy and sensitive to generational tensions and conflicts created by the shift from the Orthodox *shtetl* to the secular big city, though Freud, more than Agnon who returned to Jewish Orthodoxy after 1924, could describe himself as an 'infidel Jew'; a love for poetry and a good story (Freud revered the great writers, Shakespeare and Goethe above all, and claimed that they had anticipated his insights – he had merely presented them in systematic, 'scientific' form, though his case histories read like short stories); both were fascinated by the often-conflicting interplay of the rational mind and the emotions; both were fond of Yiddish and Yiddish jokes in particular; both had an education combining Jewish and secular knowledge, though Freud had outstanding formal secular qualifications while Agnon had none, and Agnon was far superior to Freud in practically every aspect of Jewish learning; both had a hunger to achieve something universally recognized,

DOI: 10.4324/9781003594802-8

and lifelong single-minded devotion to this goal; both were concerned with the growth of anti-Semitism from the late-19th century until the Holocaust; both were Zionists, though Agnon's Zionism was chiefly cultural, based on the revival of Hebrew language and literature, unlike Freud's Zionism, which was largely political; Freud shared with Agnon a desire to promote Jewish literary culture, and was on the board of governors of the Hebrew University.

Above all, there was Agnon's chief debt to Freud, which he shared with countless other artists: a heightened awareness of unconscious motives, the importance of childhood and early relationships in determining character and later relationships, of the significance of trauma in later life, of memories and dreams, of every detail in conversation, thought, and body language; and awareness too of the intricate subtleties in the interaction of individual psychopathology with social change.

However, in exploring the quest for wholeness in Agnon's fiction, two analysts offer especially profound insight: Carl Gustav Jung (1875–1961) in Switzerland and W.R.D. Fairbairn (1889–1964) in Scotland.

Agunot and the torn psyche

Agnon's archetypal images of unwholeness are often linked to trauma, such as bereavement, sexual difficulties, marital breakdown, or religious conflict. There are frequent Jungian echoes in the struggle to piece together the fabric of a torn psyche, to make the unwhole whole, to reconcile opposites, the false face with the true, the secular with the religious. In particular, Agnon's account in *A Simple Story* of Hirshl's breakdown and treatment by Dr. Langsam in Lemberg (Lviv), though parodic of conventional psychoanalytic practice in which the patient does the talking, has affinities with Jung.[2] Hirshl does not speak to Langsam of family dysfunction. He says nothing about his mother Tzirl, her manipulativeness and concern with social status, how quickly she weaned him, how she never sang to him, resentful at her own marriage beneath her standing, foisted on her by the stigma of madness in her family; and how Hirshl's dependence on her and vulnerability to the machinations which led to his marriage followed on from her failure to love him. Nor does Hirshl tell Langsam of the fatal moment when his mother entraps him into marriage with Mina. She sees he has fallen for Blume, his impoverished orphan cousin who lives with the family, whom Tzirl treats as a maid who works *gratis*. Hirshl goes into the dark cellar to fetch wine and she follows him creepily, closing the door behind her and, groping along, confronting her son in the dark.

> 'Hirshl, I want to talk to you. Why don't you speak?'
> Hirshl replied, 'Don't you want to talk to me? I'm waiting to hear you.'
> Pursing her lips, Tzirl replied, 'That's well put', but in a tone that said she didn't like it at all.[3]

In the dark, ominously womb-like, Tzirl traps Hirshl; whatever he does, he will suffer. His breakdown, once married, is a matter of time. Resentments and hostility previously suppressed and manageable become unbearable in marriage. Hirshl, tormented by impulses of rage and homicidal violence, can no longer live with his wife. In this state, Langsam finds Hirshl at the start of his therapy. But all this background, and much more, we learn not in the analysis but in the 'simple story'. In the therapy, it is Langsam, whose wife has abandoned him for another man, who tells his own 'simple story' to Hirshl, an endless recreation of the *shtetl* of his youth – this being, of course, Agnon's own artistic trademark!

Hirshl's treatment is highly unconventional, but the problems dealt with by Langsam and Freudian-influenced analysts – the absence of love in childhood, the failure of loved ones to love, and of the child to feel loved, a resultant sense of frustration and unwholeness – are the same.[4] The striving toward traditional Judaism governed by the Torah and aspiring to return to Zion and Jerusalem is a striving to rejoin a whole and to be whole. The Agnon hero, however, is often sorely troubled by ambivalence and guilt, in keeping with the ancient rabbinic tradition, at abandoning his religious observances and leaving the Holy Land. In *A Guest for the Night*, the semi-biographical narrator-writer confesses in language taken from Kabbalah, that 'the vessels of our souls are broken and cannot hold them. The Torah is whole but the Ark in which it is kept is broken.'[5]

Kabbalistic imagery of unwholeness appears already in '*Agunot*', with its archetypal image of the garment to depict the soul. The torn garment symbolizes not just the lovelorn *agunot* in the story but also, more broadly, as in the Midrash on Song of Songs, the Congregation of Israel since time immemorial – in quest of reparation. The story of '*Agunot*' itself, however, does not bear out the hope that the wholeness of love can be restored. It ends with all its main characters imprisoned in a state of being *agunot*. The thread remains broken, and the torn, burned or useless garment recurs in Agnon's stories, often representing troubled or unsatisfactory sexual relations: among these are 'The Legend of the Scribe', *A Simple Story*, and *Iddo and Enam*. In *A Simple Story*, Hirshl thinks of his wife, Mina, as 'a garment that covers the body but does not warm it'.[6] In *Iddo and Enam*, too, torn clothes appear to signify unhappy marital relations. The scholar Gamzu has a wife, Gemulah, who sleepwalks, endangering her life. He recalls a rabbi's advice in similar circumstances: 'I was mending a rip in my clothes and, remembering what he had said, I immediately soaked the article in water and spread it out by Gemulah's bed.'[7] This stratagem fails, and so does the marriage.

Agnon and Jung: memories of broken childhood wholeness

Agnon's images of unwholeness begin in earliest childhood, c. 1891. His preface to *Days of Awe* depicts one of the most powerful experiences of his life. It was the night of Yom Kippur, in the crowded synagogue in Buczcacz, the light and fragrance of the candles which lit the house of prayer, the men all sparkling white in the candle-light, in their *kittels* and prayer shawls and the crowns on their heads, and the old, sweet-voiced chazan, and the unity of prayer… a vision so intense that the child felt he had passed into another world, a palace of glorious holiness, *hadrat kodesh*, 'I felt at that moment the holiness of the place and of the people there'.[8]

This lovingly described epiphany and the despairing tears with which it ends, when prayer ends, rapture deflated, communal unity lost – marks the start of a quest for spiritual wholeness throughout Agnon's fiction.[9] It is present in the beautiful opening of '*Agunot*', the first story signed 'Agnon', with its allegory of a love affair like a torn garment, alluding to midrash on the Song of Songs: 'Her lover is gone, and she seeks him, crying, If you find my lover, what will you tell him? I am love-sick.'[10] The thread of tradition, the loving link with the sacred, is broken, a moment of despair recalling the loss of innocence in the Garden of Eden.[11] The story of the love triangle of Dinah, Ben Uri, and Ezekiel, is told, in the fashion of rabbinic exegesis of the Song of Songs, as an allegory of the love between the Almighty and the Congregation of Israel. The snapped thread represents the psychological state of being *agunot*. The failed marriage of Ezekiel and Dinah is a story of souls in distress who search futilely to be made whole by a loving mate. Individual tragedy is seen as archetype. The anguish of the Congregation of Israel has recurred since time immemorial. Penitence can still lead to reparation (*tikkun*). The wholeness of divine grace (*hesed*) can be restored, through the divine spirit, 'to repent and do good deeds that bring pride to their doers and resume the thread of grace and love drawn before the Lord.'[12]

Throughout his writings, Agnon returns to this image of the torn garment and other symbols of unwholeness – the damaged Ark, the whole loaf, the stopped watch, the ruined house, the shattered cup, the lost key, the broken-down bus, the locked door and garden – to portray the tattered psyche of his characters, in an intermingling of personal and national tragedy. Agnon follows the biblical tradition in which prophets such as Hosea and Jeremiah allegorize broken relations between God and Israel in terms of marriage; divorce is national exile, and the return from exile is the restoration of the loving marriage. The traditionalist element in Agnon's modernist stories is always present in the fact of writing in Hebrew – even and perhaps especially in stories about secular Weimar German Jews largely divorced from Judaism. The psyche in '*Agunot*' as in Agnon's later stories is never seen as irreparably torn, though it is never fully healed. In this respect '*Agunot*' looks forward to Agnon's return to orthodox Judaism. But in depicting spiritual unwholeness, too, Agnon seeks an artistic whole, as in the early poem mentioned in 'The Night', compared to 'a snail whose garment is an organic part of it.'[13]

Jung's memory of childhood unwholeness

The memory recounted by Agnon in *Days of Awe* may be regarded, therefore, as a 'screen memory', both expressing and disguising a whole aspect of character, relationships, and later life.[14] Jung writes of a comparable disillusionment, with similarly powerful, primordial childhood ecstasy, and a semi-mystical sense of unity with the world, shattered, foreshadowing a similar quest in his own life. Jung's earliest memories had for their backdrop the splendor of the Swiss Alps. He recalled waking to a glorious day beside Lake Constance:

> I see the sun glittering through the leaves and blossoms of the bushes. Everything is wholly wonderful, colorful, and splendid… [The lake] stretched away and away into the distance… an inconceivable pleasure to me, an incomparable splendor.[15]

Jung goes on to describe the loss of this childhood paradise, of unity in family life and in religious faith. The 'greatest defeat' of his early life was, somewhat like Agnon's, a moment of disillusionment with religious faith – his first communion, hollow and useless:

> I ate the bread; it tasted flat, as I had expected. The wine, of which I took only the smallest sip, was thin and rather sour, plainly not of the best. Then came the final prayer, and the people went out, neither depressed nor illumined with joy, but with faces that said, 'So that's that.'… I had reached the pinnacle of religious initiation, had expected something – I knew not what – to happen, and nothing at all had happened… My sense of union with the Church and with the human world, so far as I knew it, was shattered.[16]

In his autobiography, Jung gives the family background to this memory and the lifelong quest for wholeness and self-realization which followed. As in Agnon's family, Jung's father, a pastor in the Swiss reformed Church, was somewhat weak and passive alongside his mother, a stout, dynamic figure. Jung shared with Agnon the grief of having a mother who had serious illness. He was adversely affected by separations caused by his mother's mental illness, when she was treated in a hospital in Basle: 'I always felt mistrustful when the word "love" was spoken'.[17] He imagined her as having two personalities, one loving and reliable, the other frighteningly unpredictable. Jung's violent fantasies toward her were comparable to those in Agnon's writings:

> My parents were sleeping apart. I slept in my father's room. From the door to my mother's room came frightening influences. At night Mother was strange and mysterious. One night I saw coming from her door a faintly luminous, indefinite figure whose head detached itself from the neck and floated along in front of it, in the air, like a little moon. Immediately another head was produced and again detached itself. The process was repeated six or seven times.[18]

The death of this Medusa-like mother provoked in Jung conflicting emotions, in response to her duality and its lifelong effect on him. The night before she died, in January 1923, Jung dreamed that a human soul had been carried away by the Wild Huntsman, Wotan the devil: 'I awoke in deadly terror and the next morning I received news of my mother's passing'.[19] Jung went home to her on the night train:

> I had a feeling of great grief, but in my heart of hearts I could not be mournful, and this for a strange reason: during the entire journey I continually heard dance

> music, laughter, and jollity, as though a wedding were being celebrated... One side of me had a feeling of warmth and joy, and the other of terror and grief.[20]

Agnon and Jung shared a terrible loneliness, a searching for wholeness not so much in human relations as in religion, work, and ideas; an irreconcilable contradiction between *inner* and *outer*; and a concern with the struggle of the individual to gain freedom from the chains of maternal influence.[21] These psychological circumstances help explain the crushing disillusionment in their earliest childhood memories, Agnon of Yom Kippur and Jung of his first communion. This shattering of unity was emblematic of a whole world of childhood. Their *Weltanschaaung* elevates social and religious ideals to dash them on the reef of reality. Disillusionment, as we have seen, is at the heart of Flaubert, too, for whom dreams are fated to die in a bottomless pit.[22]

Shortly before World War I, Jung had visions of world calamity, of the sort which often precede schizophrenic breakdown; and Jung claimed that he had prophesied the war, evidently believing, as did Agnon, that he spoke the divine word. Like Agnon, he claimed that he merely observed facts, he did not exaggerate.[23] He wrote, as did Agnon, in an attempt to preserve or find a substitute for orthodox faith, in psychology or art.

Agnon and Fairbairn

Agnon's world, afflicted by deep pessimism and a sense of futility, corresponds to a remarkable extent with that presented by a contemporary, the Scottish psychiatrist W.R.D. Fairbairn (1889–1964). Fairbairn, seeking to understand those who describe their lives despairingly – 'I'm empty. There's nothing for me... I feel quite useless; I haven't done anything... I've gone quite cold and hard; I don't feel anything... I can't express myself; I feel futile'[24] – broadly portrays an emotional world familiar in Agnon. In part, the gloomy outlook in Agnon's works may be attributed to the forlorn state of the Eastern European Jews, the crisis of faith, and, in late writings, to the Holocaust and the difficulties faced by the fledgling state of Israel. Still, the same grinding hopelessness found in *Yesteryear* and *Iddo and Enam*, haunted by madness and violent death, is found throughout Agnon, from '*Agunot*' to *Shira*.

Fairbairn's theory of art, based on the need for wholeness and restitution, also throws light on Agnon. Agnon's quest for wholeness in religious ideals such as the land of Israel, Jerusalem, the *Shekhinah*, as well as in idealized feminine expressions of these ideals is illumined by Fairbairn's view that the drive for restitution can motivate the human striving for wholeness, for the true, the good, the beautiful, the perfect, the ideal, in art and in religion.[25] The artist creates not for others but for himself, for the inner authorities toward whom he has ambivalent feelings: in Agnon's case, these would include the image of the stern grandfather and the *Shekhinah*-like mother in his stories. Drawing on ideas of Freud, Jung, and Melanie Klein, Fairbairn sees creativity as a struggle on the part of the psyche against unconscious hostility toward these inner beings, the subject of much feeling from childhood onward.[26] As we have seen, Agnon's stories repeatedly display hostility of this nature. Creativity, with its compensatory fantasies of restitution, alleviates guilt and anxiety, Fairbairn writes. Art reassures that the threatened love object is unharmed and whole. It is both an outlet for destructive impulses toward internalized figures from childhood and also a tribute to them, relieving the tension of ambivalence. Wholeness in art requires the release of violent emotion. Agnon's characters, however, are overwhelmingly passive,[27] and the corresponding calm of Agnon's style militates against destructive urges. Yet, fantasy does at times provide an outlet where relationships do not. To the extent that Agnon's stories, such as *Betrothed* and *Iddo and Enam* are made mysterious and obscure by a load of symbols, Fairbairn would regard them as giving no genuine impression of restitution:

> Restitution is meaningless apart from the presupposition of destruction; and consequently, oversymbolization precludes the effect of restitution by excluding the impression of destruction too rigorously.[28]

Wholeness in Agnon, as in Kafka, often seems more achievable in death than in life. Kafka writes in 'Resolutions' of emotional vulnerabilities so extreme that it is best 'to throttle down whatever ghostly life remains in you, that is, to enlarge the final peace of the graveyard and let nothing survive save that'.[29] In his writings, Kafka appears to blame this death-in-life for the most part upon his father. Agnon's writings often end in irresolution and death: *Betrothed* ends by the Muslim graveyard in Jaffa ('Muslim', similar to the Hebrew '*shalem*' [whole]); *Iddo*, on the graveyard of the Mount of Olives; and Agnon ends his most despairing novel, *Yesteryear*, with Kummer's agonizing death from rabies. At best, Agnon added in a wryly cynical ending, which he wisely omitted, Kummer might have found love in the world to come.[30]

Even the wholeness sought in work is often a *fata morgana*, leading to death or a form of death-in-life. The narrator of *The Book of Deeds* confesses, 'no sooner do I stop work than I become sad, like an Ark whose scrolls have been removed, or a field eaten with worms'.[31] Work can itself be persecutory or dangerous. In 'The Legend of the Scribe', Raphael the Torah scribe devoted to his work must purify himself before finishing a scroll. He dips himself in icy water, making himself fatally ill.[32] In 'The Garment', Israel the tailor drowns absurdly, trying to save his unfinished garment from being carried off by a fish;[33] 'Forevermore' ends with the Jerusalem scholar, Adiel Amzeh, who has devoted his life to the study of a medieval town besieged in war, discovering – ironically at the last moment before submitting his life work for publication – that the local leper hospital has miraculously preserved a Scripture-like record of the war. To a death-in-life among lepers, Adiel joyfully submits, forevermore (*ad olam*).[34]

The fundamental unwholeness of Agnon's characters in their relationships with others follows from failure to satisfy their deepest emotional needs. Their inner violence undermines the satisfaction of these needs, driving them to seek distance in their attachments to others. They become trapped in an 'in and out' cycle: longing for loving relationships, they seek a way out for fear of losing either their love object or, through excessive dependence, their own independence.[35] Agnon's imagery of being tied down, stifled, hungry, swallowed up, or missing the bus, characterize the narrator's relationships. His distance from others is signified, too, in language of masks, egocentricity, coldness, superiority, mystery, and separation.[36] This oscillation in relationships, 'in and out', is one of many points of comparison between Agnon and Kafka. In *A Simple Story*, the pendulum of emotion is clear when Hirshl, trapped in marriage, is tortured both by his excessive proximity to and his distance from his wife, Mina:

> This closeness angered him most. He quarreled with Mina inwardly: didn't she feel how bad this closeness was? But when she was distant, he fumed.[37]

In Kafka, too, the need for closeness conflicts with the need for distance. In his *Letter to His Father*, Kafka laments his consequent inability to marry:

> The fundamental idea of both attempts at marriage was quite a right and proper one: to become independent. It is an idea that does after all appeal to you, only then in reality it always turns out like a children's game, where one hold's and even presses the other's hand, calling out, 'Oh, go away, why don't you go?'[38]

Samuel Beckett's world is tormented by similar emotional ambiguity, of longing both for love and distance, as in the case of the tramps in *Waiting for Godot*:

> **Vladimir**: You again! (*Estragon halts, but does not raise his head. Vladimir goes towards him.*) Come here till I embrace you.
> **Estragon**: Don't touch me! (*Vladimir holds back, pained.*)
> **Vladimir**: Do you want me to go away? (*Pause.*) Gogo! (*Pause. Vladimir observes him attentively.*) Did they beat you? (*Pause.*) Gogo! (*Estragon remains silent, head bowed.*) Where did you spend the night?
> **Estragon**: Don't touch me! Don't question me! Don't speak to me! Stay with me![39]

Restitution

In art, nevertheless, Agnon finds a semblance of restitution. Agnon's writings appear to find resolution and wholeness in art more than in human relations. The story, 'At the Outset of the Day', written after the Holocaust, repeats the situation at the start of *A Guest for the Night*, written just before the catastrophe, when the writer/narrator returns to his hometown on the eve of Yom Kippur. Then the town was in a bad way after World War I; now, it is totally destroyed and accessible only in the world of memory. The writer has brought his little daughter with him, evidently a symbol of the desire to return to childhood: '… when [the soul] takes the form of a little girl, don't imagine your soul is pure as a little girl; this but hints at the soul's yearning for the purity of her infancy when she was free of sin.'[40] An accident burns her clothes and she is left naked, and father and daughter seek refuge in the entrance to the House of Study, forge of his identity and creative soul. Standing outside, yet part of the congregation, 'at the handles of the lock' – the characteristic position in Agnon's stories – the writer, divested of the *talit* and *kittel* worn on the High Holy Days, sees the open Ark in the far distance, not damaged and fallen as in '*Agunot*' but whole and splendid. He sees to his immense astonishment and delight, his own scroll, written in memory of all that has been damaged and destroyed, included among the Torah scrolls, preserving despite his cynicism, egocentricity, and distance, a kind of unity, kinship, and harmony with the congregation of the dead:

> The ancient House of Study was full of Jews, the Ark was open, filled with old Torah scrolls and one shining new scroll, with a red cover and silver letters. This was the scroll I wrote in memory of the souls of days that had departed. A silver cover hung over the scroll, engraved with shining letters. Though I was far away, I could see them and the thick rope in front of the scroll to keep it in place.
>
> My soul fainted away; and I stood praying with those in *talit* and *kittel*. And my little girl, too, repeated the prayers in her sleep in sweet melodies no one ever heard before.
>
> I neither enlarge nor exaggerate.[41]

Notes

1 On Agnon's psychoanalytic milieu, see Falk (2018). For a study of Jungian ideas in Agnon's novel, *The Bridal Canopy*, see Ezekiel (2019).

2 On the quest for wholeness in Agnon and Jung, see Aberbach (1984). Freud and Jung are often contrasted in their attitudes to religion. As a scientist, Freud rejected the irrationality of mysticism, though he revered the great creative artists. Freud described himself as an 'infidel Jew' (Freud 1927: 170), who sought to establish psychoanalysis as a secular science, but his view of religion was inconsistent. He could even argue the existence of God and see religion as having a positive function: 'Despite his scepticism, with individual patients in treatment Freud felt that religion might serve as a constructive resolution of inner conflicts. He even sometimes regretted the increasing inability of modern man to believe in God' (Roazen 1975: 23–4). On Freud and Judaism, see Aberbach (1980, 1993a) and Appendix 2 below.

3 Agnon (CW iii 94).

4 Among the complexities of Agnon's treatment of psychanalysis in *A Simple Story* is that Langsam's 'method' reveals nothing about the vital family relationships contributing to Hirshl's breakdown; yet, the causes are clear in the narrative which in its revelations on Hirshl's childhood, and the way his early relationships have determined his later life, is, in effect, 'Freudian'. Agnon wrote *A Simple Story* at a time when his wife was undergoing treatment by Max Eitingon, a disciple of Freud; and elements in the story might reflect in fictional form the nature of the treatment. There may also be an in-joke between Agnon and Scholem in the portrayal of Hirshl's madness and 'draft-dodging': Scholem actually did pretend to be mad to avoid German army service in World War I. See p. 127 note 5. Even so, Langsam clearly understands a principle articulated by the psychoanalyst Karen

Horney who, when asked if there was any alternative to psychoanalysis in dealing with emotional problems, answered yes: 'Life.'

5 Agnon (CW iv 253). The image of the broken Ark recalls the desecrated Ark in '*Agunot*'. The quest for wholeness is often associated in Agnon's stories (e.g. 'A Whole Loaf') with deviance. See p. 99ff.

6 Agnon (CW iii 169). Hirshl's impending breakdown is hinted at in imagery of the unwhole garment, for he is literally 'losing his buttons'. Unable to sleep, Hirshl goes to see a doctor. In the waiting room, he imagines himself falling asleep: 'I thought a button came off my coat. As Mina sewed it back on, I stood chewing a thread' (CW iii 205).

7 Agnon (CW iii 371).

8 For the autobiographical memory recounted by Agnon in the preface to *Days of Awe*, see pp. 42–3.

9 In portraying spiritual deflation at the moment of greatest holiness, on the eve of Yom Kippur, Agnon brings to mind the opening of Feierberg's novella, *Whither*? (*Le'an*, 1899), whose protagonist, the son of the rabbi, blows a candle out during the service; from then on, he is regarded as a madman.

10 Agnon (CW ii 405).

11 For the opening of '*Agunot*' and the allegorical image of the ruined garment, see pp. 15–17.

12 Agnon (CW ii 405).

13 Agnon (CW vii 208).

14 On screen memories in literature, including those of Agnon and Jung, see Aberbach (1983).

15 Jung (1974: 21, 22).

16 Jung (1974: 72, 73–74).

17 Jung (1974: 23).

18 Jung (1974: 33–34).

19 Jung (1974: 344–45). On dreams of loss such as that of Jung, see Aberbach (1984a).

20 Jung (1974: 345).

21 On the mother in Agnon, see Chapter 4; in Hebrew, Appendix 1 below; on Jung, the articles, 'The Struggle for Deliverance from the Mother' and 'The Dual Mother', in Jung *Collected Works* (1956 vol. 5).

22 Baldick (1964: 13). See p. 68.

23 See 'At the Outset of the Day', quoted pp. 138–9.

24 Fairbairn (1952: 51).

25 Fairbairn (1937–38: 297ff.).

26 Fairbairn, influenced by Freud, Jung, and Klein, went on to influence later psychiatry (see Guntrip [1968], Storr [1976]), and Bowlby [1980]). For a fuller Fairbairnian interpretation of Agnon, strongly influenced also by Storr in *The Dynamics of Creation*, see Aberbach (1984). Fairbairn depicts schizoid character types, whose emotional difficulties in adult life derive in large part from problematic relationships in childhood.

27 For a detailed account of Agnon's various ways of portraying passivity, see Aberbach (1984: 31–59); and for biographical background, see Laor (1998) and Falk (2018).

28 Fairbairn (1938–39: 178).

29 Kafka (1978: 93).

30 Agnon (1971a: 213). Earlier stories, too, such as *And the Crooked Shall Be Made Straight* (*Ve-Haya he-Akov le-Mishor*, 1912) and 'The Black Canopy' (*Ha-Hupa ha-Shehora*, 1913) also reach their melancholy end in the graveyard.

31 Agnon (CW vi 223).

32 Agnon (CW ii 141).
33 Agnon (CW vii 320).
34 Agnon (CW viii 334)
35 See Guntrip (1968: 36, 48). Comparable emotional difficulties are described by Kafka (Storr 1976: ch. 3).
36 On the 'in and out' cycle in Agnon, see Aberbach (1984).
37 Agnon (CW iii 156).
38 Kafka (1978: 69).
39 Beckett (1973: 58).
40 Agnon (CW vii 175).
41 Agnon (CW vii 177). This scene has a factual side inasmuch as Agnon's anthology *Days of Awe* is often found in synagogues on the High Holy Days. Agnon's view of himself as a storyteller in the midrashic tradition is especially clear in *In the Heart of the Seas*, where he appears in person though the story is set in the early-19th century. See pp. 53–4.

In memoriam

This book was written in 2024, over 40 years after the completion of my Oxford D. Phil. on psychological themes in Agnon (1981) and the book deriving from it, *At the Handles of the Lock* (1984). Many aspects of this work which were then relatively new and controversial became familiar in the course of time. The present book, unlike the thesis, is chiefly a comparative study. Still, it owes much to the thesis, delving further into the relationship between trauma and creativity, both in relation to the solitary artist and collectively.

I would like to preserve in these pages the memory of some of the remarkable people who taught, encouraged, and helped me in many ways so long ago, in a world very different from our own today.

I spent the years 1977–1980 in Oxford and Jerusalem writing the thesis. In the succeeding years, I trained in child psychotherapy at the Tavistock Clinic, after which I taught at Oxford and Cambridge while preparing the thesis for publication by Oxford University Press. As part of my training at the Tavistock, I did a great deal of observational work in various nurseries in Oxford and London; I was employed as a nursery nurse for the London Borough of Barnet; I observed a baby and wrote reports on its development for the first two years of its life; I became acquainted with basic psychoanalytic texts, by Freud, Abraham, Klein, Bion, Bowlby, Parkes, and Winnicott, among others; and I also began a study of loss in literature (published in 1989 by Yale University Press).

During the writing of my thesis, I was in contact with Bowlby, then completing his three-volume study of *Attachment and Loss*. I was then writing about Agnon's portrayals of grief following maternal loss, and Bowlby's insights seemed valid to me then, as they still do.

My work at Oxford proved to be the basis for much later work, including books on Agnon's great predecessor, Mendele Mokher Sefarim; on literary responses to loss (for which Bowlby, who encouraged me at every stage over a decade, wrote a Preface); on Jewish patriotism and on cultural nationalism.

My thesis, being a literary study, did not depend on psychoanalytic theories, but it became clear that in understanding Agnon's psychological complexities, psychoanalysts had greater theoretical knowledge and practical experience than literary scholars. Several of my teachers at Oxford – including David Patterson,

DOI: 10.4324/9781003594802-9

my supervisor; Anthony Storr, of the Oxford Department of Psychiatry, and author of *The Dynamics of Creation*; and Richard Ellmann, of the Oxford English Department, and author of major biographies of James Joyce, William Butler Yeats, and Oscar Wilde – encouraged an open, eclectic approach to psychological interpretations of creativity, which I largely adopted in my study of Agnon.

In particular, throughout my time in Oxford, I found most compelling Ellmann's combined biographical/historical/psychological approach to James Joyce, in his classic biography and in the many lectures I attended on *Ulysses*. This background included the Austro-Hungarian milieu in which *Ulysses* was written. As a Jewish character, Leopold Bloom seemed to me then, as now, more complex and delightfully human than any creation of Agnon – both are comic writers, but Agnon's humor often has the bitter taste of satiric mockery while Joyce's is warmer and more empathetic. Ellmann, to me then, was a model of careful and thorough scholarship, and stylistic elegance, and of not-uncritical reverence for a great writer. But then, Joyce did not have Agnon's genius with the Hebrew language, his total absorption in the great texts of Jewish culture, and his ability to bring an ancient language and culture to life in a living modern world.

Storr, at the time I wrote my D. Phil., was not just an eminent scholar and teacher, he was also the leading popularizer of psychoanalytic ideas in England. I would cycle up to the Warneford Hospital, where Storr had his office, and we would have wide-ranging discussions on creativity and psychoanalysis. Storr loved and revered art and creativity – I am grateful to him, among many other things, for telling me to listen to Schubert's final works – and he also recognized, more than most analysts at the time, the value of religious tradition in the creative life. Much of Storr's reading of the interconnection of Kafka's life and works in *The Dynamics of Creation*, based on insights from Freud, Jung, Klein and especially Fairbairn, was applicable to Agnon – as, indeed, much of Agnon's own fiction is thinly disguised autobiography; and that this could be shown in a study of recurrent themes in Agnon's work in a career spanning seven decades, remains a source of fascination. There is a sense in which, as I came to realize, a *Gestalt* of works over a long period by serious novelists such as Agnon could bring their inner lives to light in ways one cannot not know even one's closest friends and family – and even oneself.

As founder of the Oxford Centre for Hebrew Studies in 1972, David Patterson created a society of scholars based in the Jacobean manor house (completed 1611, the year of the publication of the King James Bible) at Yarnton, in the countryside near Blenheim Palace. High in the attic overlooking the fields and the distant railway line to Oxford, I wrote my thesis. In this isolation, an extraordinary social world of scholars and writers emerged. Many distinguished figures visited the Manor and its beautiful grounds as well as guests and doners who came to the evening dinners and lectures. The first lecture I ever gave, on my D.Phil. in progress, was at Yarnton. In the afternoons, David was a familiar sight, going through the labyrinthine building like a *behilfer* in an Agnon story, banging on doors to remind us – don't forget dinner this evening!

While writing the thesis (copying each typewritten chapter as I completed it and depositing it in my locker at Linacre College for safekeeping), I mostly used the Bodleian library in Oxford and, in the summers, the Agnon archives in the National Library, Jerusalem. In Jerusalem, I met several friends and acquaintances of Agnon, including Gershom Scholem, Chaim Rabin, Moshe Spitzer, and Dov Sadan as well as Emunah Yaron, Agnon's daughter and editor of his posthumous works. Although my thesis was on Agnon's fiction, it became clear that those who knew him recognized much in Agnon's fiction as autobiographical.

As a teacher, David Patterson had a superb ear for the nuances of Hebrew and Agnon's sly sense of humor. His classes were often convulsed with laughter. Any comparison between Agnon and Kafka should include the hilarity with which Kafka would regale his listeners when he read his own writings. David, a leading expert on and admirer of 19th century Hebrew literature (the Haskalah) – he would confide lugubriously, 'I should have lived in the 19th century!' – stressed the importance of the historical background, both Jewish and general, even in a psychological study; of getting facts right and presenting them effectively; and in writing a thesis, the use of literary, not critical texts, as stylistic models. He thought I would write a better thesis if I read Dickens! His own aim was what is sometimes called *sod ha-tzimtzum*, the secret of brevity: he taught me to be my own editor, going through what I had written and ruthlessly leaving out every superfluous word.

An advantage of Oxford at the time, from my point of view, was that graduate thesis students were treated as an intellectual elite, with much freedom to study and write on their own. They were often expected to be guided less by supervision than by their own initiative, insight, and enterprise. I was free to attend lectures and seminars but had no obligation to do so, or to do any work other than to study in the library and write. Looking back, I doubt if I would have had comparable freedom to write it elsewhere, even under Robert Alter at Berkeley, where I was offered a place in the graduate program, which I declined.

The result was an Oxford thesis radical in its time, and perhaps still so, whose full implications have not yet been fully absorbed into Agnon criticism. Hence the need for the present book.

As a comparative study, this book follows the thesis and in some respects greatly expands it, but largely omits theoretical background, whether literary or psychoanalytic, focusing instead almost entirely on the texts. As a student in Oxford and at the Tavistock Clinic (where my teachers included Matti Harris, Shirley Hoxter, Mary Boston, Lisa Miller, and Helene Dubinsky), I was immersed in psychoanalytical literature and could write about it with some degree of knowledge and authority, and did so in a series of articles for the *International Review of Psychoanalysis* and the *International Journal of Psychoanalysis*. Today, this is no longer the case. However, throughout the past 40 years, I have studied and taught and written about Agnon; and in the studies included in this book the comparisons all involve literary similarities which do not require a theoretical framework to be comprehensible.

Drafts of material in this book first appeared in *Moznayim* (on the dead mother in Agnon's fiction), *International Review of Psychoanalysis* (on childhood memories of Kafka and Agnon), *Commentary* (on Freud), *L'Eylah* (on Agnon and Zionism), *The Times Literary Supplement* (on Agnon's *Shira*), *Jewish Book Annual* (on Agnon and Jewish tradition), my book *Surviving Trauma* (on Agnon and D.H. Lawrence); *Association for Jewish Studies Review* (on deviance in Mendele and Agnon), a *Festschrift* for David Patterson (on autobiographical uses of *aggadah* by Mendele, Bialik, and Agnon); *CCAR Journal* (on Greenberg); and *Journal of Modern Jewish Studies* (on Agnon and Flaubert, and on unrequited love in interwar German-Jewish literature).

I am indebted to my editors, Benjamin Michali, Thomas Hayley, Norman Podhoretz, Neal Kozodoy, Jonathan Sacks, Bryan Cheyette, Jacob Kabakoff, Anthony Storr, Tudor Parfitt, Stanley Nash, and especially Glenda Abramson.

The Hebrew article in *Moznayim* is reprinted as Appendix 1 in this book, and the article in *Commentary* as Appendix 2.

At Oxford, both as student and junior instructor, I had the good fortune of meeting leading Hebrew writers and scholars, whom I remember warmly: including Gershon Shaked, Shmuel Werses, Amalia Kahana-Carmon, A.B. Yehoshua, Leon Yudkin, Yoram Bronowski, Meir Gertner, Benjamin Tammuz, Ezra Spicehandler, Stanley Nash, Nicholas de Lange, Nitza Spiro, Eisig Silberschlag, Jonathan Magonet, Yehuda Friedlander, Nicholas de Lange, Alan Mintz, Arnold Band, Raphael Loewe, Benjamin Hrushovski (Harshav), and Aharon Megged as well as David Goldstein, who later skillfully edited the thesis into a book, and Louis Littmann, my publisher.

I also had much help and encouragement from various other scholars at Oxford, including John Bamborough, Isaiah Berlin, John Bayley, Nakdimon Doniach, Hyam Maccoby, Albert Hourani, Lionel Kochan, John Carey, Rupert Cecil, and Geza Vermes as well as Ron May in the Bodleian; and I was fortunate too in having friends and acquaintances of distinction who shared an enthusiasm for literature and the Humanities, including Gail Fincham, Lowri Gwilym, Michael Hilton, Hugh Loxdale, Leon Wieseltier, Philomena Nave, Martin Goodman, Deborah Maccoby, Joanna Pappworth, and Edwin (Efraim) Zicher.

Throughout my time as a university student, I lived away from home (my parents were in Baltimore, Maryland), focused totally on study, living in shabby rooms as students did, reading and attending lectures and seminars with fellow students, going out with them, having an occasional meal at Hillel House – I was very thin in those years – with no family life whatsoever; and my teachers and friends became in effect my family.

The period after the October 1973 war, when I was a BA student in English at University College, London, was especially hard for Jewish students. Israel had been invaded by several Arab armies with the aim of destroying the Jewish state, and the anti-Israel bias in the British press and on university campuses at the time was a source of grief, as was the UN designation of Zionism as racism in the aftermath of the war. Criticism of Israel was widespread in the Israeli media but the bias in England was worsened by ignorance, by a refusal to read basic world history and literature pertaining to the Jews, to learn the outline no serious historian would question, to recognize the centrality of Hebrew literature and the land of Israel not just in Jewish life from ancient to modern times but also in the history of civilization. To Israel's enemies all this is bogus. Against this dark background, the Oxford Centre for Hebrew Studies was a source of enlightenment and comfort.

To study Hebrew and Hebrew Literature is to encounter what Isaiah Berlin once described as 'an unbroken struggle against greater odds than any other human community has ever had to contend with.'

Jonathan Sacks once wrote that the Six Day War had put him on the path to the rabbinate, and the Yom Kippur War had a similar effect on me. At that time, in late-1973, I started attending Meir Gertner's evening seminars on Hebrew literature in London. One evening, Meir, whom I thought had retired from teaching (he was approaching seventy and was unwell), asked me what I planned to do when I finished my BA. I said I hoped to do graduate work in English Literature. Meir then suggested that if I wanted to work in Hebrew Literature at Oxford, he would be happy to act as my supervisor. Perhaps knowing that he did not have long to live, Meir arranged for me to meet David Patterson at Oxford. After Meir's death, David took over as my supervisor. This was how my career in Hebrew and Comparative Studies began.

My greatest debt over the years is to my wife, Miriam, and our children, Gabriella, Shulamit, and Jessica; to my grandmother, Rachel Aberbach, who taught me Hebrew; to my father, Professor Moshe Aberbach, who specialized in Jewish history and literature, and with whom I spent many hours discussing in Hebrew the subtleties of Agnon – and much else on Jewish history and literature; and to Oliver Leaman, friend and editor at Routledge, whose encouragement and wise advice in latter years have helped make the writing of this book a pleasure.

I wrote my Oxford D.Phil. on Agnon between the ages of 22 and 24 and the present book at 70. As Agnon in Hebrew is so powerfully part and expression of an ancient Jewish tradition, rooted in timeless biblical and rabbinic texts, his stories seem to self-renew within the 'seventy faces' of the tradition. The effect of returning to Agnon is to arrive at the point of starting and, as T.S. Eliot put it, 'know the place for the first time.'

10 November, 2024
9 Cheshvan, 5785

Figure 1 Iffley, 1978

Figure 2 The Sheldonian, Oxford 1981. The gown from Shepherd & Woodward, the dress from Annabelinda

Figure 3 Golders Green Park, 2024

Appendix 1

David Aberbach, Hebrew article in *Moznayim*, 'The Lost Mother in Agnon'

דוד אֲבֶרבַּך

דמות האם בכתבי עגנון

כשרונו הגאוני של ש״י עגנון התחיל לשגשג רק לאחר שהגיע לארץ־ישראל באביב 1908. אומנם גם לפני כן, בבוצ׳אץ׳, הראה סימני בגרות ספרותית, אבל ביידיש יותר מאשר בעברית. אברהם באנד מחווה דעת רבים בכתבו: ״מסיפוריו בבוצ׳אץ׳ לא היינו חושדים שש״י צ׳אצקס הוא הוא אותו הסופר המחונן ש״י עגנון ביפו. ההתקדמות בכשרונו הספרותי היא יוצאת דופן״[1].

סיפורו ״עגונות״, שנכתב רק חודשים מועטים אחרי הגיעו ליפו, הוא הישג אמנותי מפתיע לבחור בן עשרים, טבוע בסיגנונו העגנוני המיוחד, רגוע ועצוב, מלא רגש עדין וגוני שירה. המבקרים לא עוררו את השאלה מה הביא לידי מטאמורפוזה ספרותית זו, ועדיין תקופה זו בחיי עגנון עטויה מעטה סוד.

יש, כמובן, לייחס את הישגו של עגנון לאווירה התרבותית התוססת בארץ־ישראל בתחילת המאה, ביחוד לתחיית השפה המדוברת: אך האם יש בשינוי אווירה לבד הסבר מספיק לתופעה אמנותית מפליאה כמו זו שגילה עגנון? כל ימיו הסתיר הסופר את עצמו מאחורי פרגוד סיפוריו ואגדותיו. ואם מדי פעם הוא מגלה טפח, הרי הוא מכסה טפחיים, וכמקור על עצמו הוא בלתי־מהימן. מעניין, למשל, שבמכתבים ביוגראפיים הוא כותב שהגיע לארץ ישראל בל״ג בעומר תרס״ט, בעוד שלמעשה הגיע אליה שנה שלמה לפני כן[2]. מבחינת זכרונו היה עגנון ״בור סוד שאינו מאבד טיפה״ ולא ייתכן ששכח את שנת עלייתו לארץ ישראל[3]. יש למצוא

---

1. "...the Buczacz stories would hardly lead us to the suspicion that S.Y. Czaczkes had the same literaty potential as S.Y. Agnon of Jaffa. The advance in writing ability is unusual." Arnold Band: Nostalgia and Nightmare: a Study in the Fiction of S.Y. Agnon, Berkeley, 1968, p. 67.

רוב החומר הביוגראפי על עגנון במסה זו שאוב מעבודתו של באנד.

2 ״בל״ג בעומר תרס״ט זכיתי לעלות לארץ ישראל״. ש״י עגנון: ״מעצמי אל עצמי״, 1974, עמ׳ 9, 7. על אי־תיאום התאריכים, ראה תארתה של אמונה ירון, שם עמ׳ 462. לפי עדותו של עגנון, הוא נולד בתשעה באב תרמ״ח - קיץ 1888 (שם עמ׳ 9), ״בן תשע עשרה ומחצה הייתי כשעליתי לארץ ישראל״ (שם, עמ׳ 29) - כלומר, בתחילת 1908. פגישתו הראשונה עם ברנר אירעה בסוף אפריל 1908, בהיותו בדרך לארץ ישראל. ראה גרשון שקד, רפאל וייזר (עורכים): ״ש״י עגנון: מחקרים ותעודות״, ירושלים 1978, עמ׳ 39. ראה גם מאמרו של יצחק בקון: ״על שנת עלייתו של עגנון והמסתעף מזה״, ״הפועל הצעיר״, 9.4.68, עמ׳ 5–23.

3. לפי ד״ר יונה דוד, מזכירו של עגנון משך שנים רבות הוא ידע את כל סיפוריו בעל פה (הודעה פרטית מאת ד״ר יונה דוד).

הסבר פסיכולוגי לשגיאה בולטת זו בנסיבות בהן עזב עגנון את ברוצ׳אץ, שהן הרקע לגלגול הספרותי שעבר עליו.

אמו של עגנון, שאליה היה קשור באהבה עזה, סבלה שנים ארוכות ממחלת לב. כאשר עזב אותה, היתה בריאותה במצב של התמוטטות. הסיבה העיקרית לעזיבתו: הצורך להימלט משירות בצבא האוסטרי־הונגארי, אך אין ספק שסבל מרגשי אשמה שזנח את אמו לפני מותה[4]. יש לשער שרגשי אשמה אלה היו כה עזים שהיה נאלץ לדחוק אותם אל מתחת לסף ההכרה. משום כך העדיף להאמין – ורצה שגם אחרים יאמינו – שהגיע לארץ־ישראל רק לאחר מותה שחל בי״א ניסן תרס״ט (2 באפריל 1909)[5]. ״טעות״ מכוונת זו משתקפת ב״תמול שלשום״, הרומאן הגדול שלו על תקופת העלייה השנייה. גיבורו, יצחק קומר, שמכמה בחינות דומה לסופר, מגיע לארץ ישראל למעלה משנה לאחר פטירת אמו (עמ׳ 1515)[6].

סביר להניח שמחלתה הממושכת של אמו ומותה בטרם עת היו גורמים מכריעים שהבשילו את בגרותו כאמן[7]. בספרות העולמית יש מספר הגון של דוגמאות מקבילות בהן מחלה ושכול מביאים לידי יצירה אמנותית נדירה. ״קוריאולן״ (Coriolan) מאת ט.ס. אליוט, ״בחיפוש אחרי הזמן האבוד״ (A la Recherche du Temps perdu) מאת פרוסט, ״דבלינאים״ (Dubliners) מאת ג׳יימס ג׳ויס, ״אות השני״ (The Scarlet Letter) מאת הותורן, ו״קוריולנוס״ (Coriolanus) מאת שיקספיר נכתבו בתקופת האבל הדכאון והמבוכה בגלל מות אמו של הסופר. לאבל יש מוצא בתחום האמנות בו משתדל האמן להתגבר על הטראומה של אבידתו על־ידי הקמת מעין מצבה לאמו האהובה.

4. ראה אברהם באנד: שם עמ׳ 15.

5. תאריך פטירת אסתר צ׳אצקס נמסר כי״א בניסן תרס״ט. ראה גרשון שקד, רפאל וייזר (עורכים), שם עמ׳ 56.

6. כל הציטטות (אלא אם כן מצוין אחרת) מובאות מהמהדורה השניה, ״כל סיפוריו של ש״י עגנון״, תל אביב, 1953–62.

7. על נושא השכול בעגנון ראה את עבודת המחבר, A Study of Themes in the Fiction of S.J. Agnon, תזה לדוקטורט, אוניברסיטת אוקספורד, 1980. עבודה זו כוללת ניתוח פסיכולוגי מקיף של הגיבור העגנוני ודנה ביתר עמקות בנושאים המוזכרים במסה זו. ראה גם: Colin Murray Parkes, Bereavement, Penguin Books, 1976.

מעמד מיוחד בבית ההורים

בהקשר זה ראוי להוסיף כי במשפחת עגנון היתה האם דמות הדומינאנטית בעוד שהאב היה אדם פאסיבי יחסית, בעל דמיון יותר מאיש מעשה. כן יש להטעים שכבכור בין חמישה ילדים, שעלה בכשרונותיו על כולם, היה לעגנון מעמד מיוחד בבית הוריו, ביחוד בעיני אמו. בעודנו בחור צעיר היה משען לאמו במחלתה והיה מבלה זמן רב בקרבתה. יחסי האם ובנה נתהדקו גם על־ידי היעדרו של בעלה מוכר הפרוות, שלעתים קרובות היה נאלץ לנסוע לערים אחרות לרגל עסקיו. היא עודדה את שאיפותיו הספרותיות של בכורה ועוררה אותו להתעניין בסיפורי מופת של הספרות העולמית.

קשריו האינטימיים עם אמו גרמו לו לעגנון מעין אובססיה ספרותית ליחסים לא־שכיחים בין בנים לאמותיהם, וסימני הטראומה שנגרמה על־ידי מיתת האם קודם זמנה מהווה מוטיב חוזר ברוב סיפוריו החשובים. הד לאופי הביוגראפי של סיפוריו, שבהם מתאר עגנון אימהות חולניות, מוצאים אנו בנאומו בבית שוקן לרגל יום הולדתו החמישים: ״בדמי ימיה מתה עלי אמי, כבת ארבעים שנה היתה במותה, ועדיין אור נשמתה מאיר לפני במיתתה כבחייה. ואם אלף אמהות טובות אצייר – מעשיה הטובים יאירו עליהן מאורה״[8]. המשפט ״בדמי ימיה מתה אמי״ מתחיל את הסיפור ״בדמי ימיה״ המשקף את מחלתה האחרונה של אמו.

״עגונות״, שנכתב כמה חודשים לפני מות אמו, מרמז לעוגמת נפשו על פרידתו ממנה. קודם לעלייתו אף פעם לא היה רחוק מאמו זמן ממושך. פרידה במקרה זה היתה בבחינת אבידה שאינה חוזרת. אין ספק שבלבו של עגנון קוננה דאגה, ששוב לא יראה את אמו לעולם. אומנם ב״עגונות״, בדומה לכמה מסיפוריו שנכתבו לאחר מכן (כגון ״בדמי ימיה״ ו״שבועת אמונים״) מוצאים אנו שינוי בולט המראה שאפילו בתקופה זו ראה עגנון צורך להשיג ריחוק אמנותי מחוויותיו האישיות. אשה, ולא איש, סובלת את צער אבידת אמה, אך באותה שעה, ב״עגונות״, גבר – האומן בן־אורי – למרות שאבידה זו אינה נוגעת בו ישירות, שקוע בעצב, בחרטה, ביאוש, כאילו הוא עצמו נתייתם מאמו.

8. ש״י עגנון: ״מעצמי אל עצמי״, שם עמ׳ 26. ״בסיפורים רבים וחיבורים העליתי את זכרונה״ (שם).

לאחר שבן־אורי גומר את בנייתו וחריטתו של ארון הקודש, הוא דומה לאבל: הוא ״עומד ככלי שנתרוקן... דומה הוא כאבר שנקרע מתוך גופו. נדמה לו כי בזה בא הקץ לחיי רוחו... נפשו עגמה עליו והתחיל בוכה שלא מדעת... וקשה לו רצער לו וגעגועים גדולים לו... אלמלא היה יכול לפחות לראות אותה ריבה נאה, את דינה, ולשפוך לפניה שיחו!״[9]. התיאור של דינה נראה כמעט כמו אידיאליזאציה של האם המתה: ״זיו פניה כבת מלכים, צדקת ישרה כאחת מהאמהות״[10].

פרט קטן וחשוב שלכאורה אין לו כל צורך בסיפור הוא הזכרת אם דינה. דמות זו מופיעה בסיפור לאחר שדינה נתמלאה קנאה וכעס על בן־אורי, ובשצף קצף היא מפילה את ארונו ארצה. ומיד היא מתייסרת באשמה וחרטה על חטא זה ועל הפגם שהטילה באופיה. היא מודעת כי שוב אינה דומה לאמה בצדקתה ויושרה. ״על משכבה בלילה דינה שוכבת ולבה ער ומכה אותה מלקות הנפש בלי רחמים. אש של גיהנום יוצא מקרבה ושורפתה. גדולה רעתה וחטאתה מי ישאנה?... כובשת היא את פניה בכר מרוב כאב ובושה – ואינה יכולה לבכות. עומד חטאה לנגד עיניה כמלאך דומה, חרבו שלופה, וחורש הוא עליה רעה...״[11]. היא קופצת מעל מיטתה ורואה את עצמה בראי: ״ראי של אמה היה זה ולא נשאר בו כלום ממאור פניה היפות. ויודעת היא דינה שאם תעמוד כנגדו ויראה לה זה רק את פניה, פני חרטאת ופושעת: ׳אמא, אמא!׳ מצעק לבה בקרבה, והיא משתוקקת לקרבת נפש ארהבת שתיפול אליה ותשפוך מרי שיחה לפניה – ואינה מוצאת...״[12].

רגש הכעס החרטה והאשמה של דינה שנראים מוגזמים קצת – כיוון שאף ״חרליה אחת שבו Edjybe xreyuW לא נשתברה״[13] – דומים לרגשותיו של בן־אורי אחרי גמר יצירתו: גם דינה וגם בן־אורי מראים סימני אבלות. כן יש לציין שעגנון משווה את ארון הקודש לארון מתים: ״מטעי שושנים ופרחים מתנדנדים ואבלים עליו כמו על גבי קברו של מת״[14]. לפי תוכן הסיפור אין מקום לאבלות זו. יש למצוא לה הסבר בחיי הסופר עצמו.

9. ש״י עגנון: ״עגונות״, ״העומר״, תשרי־כסלו, תרס״ט, עמ׳ 56.

10. שם, עמ׳ 53.

11. שם, עמ׳ 57.

12. שם.

13. שם.

14. שם.

אהרן אבני, ״אם וילד״

הכתם הפסיכולוגי וביטויו

מ״עגונות״ ואילך תכונה בולטת של
הגיבור העגנוני היא אי־יכולתו להפריד
את זכר אמו מנשים אחרות שאיתן יש לו
קשרי אהבה. ב״בארה של מרים״ שנכתב
זמן קצר אחרי פטירתה של אסתר צ׳אצקס,
צערו של חמדת ויאושו המטורף כמעט
על אובדן אהובתו הם עזים עד כדי כך ש־
אמנות הסיפור היא משנית לאוטוביוגרא־
פיה. שלושה סיפורים כלולים כאחד: סי־
פור מסגרת המתאר את עלייתו של חמדת
לא״י, ושני סיפורים פרי עטו, האחד ״לוז״
על חמדת עצמו ועל אהובתו זהרה החול־
נית, והשני על רפאל הסופר ואשתו מרים
(נוסח ראשון, מסורבל ופרימיטיבי יחסית,
של ״אגדת הסופר״). הצד השווה בשלו־
שת הסיפורים הוא שכל אחד מתאר אמן
שאהובתו סובלת ממחלה אנושה ומתה
קודם זמנה. בשלושת המקרים ניתן לצער
ולאבל ביטוי באמנות. רפאל כותב ספר
תורה לזכר אשתו ״שהלכה לעולמה בדמי
ימיה״[15]; חמדת, לאחר פטירתה של זהרה,
כותב את הסיפור ״לוז״ ״לזכר נשמת
אהובתי״; ובסיפור המסגרת הוא מספר
על אמו כשהיא על סף הגסיסה.

קרבתו של חמדת למרים מבוססת, כ־
נראה, על נטייתו לְדַמּוֹתָהּ לאמו. בסוף ה־
סיפור, למשל, בה בשעה שהוא מתגעגע
למרים, הוא זוכר את אמו: ״בלב עגום
היה חוזר הביתה. אמו החולנית שוכבת
על מיטתה. חמדת ניגש אליה והיא תומ־
כת עליו את גופתה החביבה ומספרת לו
בין הערבים מערוב ימי נעוריה. בריאה
היתה אז וחזקה וליופי אין משלה בעירה
ומסביב. גדולי העיר היו משכימים לפת־
חה, רוצים לזכות את בניהם בה, אבל א־
ביה לא נענה להם והביא לה ממרחקים
מתנה טובה אחת, כלי מפואר מלאה תורה
וחכמה. אמנם רוב דבריה של אמו לא היו
אולי די מובנים אז לפני שנות הילד, ברם
קולה היה כל כך רך ועצוב, והיה מזלף
כשמן הטוב בעצמותיו, וריחו, שלא פג
אפילו בימי עניו, היה מעדן אותו עכ־
שיו״[16]. חמדת נכסף לימי ילדותו כשהיה
נהנה מדבקותה הנפשית, ומקרבתה הפי־
זית. הוא זוכר מה שהיתה אמו מספרת לו:
״יומם על כפים נשאתיך ובלילה היה
קשה לי להיפרד ממך, אך אביך היה מאיץ
בי, מבקש ואומר, שאשכב לנוח״[17]. לא־
חר שחמדת עזב את אמו, הוא כולו שקוע
ברגשי אבידה, וזכר האם עולה לפניו ת־
מיד, לפעמים באופן ישיר ולפעמים בצו־
רה סמלית: ״החמה כבר נתעלמה עם נר־
תיקה, רק זיקי נוגהה האחרונים עדיין
פשוטות הן כלפי העירה כידי אם רחמניה
עוברת אורח״[18].

ייתכן שהחרטה שמביע חמדת על עזבו
את זהרה ב״לוז״ משקפת את רגשי האש־
מה העמוקים יותר על שנטש את אמו. ר
הנה בתקופה זו ספר שיריו עומד לצאת
לאור: ״שלשום יצאתי ירושלימה. המה־
דורה כבר יצאה ממכבש הדפוס. בכל הד־
רך לבי אמר לי: אכזר! מי לך שָׁם ומה לך
ספרך ושיריך? לא יועילו לך ביום עֶברה.
אל ביתך שוב ושב שם על מיטתה. כי
ביום עזבך אותה מות תמות״[19]. מכאן ב־
רור שבעיני עגנון היתה נטישת חולה
גורמת למותה. ברם לזהרה אין מרפא.
בשעת גסיסתה היא מסתכלת בתמונתו
של חמדת שעליה חרז לה שיר, וברגע ה־
אחרון דם זורם מפיה ומכסה את החרוזים.

15. ש״י עגנון: ״בארה של מרים״, ״הפועל הצעיר״, 1.7.1909.

16. שם, 16.7.1909.

17. שם.

18. שם.

19. שם. כדאי לציין שלפי המדרש ״לוז״ הוא שם של עיר שבה מלאך המוות אינו שולט (בראשית רבה סט, ח); והוא גם שם של עצם הקיימת לעולם הנמצאת ביסודו של חוט השדרה (ויקרא רבה יח, א). ראוי גם לעמוד על כך שהשם ״לוז״ מתאים לסיפו־רו של חמדת, שכן בזה הוא מביע שאיפתו – שאמנם נראית כחסרת תקווה – לחיי נצח לאהובתו המתה.

הכתם הפסיכולוגי של מחלת האם ופטירתה מתפשט בכל כתבי עגנון. באותו זמן בו כתב את ״עגונות״ ו״בארה של מרים״, התחיל לכתוב את הסיפור ״הנדח״ שעליו עבד למעלה מתשע שנים[20]. בסיפור זה, הטראומה של מות אם הגיבור גרשום קודם זמנה דוחפת אותו לילדותיות מופרזת, המונעת אותו מלהפריד בין זכרונה לבין דמות ארוסתו, מנוחה[21]. בשכבו במיטת אמו, הוא מדמה את עצמו לילד השוכב בצדה. בשעה זו הוא מהרהר על מנוחה: ״ילדות היתה בו, כאילו תינוק הוא, ובצדה של אמו הוא שוכב, עד שבא בעל החלומות והעריב עליו שנתו בפסוקי שיר השירים ובדמות דיוקנה של ארוסתו״ (״אלו ואלו״, עמ׳ 37). בעגמת לבו הוא פונה לאלוהים ושופך את נפשו ״כתינוק אל חיק אמו״ (שם, עמ׳ 55) ומתוך הזיה הוא רואה את עצמו ״יושב בצלו של הקדוש ברוך הוא ויונק מן המחשבה הקדושה״ (שם).

עד כמה הוא תלוי באמו, מתחיל גרשום להבין רק לאחר מותה: ״עד מותה כפוי טובה היה ובמותה צערו צער, כאדם שהשפיעו לו לטובה ולבסוף נטרד מחיק המזל״ (שם, עמ׳ 29). מה שהיה שייך לה נראה לו כמעט מחלק מהווייתה. סידור תפילתה נהפך לו לאובייקט של רגשותיו הדתיים וכיסופיו המיניים: ״כמה הוא מחמד ומתאווה לגפף ולנשק את סידורה של אמו עליה השלום שהיו ידיה מגפפות את לוחותיו בתפילתה כידיו של משה רבנו את שתי לוחות הברית״ (שם, עמ׳ 32). ארוסתו, הקשורה בדמיונו לאמו, טהורה ותמימה היא כמוה. לא קל לו להתייחס אליה כבריה בעלת יצרים, והוא סובל מרגשי אשמה אפילו על סימני משיכתו המינית אליה: ״נראתה לו בבואה של מנוחה ארוסתו בכלי כסף זורחת כלבנה נתאדם כאדם שנתפס על עוון״ (שם, עמ׳ 36).

בדומה לסיפורו של גרשום, הסיפור ״אחות״ מתאר אדם צעיר, נעמן, אפוף ברוח יגון אחרי מות אמו. נעמן נכנס לחדר אחותו ביפו, מסתכל הוא בה, מזדעזע עד עומק לבו על־ידי דמיונה לאמו. ״על יד החלון היא יושבת. ככה ישבה אמו עליה השלום... אותן הכתפים הרועדות, אותו הראש הכפוף ואותה התוגה המיוחדת המלפפת את כל הקרב אליה״ (״על כפות המנעול״, עמ׳ 406). האחות קוראת רומאן שהיה פעם ברשות אמה. כמוה היא מניחה אותו לפני סיומו. נעמן מתמלא חמלה וכאב לזכר אמו ונושק לה על שפתיה. רמזי יחסים מקבילים מוצאים אנו גם בין שאר גיבורי עגנון. אם תלות כזאת מכוונת לדמות האחות או הבת, היא גם משקפת את יחס הגיבור לאמו.

20. גרשון שקד, רפאל וייזר (עורכים); שם, עמ׳ 56. ״הנידח״ היה מתוכנן כרומאן ארוך בעל ארבעה חלקים, אך לבסוף לא הגיע אלא לאורך נובילה. ראה Robert Alter: "S.Y. Agnon: The Alphabet of Holiness". After the Tradition, New York, 1969, p. 140.

21. על חוסר בגרותו של הגיבור, ראה התזה של המחבר, שם פרק ג.

תלות מוחלטת באם

בסיפוריו הראשונים של עגנון, שנכתבו לפני שירד מארץ ישראל לגרמניה בשנת 1912, ניכר שמחלתה ומותה של אם הגיבור משאירים בו צלקת פסיכולוגית עמוקה ומכאיבה, שיש לה השפעה שלילית מופרזת על יחסיו עם נשים. אולם הסיפורים שנכתבו לאחר שעגנון חזר לארץ־ישראל ב־1924, מראים בעליל שיחסי הגיבור לאמו חרגו מלכתחילה מן המקובל. שאם לא כן, היה מתאושש ממחלת יגונו ויוצר קשרים נורמאליים עם נשים, בלי להיות מוטרד על־ידי זכרונה. כל ימיו הוא מחפש תחליף לאמו ונמצא איפוא בנסיגה אגרצנטרית תמידית אל הילדות.

רמזים סימבוליים לתכונות אלו נמצאים ב״פנים אחרות״ שנוסחו הראשון הופיע ב־1931[22]. כאן, בדומה ל״עגונות״, נוצר קשר בין הגיבור לבין אמה המתה של ״אהובתו״. שני סמלים עיקריים בסיפור הם הכוכבות והתלולית. טוני, שבתחילת הסיפור נתגרשה ממיכאל הרטמן, נוטעת כוכבות בתלולית על קבר אמה. דרך כוכבות אלו תלולית אחרת – שממנה הרטמן זוכר את עצמו נופל בילדותו – מחוברת לאם וקשורה לטוני עצמה[23]. בחלום הזיה של הרטמן, טוני מגביהה את הכוכבות כנגד פניה ״ונתרבו הכוכבות עד שכיסו כל אותה תלולית״ (״על כפות המנעול״, עמ׳ 468). יש לראות את נפילתו של הרטמן מהתלולית כזכרון־מסך (Screen Memory) של קשריו החולניים עם האם המתה – ועם טוני.

22. נוסח זה של ״פנים אחרות״ מופיע גם בספרו של הלל ברזל ״סיפורי אהבה של ש״י עגנון״, רמת גן, 1975.

23. להזכרת הנפילה של הרטמן יש הקבלה בולטת בזכרון של סטיבן דדלוס בסיפור A Portrait of the Artist as a Young Man מאת ג׳ימס ג׳ויס. בשני המקרים יש רמזים שהזכרונות מסתירים מעין יחסי ערוות של הגיבור עם אמו.

מה שנרמז ב״פנים אחרות״ מופיע בגלוי ב״סיפור פשוט״ שנכתב שנתיים־שלוש לאחר מכן. רומאן זה הוא הסיפור הארוך היחיד של עגנון המתאר בחור הגדל בבית הוריו. נישואיו העלובים של הירשל למינה וכיסופיו האסורים לבלומה בת דודתו, מביאים אותו לידי טירוף סכיזופרני המצריך טיפול פסיכיאטרי לזמן ממושך. מחלתו נגרמת, במִדה מסוימת, על־ידי אמו השתלטנית, הכופה על בנה את עול נישואיו ומאלצת אותו להאמין – כמו כל גיבורי עגנון – ש״הכל בידי האשה״ (״על כפות המנעול״, עמ׳ 98).

הציניות בתיאור האם ב״סיפור פשוט״ עומדת בניגוד לאידיאליזאציה הטהורה בסיפורים הקודמים. אמו של הירשל עושה אותו לנכה רגשי, שכן היא מונעת ממנו אהבה שיש בה כדי לעודד את עצמאותו, ומשתמשת בו למטרות אנוכיות. התוצאה היא שהוא נשאר במצב של תלות באמו אפילו אחרי חתונתו. אף־על־פי שבתת־הכרתו הירשל שונא את אמו, תלותו בה מוחלטת עד כדי כך ששנאתו אינה מוצאת לה פורקן. עם זה הוא מעביר את רגשותיו השליליים מאמו לאשתו.

מ״סיפור פשוט״ אפשר להבין את יסוד רגשי אשמתו הכבדה של הגיבור העגנוני ביחס לאמו ואת האידיאליזאציה הבלתי־נורמאלית של האשה. רגשותיו האמביוואלנטיים של הירשל לגבי אמו מוצאים ביטוי בקרע שנוצר בדמיונו בין בלומה, האשה ״האהובה״, ומינה, האשה ״השנואה״. רגשותיו הרצחניים אל אמו מתבטאים על פי רוב בהזיותיו ודחפיו הסאדו־מאזוכיסטיים לאשתו. אך לבסוף התלבטותו של הירשל בסבך דחפיו היא למעלה מכוחותיו הנפשיים ומביאה אותו לידי טירוף הדעת.

״סיפור פשוט״ הוא יצירה מיוחדת במינה, שבה הדינאמיקה של אופי הגבור העגנוני מתוארת במלוא היקפה. עגנון לא כתב סיפור מסובך וריאליסטי כמו ״סיפור פשוט״, אף כי ״שירה״ מבחינה פסיכולוגית מהווה מעין המשך לרומאן זה. בסיפורים וברומנים הבאים בעקבות ״סיפור פשוט״ – כגון ״אורח נטה ללון״, ״שבועת אמונים״ ו״תמול שלשום״ – חוזר עגנון להטעים את מחלת האם ומותה, אך מתוך עמקות הולכת וגדלה הוא חושף את ליקוייו הפסיכיים של גיבורו.

רמז לשארית האשמה

ברומאן ״אורח נטה ללון״ הגיבור, שמואל, חוזר לעיירת מולדתו, שיבוש; שם הוא נמשך לאהוב את רחל, בתו של

בעל האכסנייה. ברוך קורצווייל[24] מפנה את תשומת ליבנו לסמיכות פרשיות חשובה: מייד לאחר ששמואל מגלה לנו את רגשותיו לרחל הוא מאבד את מפתח בית־המדרש. בדומה לגרשום ב״הינדה״ אין ביכולתו של שמואל להתייחס אל רחל אלא כאל אידיאל הנראה מרחוק, ולא כאל אשה מציאותית ומינית, בעלת תכרנות רעות וטובות. כשם שבית־המדרש נעול בפניו, כך גם הוא עומד תמיד ״על כפות המנעול״, ולא בפנים, ביחסיו עם נשים. כנראה, מבחינה ממשית קיים אצלו מעצור פסיכולוגי המונע אותו מלהתקרב אל רחל קירבה מוחשית. אך קורצווייל מתעלם מהמשך הפרשה, הוא הפרק שבו מבקר שמואל אצל קבר אמו. בסמיכות פרקים אלו מדגיש עגנון את הקשר בין רחל לאמו של שמואל ומשקף את תיסכול רגשותיו לרחל משום שהיא מופיעה אצלו כדמות אם (גם שמה מרמז על קשר זה, שכן ״רחל אמנו״ היה מושג פופולארי ביותר בעולם היהודי של העיירה).

בפרשה זו, כבסיפורים הקודמים, עגנון רומז על שארית אשמתו המעיקה עליו שנטש את אמו במחלתה האחרונה. בדרך לקבר אמו, שמואל פוגש את מיניקתה הקשישה, פרידה קיסר, שגם בנה הניח אותה והלך לו. היא מלאה מרירות עד כדי כך שאבד לה חפץ החיים: ״וכי לא מוטב היה, שהיה נוטל סכין ושוחטני״ (עמ׳ 79). היא אומרת לשמואל שאילו היה בנה חוזר, היתה לועגת למוות, אך יודעת היא שסופה להיקבר על־ידי זרים. כשפונה שמואל ללכת אל קבר אמו, עיניו מתמלאות דמעות: דבריה של פרידה קיסר כמחט בבשרו החי. חש הוא בליבו שאלו הם הדברים שהיתה אמו אומרת אילו היתה חוזרת מעולם האמת.

הסיפור ״שבועת אמונים״, בדומה ל״תמול שלשום״ (שנכתב בערך באותו זמן, בשנות מלחמת העולם השנייה), חוזר לתקופת העלייה השנייה, ולמוטיב המוכר של אדם צעיר הקשור בתלות מחניקה לאמו. אהבתו של יעקב רכניץ, לאצות הים – הוא ביולוג ימי – משקפת את יחסיו לאמו ולשושנה אהובתו. התלהבותו בחיפושיו אחרי. אצות וניתוחן יש בה אספקט מיני: למעשה האצות דומות ל״בשר חי״ וחוא ״דבק בים״ כאדם שדבק באשה (״עד הנה״, עמ׳ 218)[25].

דמותה של שושנה נאחזת בסבך דמיונו בגרטרוד, אמה המתה, שאליה הוא קשור באופן מסתורי כמו אל הים. אחרי מותה היא נשארת חרותה בזכרונו, למרות ששושנה לוקחת את מקומה כ״מין פעולה חדשה מפעולות הנפש, כשהנפש כוללת עצמה עם הנעדר ועם המצוי ונכללת בשניהם כאחד״ (שם, עמ׳ 225). רכניץ מסתכל על־ידי שושנה ״כדרך שהיה מביט על אצבעותיה של אמה, כשהיתה משימה ידיה על השולחן היה פיו מתרגש והיה מבקש לתת שפתיו עליהן״ (שם, עמ׳ 268). בסוף הסיפור בשעה ששושנה רצה על חוף הים, רכניץ רואה בדמיונו את החלפת הנעדר והמצוי – שושנה, גרטרוד ואמו.

גם ב״תמול שלשום״ נמצא המוטיב של פטירת אם הגיבור, הממלאה את חייו ביגון. יצחק קומר (בגרמנית: יגון) מחפש לו תחליף: ״היה ברור בעיניו שאין בעולם אשה כאמו. וכיוון שמתה אמו עתידה אשה אחרת שתבוא במקומה צנועה וחסודה כאמו״ (עמ׳ 90). כשבחורה נותנת לו תפוז הוא זוכר את אמו; כשהוא מנשק לה הוא זוכר את הנשיקה שנשתמרה בפיו משעת גסיסתה. ראוי לציין גם שביום השנה לפטירת אמו מתחיל יצחק קומר לחזור בתשובה – ואמונתו שהתרופפה מאז בואו ליפו מתחדשת. הוא נכנס לבית כנסת לומר קדיש: ״וכיוון שנזכר באמו נזכר באותם הימים שהיה תינוק והיתה אמו עומדת אצל מיטתו ומקריאה את קריאת שמע. ושתי אהבות, אהבת השם ואהבת אמו, הרגישו את לבו״ (עמ׳ 342).

רגשות כמוסים ודחפים אסורים

כפי שאנו רואים, אפילו כשהגיע לשנות החמישים של חייו, שלושים שנה אחרי ״עגונות״, אי־אפשר היה לו לעגנון להיפרד ממוטיב מרכזי זה – יצירת גיבור קשור לאמו עד כדי כך שזכרונה מונע אותו מליצור יחסים נורמאליים עם נשים. עובדה היא: גם ב״שירה״, הרומאן שנשאר בלתי גמור בשעת מותו ב־1970, הוא עודנו מתלבט בבעיות אלו. ברומאן זה יחסיו של הרבסט לאחות שירה הם כמעט בלתי מובנים אלא אם כן רואים בה דמות־אם שבה הוא תלוי. לא מקרה הוא במבנה הרומאן שפגישתו הראשונה עם שירה מתרחשת כמעט בדיוק ביום השנה למיתת אמו, ושהרבסט מודאג מאוד מהתאמה זו. יש לציין גם ששמה של שירה הוא שינוי קל של שמה של אמו, שרה.

ב״שירה״, בפעם הראשונה בחייו, עגנון מייצג גיבור שדחפיו הרצחניים לדמות־אם אידיאלית אינם מאופקים או מוסווים על־ידי המספר. הרבסט שנא את שירה תכלית שנאה, אפילו בטרם הכיר אותה. בדמיונו שירה נדרסת על־ידי מכונית, היא סובלת ממחלה ממארת, היא נחבטת, נאנסת, ואבריה נחתכים ממנה. התכונה הבולטת ברומאן היא תיאור אופיו הילדותי של הרבסט שנמצא תמיד בחיפוש אחרי אהבה שלעולם לא ישיגנה. אין חוסר ברמזים שטראגדיה פסיכולוגית זו תוצאה היא של קשריו הפגומים עם אמו. היגון הגולמי של ״עגונות״, ״בארה של מרים״, ו״הנידח״ חלף עבר. מה שנשאר הוא הצורך להתיר רגשות כמוסים ודחפים אסורים.

האובססיה של עגנון לגבי האם או דמות־האם החולנית והמתה, שהתחילה בתקופת פטירת אמו בשנת 1909, רדפה אותו כל ימיו. יש לראות בסיפוריו הקודמים את הביטוי הברור והחזק ביותר של הלם אבידתו ותהליך האבלות, הכעס, החיפוש אחרי תחליף ושאיפה להשלמה אחרי מותה. אך גם בסיפוריו המאוחרים – כגון ״פנים אחרות״, ״שבועת אמונים״ ו״עידו ועינם״ – מוצאים אנו צלילים רפים של אבידה וחיפוש, כמעט לא ניכרים, כאילו התכווץ הכאב והשאיר רק שרידים דקים של צער.

אחד הצדדים השווים בסיפורים הקדמים והמאוחרים הוא, כפי שראינו, אי־יכולתו של הגיבור להימלט מצל השפעת אמו ביחסיו עם נשים. אי־יכולת זו נגרמת לא רק על־ידי הטראומה של מחלת האם ופטירתה, אלא גם על־ידי עצם קשריו המעיקים עם אמו. ב״סיפור פשוט״ בלבד, בין כל סיפוריו, מתאר עגנון מציאות עכורה זו. חפצו האדיר ליצור יחס אמביוואלנטי לאמו נגלה בביטוי מוחלט ומפורט עשרים־וחמש שנים אחרי הופעת ״עגונות״. אין ספק שפרידתו של עגנון מאמו, מחלתה האחרונה ומותה בדמי ימיה, העניקו לו חומר סיוטי שהטריד אותו כל ימיו.

---

*מחבר המאמר, ד״ר דוד אברבך, הוא יליד לונדון. בילדותו עבר עם משפחתו לבלטימור שבארה״ב, שם קיבל חינוך עברי מעולה. בנעוריו חזר לאנגליה. באוניברסיטת לונדון זכה לתואר ראשון בספרות אנגלית. עתה הוא עוסק בספרות השוואתית (עברית ואנגלית) באוקספורד. בשנה שעברה הוענק לו תואר דוקטור באוקספורד על דיסרטאציה שלו ״נושאים פסיכולוגיים בכתבי עגנון״.

24. ברוך קורצווייל: ״מסות על סיפורי ש״י עגנון״, 1970, עמ׳ 59 וכו׳.

25. ראה בראשית ב, כד, ״ודבק באשתו״.

Appendix 2

David Aberbach, article in *Commentary*, 'Freud's Jewish Problem'

Freud's Jewish Problem

David Aberbach

ALL psychological systems, Sigmund Freud's included—indeed, all systems of thought—are stamped with the limitations of their creators. This might seem a gloomy and cynical way of looking at the history of ideas, yet in most cases, the limitations not only spur the creation of the system but also constitute its very stuff. The biases of a man, with their traumatic origin, make him think, force him to rummage through his world, discovering why he burns with the need to understand, to illuminate, why he thinks and acts in a particular way. To ask why ideas come into existence is a step toward learning their meaning and application.

On October 15, 1897, during the self-analysis that led to *The Interpretation of Dreams*, Freud wrote to his friend and colleague, Wilhelm Fliess, that he had discovered in himself what he was later to call the Oedipus complex: "I have found love of the mother and jealousy of the father in my own case too." The development of psychoanalysis was thus determined, and centered on incest and aggression. Freud's accounts of his complex are sketchy, but the main cause is touched upon in Ernest Jones's biography, namely, an incestuous dependence upon a domineering mother. This dependence was encouraged by her strong affection for him as her first-born and favorite child; by her beauty and extreme youthfulness in comparison with his father, Jakob Freud, who was twenty years older and had been married before; by the death of her second child when Freud was eighteen months old; by her affliction with tuberculosis which required confinement in a sanatorium; and by the overly demonstrative and excessive protection that Jewish mothers have often given their children, perhaps to inure them against hardships that they have been liable to suffer as Jews.

But if incestuous dependence can account for Freud's unconscious attachment to his mother, incestuous rivalry alone cannot account for the virulence of Freud's unconscious hostility toward his father. Jakob Freud was by no means an overbearing or indifferent father; on the contrary, he was kind, affectionate, and proud of his son, though he was somewhat detached by his age and temperament from the rest of the family. Yet in Freud's dreams his father is constantly degraded by association with illiteracy, feeble-mindedness, sexual immorality, drunkenness, urination, or defecation. A death-wish against his father is expressed in a dream in which Freud hands him a urinal shaped like a poisoned chalice belonging to Lucrezia Borgia. Interpreting another of his dreams, Freud writes, "I have broken off at thoughts which would have contained an unfriendly criticism of my father." No doubt he exercised his censorship elsewhere as well.

Some of Freud's theories about fathers are cruelly defamatory and obscene. For over four years (1893-97), he held to the theory that hysteria in women is the result of seduction by their fathers. According to Jones, Freud believed that his own father, too, was guilty of such acts. Similarly, he thought at first that neurotics had syphilitic fathers. Aggression against the father appears in Freud's stress upon the Oedipus complex (which he first called the "father complex"), as the father stands accused of causing castration-anxiety and neurosis.

Freud was suspiciously eager to lend support to far-fetched theories involving the murder of the father, or father-image. He believed, for example, that in primitive times sons murdered their fathers in order to have the women. Likewise, he thought that the Jews had murdered their father-figure, Moses, in the desert. Still, it is interesting that although Freud generally had few inhibitions about publishing his work, precisely those books in which the theme of parricide figures most strongly—*The Interpretation of Dreams, Totem and Taboo, Moses and Monotheism*—were published only after hesitation and delay. After reading *Totem and Taboo*, Jones and Sandor Ferenczi suggested to Freud that his work was a sublimation of parricidal impulses, that "he had in his imagination lived through the experiences he described in his book, that his elation represented the excitement of killing and eating the father, and that his doubts were only the reaction."

Errors in Freud's dreams often signify hostility to the father. Interpreting one of his own dreams containing an error, Freud reveals that in it he was identifying himself with a patient who, as a result

DAVID ABERBACH, a new contributor, is a young Englishman who has recently completed his doctorate in literature at Oxford University and will soon start work in child therapy at the Tavistock Clinic of London. Since 1978 he has held a Fellowship at the Oxford Center for Postgraduate Hebrew Studies.

of his desire to murder his father, "was unable to go out into the street because he was tortured by the fear that he would kill everyone he met." His dream confusion of Hasdrubal with Hamilcar, in which he put the brother's name instead of the father's, seems to him to expose "dissatisfaction with my father's behavior toward the 'enemies of our people' " and fantasies of being the son not of his father, but of his half-brother, Emanuel.

In another dream, Freud is overcome with hostility and says of a deceased colleague, Josef Paneth, *non vixit* (he did not live) rather than *non vivit* (he is not alive). Marthe Robert, in her book *From Oedipus to Moses*, interprets this to indicate a desire by Freud that his father had never lived, a surmise given added credibility by the fact that the dream occurred during the week of the second anniversary of Jakob Freud's death. Another error in this dream, the substitution of *patriae* for *publicae* on an inscription, reveals more directly that Freud's underlying concern is the father. In the dream, Freud discovered that by looking straight at apparitions of the dead he could make them disappear. No doubt he wanted his father's memory, too, and all that he stood for, to stop haunting him.

FREUD was himself shocked by his discovery, precipitated by the death of Jakob Freud in 1896, that he hated his father. The crisis which followed lasted for several years and is reflected in Freud's major work, *The Interpretation of Dreams*. In this period, he was afflicted by an exacerbation of neurotic symptoms which drove him to self-analysis. He was much sicker, especially at this time, than Jones's biography leads us to believe. His moods fluctuated intensely between despair and optimism; he had severe migraines and nasal catarrh, chronic indigestion, anxiety attacks, a dread of dying, particularly through heart failure, and impaired potency. From studying his illnesses, believing that by penetrating to their causes he could cure himself, Freud concluded that his symptoms were partly a self-punishment because he had unconsciously wanted his father's death. What caused these parricidal tendencies and self-punishment? According to Freud, it was incestuous rivalry for the mother.

Incestuous rivalry is, presumably, a universal cause of the animosity sons feel toward their fathers. However, Freud's own difficulties also had other, more circumstantial causes, involving Jewishness and anti-Semitism. Jones does not give these factors the attention they deserve. A major cause of tension between father and son was the fact that Freud went much further than his father along the path of assimilation from a deeply religious Eastern European environment into a non-Jewish Western milieu.

Jakob Freud was born in 1815, the year of Waterloo, in the Galician *shtetl* of Tysmenitz. Until he was about twenty, when he moved to Freiburg, he was as observant as a modern Hasid in Williamsburgh. His father, who died shortly before Freud was born in 1856, had been a hasidic rabbi (Freud was named Shlomo in his memory). His family background and the cultural environment in which he was raised meant that Jakob Freud was steeped in Jewish learning and rituals.

By 1855, when he reached Vienna, Jakob Freud had dispensed with many of his early religious observances. Nevertheless, he was Jewish to the core. That he was able to conduct by heart the Passover *seder*—which is recited only twice a year in the Diaspora—indicates how deeply engrained was his Jewish education. He regularly studied Talmud and Hebrew literature. In some ways he was a typical Jew of the Haskalah (the period of the Enlightenment), disillusioned with a traditionally religious way of life (and preferring Hebrew or German to Yiddish), but unable to abandon it completely or find anything to take its place. When he gave his son a Bible for his thirty-fifth birthday, he wrote a Hebrew inscription which could have been written by a more observant Jew than the one he had become: "Thou hast seen in this Book the vision of the Almighty, thou hast heard willingly, thou hast done and hast tried to fly high upon the wings of the Holy Spirit."

Still, the religious feeling behind these words had apparently faded long before. T.S. Eliot's observation on the Elizabethan dramatist Philip Massinger has relevance to Freud's father and, in general, to German-speaking Jews of the 19th century: "As soon as the emotion disappears, the morality which ordered it appears hideous." Hideous indeed were Jewish rituals to Freud, for as he usually saw them observed at home and by other assimilated Viennese Jews, they were empty and meaningless.

Freud came to despise Jewish religion, indeed, all religion, as a form of psychological illness, a compulsive neurosis, a sign of communal immaturity. He did not hold to this rigidly, but it was his view. The vehemence of his rejection of religion was a symbolic rejection of the father who represented, though he did not properly observe or teach, a traditional Jewish way of life. Although ritualistic elements are part of psychoanalysis, Freud placed little emphasis upon the fact that ritual may have a positive function in life. The fearful and defensive side of religion, rather than the loving side, loomed largest in his mind.

IT IS likely that the poverty of his Jewishness helped to generate Freud's anger at his father. Judaism as Freud learned it from his father was a thing of shreds and patches to which one paid lip-service. The hypocrisy of it was abhorrent to Freud. His sense of what it meant to be Jewish was inauthentic and confused. It is true that the closest adult friend of Freud's youth was his beloved teacher, Samuel Hammerschlag, who for many years taught him Hebrew and Bible. But Freud also had a Catholic nanny who frequently took him to church. Afterward he would deliver imitations of sermons. From childhood, Freud was fascinated by Jesus and Paul. He chose to open his medical practice on Easter Sunday, presumably as a gesture of identification with Jesus, and confessed to the Protestant theologian Oskar Pfister a special sympathy for Paul as "a genuinely Jewish character." Such interests were utterly foreign, and probably anathema, to Jakob Freud.

Freud's distorted view of Judaism betrays an unmistakable Oedipal bias. His rejection of the father and of the "Father religion" went side by side: "The Mosaic religion had been a Father religion: Christianity became a Son religion. The old God, the Father, took second place; Christ, the Son, stood in his place, just as in those dark days every son had longed to do. . . . From now on Jewish religion was, so to speak, a fossil" (*Moses and Monotheism*). Upon the stage of Jewish ritual, the drama of Freud's troubled relationship with his father was enacted. While Jakob Freud continued to observe the vestiges of an Orthodox Jewish life, his son emphatically refused to do so. He wrote to Martha Bernays during their engagement: "Am I to fast on Yom Kippur? . . . Surely not."

Characteristically, Freud opposed having a traditional Jewish burial service for his father. His late arrival at the funeral, a dream of his suggests, aroused strong compunction. (For himself he chose cremation, a final act of defiance against his father, as it is a violation of Jewish law.) The idea of being married under a *chupa* (canopy) was loathsome to Freud; rather than undergo this ordeal, he went so far as to discuss with Josef Breuer the possibility of conversion to Christianity. He once went to a Jewish wedding and, as Jones tells it, "gazed at the scene with fascinated horror and then wrote a letter of sixteen pages describing all the odious details in a spirit of malign mockery."

Freud's life as a husband and father involved a defiance of Jewish tradition. That he married a strictly Orthodox Jewish girl, the granddaughter of a famous rabbi, shows how strong was the influence of his background. During their engagement, he promised Martha that "something of the core, of the essence of this meaningful and life-affirming Judaism will not be absent from our home." But after marrying her, he persuaded her, somewhat against her will, to become as completely non-Orthodox as himself. Isaiah Berlin has recalled that Freud at the end of his life was still bickering with Martha about whether to light candles on Friday nights (he was against it).

Freud had not learned from his father "meaningful and life-affirming Judaism," and he could not give this to his children. He raised them in abysmal ignorance of their heritage. They were aware that something was missing. Martin, his son, tells a revealing anecdote about Martha's mother, Emmeline: "On Saturdays we used to hear her singing Jewish prayers in a small but firm and melodious voice. All of this, strangely enough in a Jewish family, seemed alien to us children who had been brought up without any instruction in Jewish ritual."

Raised in an environment which taught him both to look askance upon his religious heritage and to struggle to gain advancement in a hostile Gentile world, Freud had little to shield him from feeling that the religion of his fathers was an odious handicap. He wished at times that he were not his father's son, and not the son of any Jew. His dreams betrayed the wish for better origins: "If only I had been the second generation, the son of a professor or court counselor, I would certainly have *got on faster*." He had fantasies of how different things would have been had he been born the son of his half-brother, Emanuel, who had gone to England to escape the clutches of anti-Semitism. To his colleague, Karl Abraham, he complained, "If my name were Oberhüber, in spite of everything, my innovations would have met with far less resistance."

Perhaps out of disdain for the humble Jewish background of his father, Freud had a preference for noble origins. He subscribed to the theory that the works attributed to Shakespeare were actually written by the Earl of Oxford, and to the theory that Moses was not a Jew but an Egyptian prince. While Freud greatly admired the heroic side of Jewish history, he could not but feel, living in one of the most virulently anti-Semitic countries in the world, that his Jewishness was a millstone around his neck.

As in the case of many Jewish families at the time, a touchstone of conflict between father and son was education. Jakob Freud's early life in the *shtetl* was one in which only the Bible, the prayer book, and Jewish legal texts—especially the Talmud—were thought to have real value. Jakob Freud probably did not consciously preserve this attitude, but evidently he did not altogether respect secular learning. Freud recalled that as a child he had once been handed a book by his father to destroy: "Not easy to justify from an educational point of view!" He mentions in *The Psychopathology of Everyday Life* that his hostility toward his father was connected with books. As Jakob Freud's education was predominantly talmudic, he was unable to advise his son in his career. The contrast in education between father and son, not so unusual for the period, was nevertheless striking: while Jakob Freud studied the legal discourses of the Talmud, his son kept a diary in Greek. Freud, enlightened and university-educated, abhorred his father's continuing interest in the Talmud, considering it backward. Jones tells us that the only examination which Freud ever failed was in medical jurisprudence. This failure, from a Freudian viewpoint, might indicate an unconscious rejection of the father whom Freud identified with law.

Jakob Freud's defective education and his consequent limitations rankled with Freud, all the more so as Jakob Freud was an ineffectual provider and the family was impoverished. Freud's own success gave rise to a sense of guilt. At the end of his life he wrote of people "wrecked with success" who "fall ill or even go entirely to pieces, because an overwhelmingly powerful wish of theirs has been fulfilled." He omits mention of the great crisis in his life after his own "overwhelmingly powerful wish," the death of his father, had come about, but gives a related example—a mysterious depression which he felt before visiting the Acropolis in 1905, and a reaction at the site that "what I see is not real." He explains:

> A sense of guilt was attached to the satisfaction in having gone such a long way: there was something about it that was wrong, that from earliest times had been forbidden. It was something to do with a child's criticism of his father, with the undervaluation of earlier childhood. It seems as though the essence of success was to have got further than one's father, and as though to excel one's father was still something forbidden. . . . The very theme of Athens and the Acropolis in itself contained evidence of the son's superiority. Our father had had no secondary education, and Athens could not have meant much to him. Thus what interfered with our enjoyment of the journey to Athens was a feeling of *filial piety*.

With his father's encouragement, Freud had achieved the intellectual perspective which made criticism of his way of life and even hatred of it almost inevitable. In the non-Jewish world (symbolized by Athens or Rome), Freud went much further than his father. His superiority was at times a distressing burden. In *The Interpretation of Dreams* he tells of waking in a fright after dreaming that children can achieve what their fathers fail to do.

HERE it might be asked whether the urge to go further than one's father necessarily gives rise to guilt or fear. Traditionally in Jewish life sons are encouraged to achieve as much as possible and thereby bring honor to their parents. According to a rabbinic saying, "No father envies his son." Then what was the source of Freud's pathological desire to outdo his father (which, after all, was not so very difficult), and make intellectual conquests? Once again his relation to his own Jewishness provides the key. In *The Interpretation of Dreams* Freud tells of a turning point in his early life, his deep hurt and disillusionment upon hearing of his father's unheroic conduct when humiliated by an anti-Semite. From then on, he was obsessed with Rome as a symbol of the Catholic Church and of anti-Semitism, and he worshipped Hannibal, the Semitic general who, unlike Jakob Freud, fought Rome courageously. Inwardly he raged against qualities which he associated with his father and his Jewishness—passivity, cowardice, ignorance.

Unlike his father, Freud was never passive in the face of anti-Semitism. This cost him a good deal of strain as he was himself a rather shy, unobtrusive man. Through intense yearning for heroism and lifelong hero worship, Freud reacted against his father's—and his own—powerlessness, and the traditional, powerless life of the Jews. To Martha he wrote during their engagement: "I have often felt as though I had inherited all the passion and all the defiance with which our ancestors defended their Temple and could gladly sacrifice my life for one great moment in history. And with all that I was always so powerless and could not express my flowing passions." Freud's sympathy for Zionism was owing partly to the fact that the Zionists, unlike most traditional Jews at that time, were prepared to fight and if necessary give up their lives for their land.

Military heroes, especially those whom he identified as or associated with Jews, such as Moses, Hannibal, Oliver Cromwell (after whom he named one of his sons), and Napoleon, received Freud's highest admiration. These men, unlike his father, could fight back. In his youth, Freud had ambitions of being a great general and was responsible, at the age of ten, for naming his brother Alexander, after Alexander the Great. His very system of thought, with its frequent use of the language and imagery of warfare, was a kind of intellectual military operation—he described himself once as a "conquistador." At the end of his life, during the night journey across the Channel to England, Freud dreamed that he was landing at Pevensey. When he related this dream to his son, he explained that Pevensey was where William the Conqueror had landed in 1066. These heroes and their bravery were as far removed from the character and life of Jakob Freud as is imaginable.

BUT Freud was more like his father than he dared admit. For all his unconscious quarrels with his father, he loved him deeply. His anger at his father for remaining passive in the face of anti-Semitism is, in a deeper sense, an assertion of love; the thought of his father humiliated was unbearable to Freud. Moreover, his love for his father was bound up inextricably with the issue of Jewishness. As he himself suffered from anti-Semitic prejudice, it is probable that, to some extent, feelings and thoughts which Freud interprets as signs of hostility toward his father, and which he generalizes into a universal human problem, reflect the peculiar conditions of being Jewish in antipathetic surroundings. Freud's very theories can be seen as an implicit attack upon anti-Semitism, and upon human prejudice in general, for his central assumption is that all men are driven by the same impulses and are, in a sense, equally wicked; therefore, it is ludicrous for any set of men to regard themselves as racially superior.

Freud believed that the Gentile world was, on the whole, anti-Semitic. (This, ironically, more than anything else, gave him a sense of identity as a Jew.) After seeing Herzl's play, *Das Neue Ghetto*, Freud had the following dream: "On account of certain events which had taken place in the city of Rome, it had become necessary to remove the children to safety, and this was done. . . . I was sitting on the edge of a fountain and was greatly depressed and almost in tears." Freud comments that the dream alludes to the Psalm beginning, "By the waters of Babylon, there we sat down, yea, we wept, when we remembered Zion," and that the dream-thoughts involve "the Jewish question, concern about the future of one's children to whom one cannot give a country of their own." Freud was deeply moved by a dream in which the apparition of Herzl appeared to him and spoke of the perilous condition of the Jewish people, and the need to act immediately if they were to be saved.

Freud's famous "revolutionary" dream shows how hatred of the father and the effects of anti-Semitism are intertwined. According to Freud, this dream goes back to his rebellion against his father. Nevertheless, certain aspects of it point more directly to problems caused by anti-Semitism. During the dream, Freud, to his surprise, expresses fierce German nationalist feeling. He then finds that the gates to the university and the main train station are "cordoned off." He can use only the local railroad. The dream ends with Freud standing at a main-line station, hoping to "get away" with the help of his invalid father, while giving vent, through association, to immense hostility toward him.

In the dream, Freud's surprise at showing patriotic feeling can be explained by the fact that he is a Jew whose country sanctions discriminations which "cordon" him off from a normal life and from gaining advancement and recognition. In the dream he can use only the local line (indeed, the local Jews of Vienna, especially the B'nai B'rith, were the only ones who valued his work at the start). Freud's aggresssion toward his father later in the dream might, therefore, be caused partly by anti-Semitism which embittered his life, frustrated his ambitions, and worsened the conflict with his father. Ironically, the discovery of this aggression did enable Freud to "get away," and gain international recognition along the "main line" of Western thought. He himself interpreted the aggression as a symptom of the Oedipus complex, a universal phenomenon, but in doing so he suppressed the "local" or circumstantial factors having to do with his Jewish background.

Freud's sensitivity about his origins was so acute that he hardly spoke of them, even to his children. Like his Viennese contemporary, Gustav Mahler (who, however, was a convert to Christianity), he obliterated practically everything pertaining to his early life. This is astonishing in view of the importance which Freud attached to childhood and family background. His entire life was a denial of his roots. While he often admitted the general social and psychological importance of his Jewishness, he never acknowledged the normative and healthy aspects of the tradition which he rescinded, or publicized his enormous debt to it.

In utterly rejecting Jewish ritual, Freud protested too much. He ignored the practical importance of the talmudic background to his way of thinking. He did not openly concede that he had probably inherited his prodigious memory and analytical ability from his rabbinic ancestors. He did not consider seriously that the psychoanalytic role he had created for himself was in some ways similar to that of the Eastern European rabbi, who often advised members of his congregation in their personal lives. And, while he was highly critical of his father's education, he did not mention how much he owed to the educational tradition sustained by the Jewish religion, which for hundreds of years had made the Jews the only large group in Europe among whom illiteracy was practically unknown.

It is impossible to escape the conclusion that Freud probably chose to downplay his Jewishness and the role of anti-Semitism and Jewish self-hatred in stimulating conflict with his father for fear of diverting attention from the allegedly universal nature of the Oedipus complex. Yet the fact remains that Freud's hatred of his father was caused not only by incestuous rivalry, but also by the extraordinary social conditions of the Jews in 19th-century Europe, and the vast cultural and psychological changes that they underwent in the passage to modernity.

Bibliography

Aberbach, David (1980) 'Freud's Jewish Problem', *Commentary* 69(6): 35–9.

Aberbach, David (1982) '*Dmut ha-em be'khitve Agnon*' (The Lost Mother in Agnon), *Moznayim* 54: 52–6.

Aberbach, David (1983) 'Screen Memories of Writers', *International Review of Psycho-Analysis* 10(1): 47–62.

Aberbach, David (1984) *At the Handles of the Lock. Themes in the Fiction of S.J. Agnon*. Oxford: Oxford University Press.

Aberbach, David (1984a) 'Loss and Dreams', *International Review of Psycho-Analysis* 11(4): 393–98.

Aberbach, David (1988) 'Agnon and the Need for Tradition', in *Jewish Book Annual*, J. Kabakoff (ed.). New York: Jewish Book Council of America.

Aberbach, David (1989) *Surviving Trauma: Loss, Literature, and Psychoanalysis*. New Haven and London: Yale University Press.

Aberbach, David (1990) 'Speaking for the diseased in spirit' (on Agnon's *Shira*), *Times Literary Supplement*, April 20–26: 428.

Aberbach, David (1993) *Realism, Caricature and Bias: The Fiction of Mendele Mokher Sefarim*. Oxford: Littman Library.

Aberbach, David (1993a) 'Infidel Jew: Freud, Jewish Ritual and Psychoanalysis', in *Psychoanalysis and Tradition*, L. Spurling (ed.). London: Routledge & Kegan Paul, pp. 40–8.

Aberbach, David (1994) 'Fantasies of Deviance in Mendele and Agnon', *Association for Jewish Studies Review* 19: 45–60.

Aberbach, David (1995) 'Aggadah and Childhood Imagination in the Works of Mendele, Bialik and Agnon', in *Jewish Education and Learning, Festschrift* for Dr. David Patterson, G. Abramson & T. Parfitt (eds.). Chur, Switzerland: Harwood Academic Publishers.

Aberbach, David (2003) *Major Turning Points in Jewish Intellectual History*. Basingstoke, UK: Palgrave Macmillan.

Aberbach, David (2003a) 'Fanatic Heart: The Poetry of Uri Zvi Greenberg', *Central Conference of American Rabbis Journal*, Spring: 16–32.

Aberbach, David (2004) 'Enlightenment and Cultural Confusion: Mendele's *The Mare* and Dangarembga's *Nervous Conditions*', *Comparative Literary Studies* 41: 214–30.

Aberbach, David (2006) 'Nationalism, Reform Judaism and the Hebrew Prayer Book', *Nations and Nationalism* 12(1): 139–59.

Aberbach, David (2008) 'Beggars of Love: Agnon and Flaubert', *Journal of Modern Jewish Studies*, 7(2): 157–174.

Aberbach, David (2008a) *Jewish Cultural Nationalism*. London and New York: Routledge.

Aberbach, David (2009) 'Holocaust Literature: Foreshadowings and Shadowings' in *Arguing the Modern Jewish Canon: Essays on Modern Jewish Literature in Honor of Ruth Wisse*', J. Cammy et al. (eds.). Harvard Center for Jewish Studies, Harvard University Press.

Aberbach, David (2009a) 'Zionist Patriotism in Europe, 1897–1942: Ambiguities in Jewish Nationalism', *International History Review* xxxi(2): 268–298.

Aberbach, David (2009b) 'Patriotism and Antisemitism: The Crisis of Polish Jewish Identity between the Wars', *Polin* xxii: 368–88.

Aberbach, David (2013) *The European Jews, Patriotism and the Liberal State 1789–1939*. London and New York: Routledge.

Aberbach, David (2015) '"A One-Sided Love Affair": German Jewish Literature 1789–1939', *Journal of Modern Jewish Studies* 14(3): 1–19.

Aberbach, David (2023) *Bialik, the Hebrew Bible and the Literature of Nationalism*. London and New York: Routledge.

Agnon, S.J. (1908) 'Agunot' (Hebrew), *Ha-Omer* 2(1): 53–65.

Agnon, S.J. (1909) 'The Well of Miriam' (*Be'era shel Miryam*) *Ha-Poel ha-Tzair* 2, 14–18 (21 May, 3 June, 17 June, 1 July).

Agnon, S.J. (1946) *Yamim Nora'im* (Days of Awe). Tel Aviv: Schocken.

Agnon, S.J. (1953–62) *Kol Sippurav shel Shmuel Yosef Agnon* (Collected Works), 8 vols. Tel Aviv: Schocken. Reprinted with corrections and additions, 1998.

Agnon, S.J. (1970) *Twenty-One Stories*. N. Glatzer (ed.). New York: Schocken Books.

Agnon, S.J. (1971) *Shira*. E. Yaron (ed.). Tel Aviv and Jerusalem: Schocken.

Agnon, S.J. (1971a) 'Epilogue to *Yesteryear*' (Hebrew) *Moznayim*, Vol. 32 (February 1971).

Agnon, S.J. (1973) *Ir uMelo'ah* (A City in its Fullness). E. Yaron (ed.). Tel Aviv/Jerusalem: Schocken.

Agnon, S.J. (1974) *Ba-Hanuto shel Mar Lublin* (In the Shop of Mr. Lublin). E. Yaron (ed.). Tel Aviv/Jerusalem: Schocken.

Agnon, S.J. (1976) *Me-Atzmi el atzmi* (From Myself to Myself). E. Yaron (ed.). Tel Aviv/Jerusalem: Schocken.

Agnon, S.J. (1983) *Esterlein Yakirati* (Letters to and from Esther Agnon). E. Yaron (ed.). Tel Aviv/Jerusalem: Schocken.

Agnon, S.J. (1989) *Shira*. Z. Shapiro (transl.). New York: Schocken Books.

Agnon, S.J. and S.Z. Schocken (2003) *Hilufe Iggrot* (Letters 1916–1959). Tel Aviv/Jerusalem: Schocken.

Alter, Robert (ed.) (1975) *Modern Hebrew Literature*. New York: Behrman House Inc.

Alter, Robert (1985) 'Blind Beggars and Incestuous Passions', *New York Times Book Review*, 22 December 1985.

Alter, Robert (1989) 'Afterword' to Agnon's *Shira*, Z. Shapiro (transl.). New York: Schocken Books.

Aschheim, Steven E. (2001) *Scholem, Arendt, Klemperer: Intimate Chronicles in Turbulent Times*. Bloomington and Indianapolis: Indiana University Press.

Bakon, Yitzhak (1989) *Agnon ha-Tza'ir* (The Young Agnon). Beer Sheba: Ben-Gurion University Press.

Baldick, Robert (1964) Introduction to Gustav Flaubert, *Sentimental Education*. R. Baldick (transl.). Harmondsworth: Penguin.

Band, Arnold J. (1968) *Nostalgia and Nightmare: A Study in the Fiction of S.Y. Agnon*. Berkeley, CA: University of California Press.

Band, Arnold J. (1994) 'Negotiating Jewish History: The Author, His Code and His Readers', *Tradition and Trauma: Studies in the Fiction of S. J. Agnon*, Glenda Abramson and David Patterson, eds. Boulder, CO: Westview Press.

Barzel, Hillel (1975) *Sippure ahavah shel S.Y. Agnon* (Agnon's Love Stories), 2nd edn. Ramat Gan: Bar Ilan University Press.

Barzilay, Isaac E. (1959) 'National and Anti-National Trends in the Berlin Haskalah', *Jewish Social Studies* 21: 165–92.

Becker, Hans-Jürgen and Hillel Weiss (eds.) (2010) *Agnon and Germany: The Presence of the German World in the Writings of S.Y. Agnon*. Ramat Gan: Bar Ilan University Press.

Beckett, Samuel (1973, orig. 1956) *Waiting for Godot*. London: Faber and Faber.

Be'er, Hayyim (1993) *Bialik, Brenner, Agnon* [Hebrew]. Tel Aviv: Am Oved.

Bialik, C.N. (1935) *Devarim She-Be'al Peh* (Speeches). 2 vols. Tel Aviv: Dvir.

Bialik, C.N. (1975) *Stories* (Hebrew). Tel Aviv: Dvir.

Bialik, C.N. (2004) *C.N. Bialik: Selected Poems*. D. Aberbach (ed. & transl.). Overlook Press/Duckworth.

Bowlby, John (1980) *Loss: Sadness and Depression*, vol. 3 of *Attachment and Loss*. London: The Hogarth Press and The Institute of Psycho-Analysis.

Brenner, Y.H. (1955, 1960, 1967) *Collected Works* (Hebrew). 3 vols. Tel Aviv: Hakibbutz HaHameuchad.

Brenner, Y.H. (1983, orig. 1909) *Nerves*, in A. Lelchuk and G. Shaked (eds.) *Eight Great Hebrew Short Novels*. New York: New American Library.

Buber, Martin (1970) *I and Thou*. W. Kaufmann (transl.). Edinburgh: T. & T. Clark.

Buber, Martin (1974, orig. 1923) *Ich und Du*. Heidelberg: Lambert Schneider.

Canaani, David (1971) *S.Y. Agnon Be'al Peh* [Agnon in Conversation]. Merhavia: Ha-Kibbutz Hameuchad.

Canetti, Elias (1978) 'Kafka's Other Trial', in Franz Kafka, *Letters to Felice*. C. Middleton (transl.). Harmondsworth, Middlesex: Penguin Books.

Coleridge, S.T. (1975, orig. 1963) *Poems*. J. Beer (ed.). Everyman's Library. London: Dent; New York: Dutton.

Davidson, Israel (1966, orig. 1907) *Parody in Jewish Literature*. New York: AMS Press.

Ellmann, Richard (1983) *James Joyce*. 2nd edn. Oxford University Press.

Elon, Amos (1975) *Herzl*. London: Weidenfeld & Nicolson.

Ezekiel, Sarit (2019) *Where Agnon and Jung Meet: Travels along an External and Internal Path in the novel The Bridal Canopy*. Newcastle: Cambridge Scholars Publishing.

Fairbairn, W.R.D. (1937–38; 1938–39) 'Prolegomenon to a Psychology of Art' and 'The Ultimate Basis of Aesthetic Experience', *British Journal of Psychology*, vols. 28, 29.

Fairbairn, W.R.D. (1952) *Psycho-Analytic Studies of the Personality*. London: Tavistock Publications.

Falk, Avner (2018) *Agnon's Story: A Psychoanalytic Biography of S.Y. Agnon*. Leiden: Brill.

Feierberg, M.Z. (1973) *Whither? and Other Stories*. H. Halkin (transl.). Philadelphia: Jewish Publication Society of America.

Field, Geoffrey G. (1981) *Evangelist of Race: The Germanic Vision of Houston Stewart Chamberlain*. New York: Columbia University Press.

Fisch, Harold (1975) *S.Y. Agnon*. New York: Frederick Ungar.

Flaubert, Gustav (1961, orig. 1878) *Three Tales*. R. Baldick (transl.). Harmondsworth: Penguin.

Flaubert, Gustav (1964, orig. 1869) *Sentimental Education*. R. Baldick (transl.). Harmondsworth: Penguin.

Flaubert, Gustav (1976, orig. 1881) *Bouvard and Pecuchet*. A.J. Krailsheimer (transl.). Harmondsworth: Penguin.

Flaubert, Gustav (1977 [1950], orig. 1857) *Madame Bovary*. A. Russell (transl.). Harmondsworth: Penguin.

Flaubert, Gustav (1977a, orig. 1862). *Salammbo*. A. Krailsheimer (transl.). Harmondsworth: Penguin Classics.

Freud, Ernst (ed.) (1960) *The Letters of Sigmund Freud*. T. & J. Stern (transl.). New York: Basic Books.

Freud, Martin (1957) *Glory Reflected*. London: Angus & Robertson.

Freud, Sigmund (1914) 'The Moses of Michelangelo', in *Standard Edition of the Complete Psychological Works of Sigmund Freud*, 24 vols, 1953–74, J. Strachey (transl.). London: Hogarth Press, 13: 211–36.

Freud, Sigmund (1927) *The Future of an Illusion*. J. Strachey (ed. & transl.). *Standard Edition of The Complete Psychological Works of Sigmund Freud*, Vol. 21, pp. 5–56. London: Hogarth Press.

Freud, Sigmund (1976, orig. 1900) *The Interpretation of Dreams*. Transl. J. Strachey. Harmondsworth, Middlesex: Penguin.

Friedman, Maurice (1981) *Martin Buber's Life and Work*. Vol. 1. New York: E.P. Dutton.

Fromm, Bella (1942) *Blood and Banquets: A Berlin Social Diary*. New York and London: Harper Brothers.

Gardiner, Muriel (ed.) (1972) *The Wolf-Man and Sigmund Freud*. London: Hogarth Press and Institute of Psycho-Analysis.

Gavron, Daniel (1997) *Saul Adler, Pioneer of Tropical Medicine*. Rehovot: Balaban.

Gay, Peter (2001) *Schnitzler's Century*. London: Allen Lane, The Penguin Press.

Gogol, Nikolay (2005, orig. early 19th century) *Diary of a Madman, The Government Inspector, and Selected Stories*. R. Wilks (transl.). Harmondsworth: Penguin.

Greenberg, Uri Zvi (1990–98) *Kol Ketavav* (*Collected Works*). 13 vols. D. Miron et al. (eds.). Jerusalem: Bialik Institute.

Guntrip, Harry (1968) *Schizoid Phenomena, Object Relations and the Self*. London: Hogarth Press and Institute of Psycho-Analysis.

Habermann, A.M. (1976) 'Conversations with Agnon' (Hebrew). *HaDo'ar* 8 Tevet.

Hawthorne, Nathaniel (2008, orig, 1859) *The Scarlet Letter*. B. Harding and C. Weinstein (eds.). Oxford University Press.

Heine, Heinrich (1961–64) *Werke und Briefe*. 10 vols. H. Kaufmann (ed.). Berlin: Aufbau-Verlag.

Hemingway, Ernest (1984) *The Essential Hemingway*. London: Granada.

Herzl, Theodor (1896) *Der Judenstaat*. Leipzig and Vienna: M. Breitenstein.

Hochman, Baruch (1970) *The Fiction of S.Y. Agnon*. Ithaca, NY: Cornell University Press.

Hoffman, Anne Golomb (1991) *Between Exile and Return: S.Y. Agnon and the Drama of Writing*. Albany, NY: State University of New York Press.

Horwitz, Rivka (1988) 'Voices of Opposition to the First World War among Jewish Thinkers' in *Leo Baeck Institute Year Book*, 33, 233–259.

Ibsen, Henrik (1973, orig, 1881) *Ghosts*. M. Meyer (transl.). London: Eyre Methuen.

Isherwood, Christopher (1958, orig. 1939) *Goodbye to Berlin*. Harmondsworth, Middlesex: Penguin Books.

Janouch, Gustav (1971) *Conversations with Kafka*. G. Rees (transl.). London: Andre Deutsch.

Joll, James (1960) *Intellectuals in Politics: Three Biographical Essays*. London: Weidenfeld and Nicolson.

Jones, Ernest (1953, 1955, 1957) *Sigmund Freud: Life and Work*. 3 vols. London: Hogarth Press.

Joyce, James (1993, orig. 1922) *Ulysses*. J. Johnson (ed.). Oxford University Press.

Jung, C.G. (1956) *Symbols of Transformation*, in *Collected Works of C.G. Jung*, vol. 5, G. Adler et al. (eds.), R.F.C. Hull (transl.). London: Routledge.

Jung, C.G. (1974) *Memories, Dreams, Reflections*. A. Jaffé (ed.), R. & C. Winston (transl.). London: Collins, The Fontana Library.

Jungk, Peter Stephan (1990) *Franz Werfel: A Life in Prague, Vienna, and Hollywood*. A. Hollo (transl.). New York: Grove Weidenfeld.

Kafka, Franz (1926) *Das Schloss*. Leipzig: Poeschel & Trepte.

Kafka, Franz (1953) *Letters to Milena*. T. & J. Stern (transl.). London: Secker and Warburg.

Kafka, Franz (1975) *The Diaries of Franz Kafka*. Max Brod (ed.). J. Kresh & M. Greenberg. (transl.). Harmondsworth, Middlesex: Penguin Modern Classics.

Kafka, Franz (1977, orig. 1925) *The Trial*. E. & W. Muir (transl.). Harmondsworth, Middlesex: Penguin Books.

Kafka, Franz (1978) *Wedding Preparations in the Country and Other Stories*. E. Kaiser, E. Wilkins et al. (transl.). Harmondsworth, Middlesex: Penguin.

Kafka, Franz (1978a) *Letters to Felice*. J. Stern & E. Duckworth (transl.). Harmondsworth, Middlesex: Penguin.

Kafka, Franz (1983) *Letters to Milena*. W. Haas (ed.), T. & J. Stern (transl.). New York: Penguin.

Kafka, Franz (1994, orig. 1926) *The Castle*. W. & E. Muir (transl.). New York: Schocken.

Katz, Jacob (1980) *From Prejudice to Destruction: Anti-Semitism 1700–1933*. Cambridge, MA: Harvard University Press.

Kermode, Frank (1973) *Lawrence*. Modern Masters series. Bungay, Suffolk: Fontana/ Collins.

Laor, Dan (1998) *Haye Agnon: Biografia* [S.Y. Agnon: A Biography]. Jerusalem/Tel Aviv: Schocken.

Laor, Dan (2008) *S.Y. Agnon* (Hebrew). Jerusalem: Merkaz Zalman Shazar.

Lasker-Schüler, Else (2001) *Werke und Briefe*, vol. 4.1 (*Prosa 1921–1945*). Eds. K.J. Skrodzki and I. Shepletzky. Frankfurt am Main: Jüdischer Verlag.

Lawrence, D.H. (1916) *Amores*. New York: B.H. Huebsch.

Lawrence, D.H. (1972, orig. 1964) *Collected Poems*, 2 vols. V. de Sola Pinto, W. Roberts (eds.). London: Heinemann.

Lawrence, D.H. (1975, orig. 1923) 'The Fox', in *Three Novellas*. Harmondsworth, Middlesex: Penguin Books.

Lawrence, D.H. (1976, orig. 1913) *Sons and Lovers*. Harmondsworth, Middlesex: Penguin.

Lawrence, D.H. (1979) *Letters*, vol. I, J.T. Boulton et al., eds. Cambridge University Press.

Lelchuk, A and G. Shaked (eds.) (1983) *Eight Great Hebrew Short Novels*. New York: New American Library.

Leoussi, Athena and David Aberbach (2002) 'Hellenism and Jewish Nationalism: Ambivalence and Its Ancient Roots', *Ethnic and Racial Studies* 25(5): 1–23.

Levy, Richard S. (2010) 'Political Antisemitism in Germany and Austria, 1848–1914', in A.S. Lindemann and R.S. Levy (eds.) *Antisemitism: A History*. Oxford: Oxford University Press.

Macaulay, Lord Thomas (1963) *Macaulay's Essays*. H. Trevor-Roper (ed.). London and Glasgow: Collins, Fontana.

Margaliot, Abraham (1988) 'Remarks on the Political and Ideological Development of the C.V. before 1914', *Leo Baeck Institute Year Book* XXXIII: 101–6.

Marrus, Michael R. (1980) *The Politics of Assimilation: A Study of the French Jewish Community at the Time of the Dreyfus Affair*. Oxford: Clarendon Press.

Mazor, Yair (1987) *The Triple Cord: Agnon, Hamsun, Strindberg: Where Hebrew and Scandinavian Literature Meet*. Tel Aviv: Papyrus, Tel Aviv University.

McCourt, John (2000) *The Years of Bloom: James Joyce in Trieste 1904–1920*. Dublin: the Lilliput Press.

Meirtchak, Benjamin (2004) *Jews-Officers in the Polish Armed Forces 1939–1945*. 2nd edn. Tel Aviv: Solomon Levy Ltd.

Mendele Mokher Sefarim (1947) *Collected Works* (Hebrew). 1 vol. Tel Aviv: Dvir.

Mendelsohn, Ezra (1993) *On Modern Jewish Politics*. New York and Oxford: Oxford University Press.

Mendes-Flohr, Paul R. and Jehuda Reinharz (eds.) (1995) *The Jew in the Modern World: A Documentary History*. 2nd edition. New York and Oxford: Oxford University Press.

Mintz, Alan (2022) *American Hebraist: Essays on Agnon and Modern Jewish Literature*. B. Bailis & D. Stern (eds.). Penn State University Press.

Miron, Dan (1973) *A Traveller Disguised: A Study in the Rise of Modern Yiddish Fiction in the Nineteenth Century*. New York: Shocken.

Miron, Dan (1987) *Bodedim be-Mo'adam* (When Loners Come Together: A Portrait of Hebrew Literature at the Turn of the Twentieth Century). Tel Aviv: Am Oved.

Miron, Dan (1992) 'The Domestication of the Foreign Genre: On the Problem of Agnon's Novelistic Art' in *Shai Agnon Babikoret Ha'ivrit* (Critical Essays on S.Y. Agnon), Avinoam Barshai (ed.). Tel Aviv: Open University.

Moore, H.T. (ed.) (1965) *The Collected Letters of D.H. Lawrence*, 2 vols. London: Heinemann.

Musil, Robert (1930–1943) *Der Mann ohne Eigenschaften*. Berlin: Ernst Rowohlt Verlag.

Nietzsche, Friedrich (1968, orig. 1901) *The Will to Power*, W. Kaufmann (ed.), W. Kaufmann & R.J. Hollingdale (transl.). New York: Vintage, Random House.

Patai, Raphael (1996) *The Jews of Hungary: History, Culture, Psychology*. Detroit: Wayne State University Press.

Pauley, Bruce F. (1992) *From Prejudice to Persecution: A History of Austrian Anti-Semitism*. Chapel Hill & London: The University of North Carolina Press.

Petuchowski, Jakob J. (1968) *Prayerbook Reform in Europe: The Liturgy of European Liberal and Reform Jews*. New York: World Union for Progressive Judaism.

Plessix Gray, Francine du (2001) *Simone Weil*. London: Weidenfeld & Nicolson.

Prawer, S.S. (1983) *Heine's Jewish Comedy*. Oxford: Clarendon Press.

Rabin, Chaim (1979) *A Short History of the Hebrew Language* (Hebrew). Jerusalem: World Zionist Organization, Department for Education and Culture.

Rathenau, Walther (2006) *Briefe*. 2 vols. A. Jaser, C. Picht, & E. Schulin (eds.). Düsseldorf: Droste Verlag.

Rawidowicz, Shimon (1983) *Conversations with Bialik* (Hebrew). Y. Friedlander & B.C.I. Ravid (eds.). Tel Aviv: Dvir.

Rechter, David (2001) *The Jews of Vienna and the First World War*. London and Portland, OR: Littman Library of Jewish Civilization.

Reinharz, Jehuda (1975) *Fatherland or Promised Land: The Dilemma of the German Jew, 1893–1914*. Ann Arbor: University of Michigan Press.

Roazen, Paul (1975) *Freud and His Followers*. New York: Alfred A. Knopf.

Robert, Marthe (1976) *From Oedipus to Moses: Freud's Jewish Identity*. R. Manheim (transl.). Garden City, New York: Anchor Books.

Roth, Joseph (2002, orig. 1932) *The Radetzky March*. M. Hofmann (transl.). London: Granta.

Roth, Joseph (1970) *Briefe 1911–1939*. H. Kesten (ed.). Koln, Berlin: Kiepenheuer & Witsch.

Roth, Joseph (1975 76) *Werke*. 4 vols. H. Kesten (ed.). Koln, Berlin: Kiepenheuer & Witsch.

Roth, Philip (2004) *The Plot Against America*. Boston & New York: Houghton Mifflin Harcourt.

Ruppin, Arthur (1913) *The Jews of To-Day*. M. Bentwich (transl.). London: G. Bell and Sons, Ltd.

Sadan, Dov (1978) *Masot u-Ma'amarim al S.Y. Agnon* (Essays and articles on Agnon). Tel Aviv: Hakibbutz Hameuchad.

Schnitzler, Arthur (2001, orig. 1926) *Traumnovelle*. Frankfurt: Fischer.

Schnitzler, Arthur (1999, orig. 1926) *Dream Story*. J.M.Q. Davies (transl.). Harmondsworth, Middlesex: Penguin Books.

Schocken, Gershon (1978) *'Motif hatzara'at beShirah uve-Ad Olam'* (On Leprosy in Shira and 'Forevermore') in *S.Y. Agnon: Mekhkarim u-te'udot* (S.Y. Agnon: Studies and Documents), Shaked & Weiser (eds.). Jerusalem: Bialik Institute.

Scholem, Gershom (1976) *On Jews and Judaism in Crisis*. W.J. Dannhauser (ed.). New York: Schocken Books.

Shaked, Gershon (1977) *Hebrew Narrative Fiction 1880–1970: Vol 1: In Exile*. Tel Aviv: Hakibbutz Hameuchad and Keter.

Shaked, Gershon (1989) *Shmuel Yosef Agnon: A Revolutionary Traditionalist*. J.M. Green (transl.). New York: New York University Press.

Shaked, Gershon and Raphael Weiser (eds.) (1978) *S.Y. Agnon: Mehkarim u-Te'udot* (Studies and Documents). Jerusalem: Mossad Bialik.

Shamir, Ziva (2017) *Me-Ohev le-Oyev* (From Friend to Foe). Tel Aviv: Ha-Kibbutz Hameuchad.

Sholom Aleichem (1987) *Tevye the Dairyman and The Railroad Stories*. H. Halkin (transl.). New York: Schocken Books.

Storr, Anthony (1976) *The Dynamics of Creation*. Harmondsworth, Middlesex: Pelican Books.

Storr, Anthony (1977) *Sexual Deviation*. Harmondsworth, Middlesex: Penguin Books.

Svevo, Italo (1954) *Opere di Italo Svevo* (Collected Works). Milan: dall'Oglio.

Svevo, Italo (1965, orig. 1898) *As a Man Grows Older* (*Senilità*). B. de Zoete (transl.). Harmondsworth, Middlesex: Penguin Books.

Toller, Ernst (1933) *Eine Jugend in Deutschland*. Amsterdam: Querido.

Toller, Ernst (1934) *I Was a German: an Autobiography*. E. Crankshaw (transl.). London: John Lane, The Bodley Head.

Turgenev, Ivan (1977, orig. 1860) *First Love*. I. Berlin (transl.). Harmonsdsworth, Middlesex: Penguin Classics.

Vital, David (1999) *A People Apart: The Jews in Europe 1789–1939*. Oxford University Press.

Vogel, David (1986, orig.1929–30) *Hayei Nisuim*. Tel Aviv: Hakibbutz Hemeuchad; Jerusalem: Keter.

Vogel, David (1988, orig.1929–30) *Married Life*. D. Bilu (transl.). London: Peter Halban.

Wassermann, Jakob (1921) *Mein Weg als Deutscher und Jude*. Berlin: Fischer.

Wassermann, Jakob (1933, orig. 1921) *My Life as German and Jew*. S.N. Brainin (transl.). New York: Coward-McCann, Inc.

Weisgal, Meyer (1971) *So Far: An Autobiography*. London: Weidenfeld and Nicolson.

Weizmann, Chaim (1949) *Trial and Error: The Autobiography of Chaim Weizmann*. New York: Harper and Brothers.

Werfel, Franz (1947, orig. 1933) *Die Vierzig Tage des Musa Dagh*. 2 vols. Stockholm: Bermann- Fischer.

Werfel, Franz (2012, orig. 1933) *The Forty Days of Musa Dagh*, G. Dunlop & J. Reidel (transl.). Boston: Verba Mundi.

Werses, Shmuel (2000) *Shai Agnon kifshuto* (S.Y. Agnon Literally). Jerusalem: Bialik Institute.

Whitman, Walt (1949, orig. 1855) *Leaves of Grass and Selected Prose*. S. Bradley (ed.). New York: Holt, Rinehart and Winston Inc.

Wilde, Oscar (1891) *Intentions*. Leipzig: Heinemann and Balestier.

Wistrich, Robert S. (1990) *The Jews of Vienna in the Age of Franz Joseph*. Oxford: Littman Library, Oxford University Press.

Yaron, Emunah, Rafael Weiser, Dan Laor and Reuven Merkin, eds. (1994) *Kovets Agnon* (An Agnon Miscellany). Jerusalem: Hebrew University/Magnes Press.

Young-Bruehl, Elizabeth (1982) *Hannah Arendt: For Love of the World*. New Haven and London: Yale University Press.

Zborowski, Mark and Herzog, Elizabeth (1974, orig. 1952) *Life Is With People: The Culture of the Shtetl*. New York: Schocken Books.

Zechlin, Egmont (1969) *Die Deutsche Politik und die Juden im Ersten Weltkrieg* (German Politics and the Jews in World War I). Göttingen: Wandenhoeck & Ruprecht.

Zuckmayer, Carl (1934) *Eine Liebesgeschichte*. Berlin: S. Fischer.

Zweig, Stefan (1934, orig. 1922) *Letter from an Unknown Woman*. E. & C. Paul (transl.). New York: The Viking Press.

Zweig, Stefan (1981, orig. 1922) *Brief einer Unbekannten*. Utrecht: De Roos.

Index

Note: **Bold** denotes a quote or significant passage.

I Agnon

(a) *Works cited*

***(b)** Psychoanalytic Themes*

II General Index

FSC
www.fsc.org
MIX
Papier | Fördert gute Waldnutzung
FSC® C083411

Kolibri 360 GmbH
Ferdinand-Jühlke-Straße 7
99095 Erfurt, Deutschland
produktsicherheit@kolibri360.de